D0886566

Ex Libris

Indiana-Purdue University Library

Gift Presented By

Mary Waller Gift Fund

Becoming Benjamin Franklin

BECOMING BENJAMIN FRANKLIN

The *Autobiography* and the Life

Ormond Seavey

E
302.6
.F7
A2
1988

THE PENNSYLVANIA STATE UNIVERSITY PRESS
University Park and London

Indiana
Purdue
Library
Fort Wayne

Frontispiece: Robert Feke, *Benjamin Franklin*, c. 1746, oil on canvas. Courtesy of The Harvard University Portrait Collection, Bequest of Dr. John C. Warren, 1856.

INDIANA-P
PURDUE
LIBRARY
WITHDRAWN
FORT WAYNE

Library of Congress Cataloging-in-Publication Data

Seavey, Ormond.
  Becoming Benjamin Franklin.

  Includes index.
  1. Franklin, Benjamin, 1706–1790. Autobiography.
  2. Franklin, Benjamin, 1706–1790. 3. Statesmen—United States—
  Biography—History and criticism.
  I. Title.
  E302.6.F7A23 1988   973.3′092′4   87–43125
  ISBN 0-271-00627-7

Copyright ©1988 The Pennsylvania State University
All rights reserved
Printed in the United States of America

7-13-90

TO MY FATHER AND THE MEMORY OF MY MOTHER
AND TO NINA

Contents

Preface

This study attempts to describe Benjamin Franklin's sense of personal and national identity as it appears in his *Autobiography* and as it developed in his life. No American of the eighteenth century was more alert to psychological complexities than Franklin, and no one was better equipped to describe them. He employed his considerable powers of description and analysis most of all in his *Autobiography*, by far the longest piece he ever wrote. But the *Autobiography* mobilizes Franklin's psychological insight to serve a particular rhetorical purpose, the depiction of a model of human existence which Franklin claimed to understand and in part to have fulfilled. Because of the resulting discrepancy between the *Autobiography* and the life itself—a discrepancy between an ordered, directed presentation of experience and the mixture of purposes and impulses characteristic of the lives we know—this study is divided into two parts. I begin with an examination of the *Autobiography* for its rhetoric and its adoption of certain Enlightenment notions about character and the self. The second part of the study is devoted to Franklin's life itself, the experience which his own account professes to describe. I attempt in that part to set forth the costs and rewards Franklin found in trying to be the sort of self depicted in the *Autobiography*.

This book is therefore not a biography in the conventional sense, nor is it purely a literary study. No single methodology will provide access to the Franklin who so successfully concealed the history of his identity by the act of revealing it. Unlike those figures who have left behind only confused and suggestive written records of themselves, Franklin converted his experience into a book, so certain questions about the structure and rhetoric of his presentation must arise first. As for the life itself, I employ the methods of psychohistory, a discipline that investigates the intersections between an inner self and the political, social, and cultural environment which surrounds it. In asking psychohistorical questions, I am not assuming that there was something pathological about Franklin's inner state. Rather, I believe that his own claims to self-mastery and his own capacity for psychological insight deserve a treatment commensurate with his own acuteness.

Franklin's own self-understanding has posed a particular challenge to the students of his life. The great impediment to biographies of Franklin is that he took charge of the territory first. Because of the primacy of his *Autobiography*, conventional biographers have been characteristically reduced to echoing or embellishing his own story. Only in the last half of his life, where his narrative does not reach, do they have space for an independent account, and by then his life is involved in large political questions of a sort that have their own gravitational pull. The biographer becomes a minor adjunct to the historians of the Revolution and the early Republic. What might have been perceived as troublesome choices or personal crises become enveloped in a historical momentum in which he seems more an exemplar than a separable voice and will.

By writing his *Autobiography* Franklin asserted that his experiences and perceptions reflected a unified and indentifiable mode of consciousness, which others might borrow from or adopt for themselves. In the first part of this study I take Franklin at his word, treating him as the author and principal character of his book as if he were a novelist. As a literary form, autobiography is an odd sort of hybrid; it is necessarily a type of fiction, a schematized and selective ordering of the varied materials of experience. (I assume that experience is inevitably beyond our capacity either to control or to fully understand.) Yet like other fictions autobiography aspires to a truth of its own, in its own terms. Those terms, in this case, derive from certain Enlightenment ideas about the self, so that cultural background is also treated in the first part.

The basic question of the second part is why and how Franklin tried to be what the *Autobiography* describes. There was nothing natural or inevitable about becoming Benjamin Franklin. To convert such an unusual history into a representative model for his young countrymen required a considerable and sustained imaginative transformation, but Franklin carried it off so well that his extraordinary claims for himself are routinely accepted by his readers. To recover the real achievement requires a different use of the *Autobiography* and recourse to the large body of letters, papers, and other materials which in some cases corroborate and in other cases undercut his authorized account.

The Franklin who finally emerges from my treatment is preeminently a writer, one preoccupied all his life with the presentation of selves to an audience. The audiences he found at first were far too small for what he knew to be his talents, so he set about enlarging that audience—a process directly linked to the establishing of something recognizable as America. He felt that the social scenes in which he found himself could be remodeled to suit his own notions about life, so he employed his own subtle powers of persuasion to encourage the remodeling. This study cannot presume to measure his success; it looks instead for the will that would attempt to mold his posterity, his countrymen, in his own image.

Traditional scholarly approaches to Franklin have divided him into areas of special interest. There are studies, for example, on Franklin as scientist, Franklin as economic theorist, Franklin as spelling reformer, Franklin on foreign policy or political philosophy, Franklin as religious thinker, Franklin as printer. The kind of division of labor implied by these studies is inevitable, so wide-ranging were his interests and so fresh and responsive his intelligence. The problem with such studies, though, is that Franklin's thinking on most subjects was sporadic and extemporaneous; he was always moving on to a new scheme and playing by ear. Focusing narrowly on some aspect of his life is likely to suggest simplistic or misleading conclusions about the man as a whole.[1]

It is Franklin's wholeness, his sense of identity, that is my subject— the subject of his *Autobiography* and the preoccupation of a lifetime of close self-scrutiny. Describing that wholeness does not require an exhaustive enumeration of the events of his life. I offer no extended discussion of his scientific, economic, or political ideas or activities, except insofar as those are connected to certain inner needs. For example, the negotiations he carried out with the Penn brothers, the Proprietors of Pennsylvania colony, though full of complicated legal and political ramifications, appear here as an episode in which Franklin found himself treated abusively by persons in power. Fortunately I am not alone in asking questions about Franklin's motivations. Important brief studies of Franklin, such as those of Richard Bushman, John Lynen, David Levin, and James Cox, have provided important suggestions about the complexities of his identity. The *Autobiography* itself cheerfully invites its readers to scrutinize Franklin's life and acknowledge his success as a whole. Its subtleties will not be exhausted by this study, nor will Franklin's greatness be diminished by looking beyond the genial, avuncular role he played so successfully.[2]

This book is also intended as a contribution to a growing body of studies on the consciousness of the eighteenth century. The works of Leo Braudy, Peter Shaw, Fred Weinstein and Gerald M. Platt, Edwin Burrows and Michael Wallace, Jay Fliegelman, and Mitchell Breitwieser, in particular, seem to me to explore the intersections between character and political or ethical thinking in the eighteenth century.[3] An age of such immense redirections of thought and feeling could not have accomplished its imaginative work without psychic turmoil. Franklin was eager to adapt its possibilities for himself. In turn he was heir to its troublesome ambiguities.

Acknowledgments

One of the satisfactions of completing a book that has required years of effort is the pleasure of thanking the people who have helped to sustain its becoming. The reader of this book will easily see the debt I owe, in common with other Franklin scholars, to the great Yale edition of *The Papers of Benjamin Franklin*. Sacvan Bercovitch and Quentin Anderson read the earliest version, and I profited from the encouragement they gave me. James Maddox, Leo Braudy, and Peter Shaw have been generous with their time. Earlier drafts have benefited from readings by Norman Fiering and Victoria Arana Robinson. I have also received small stipends from the Graduate School of Arts and Sciences at George Washington University. As it all came closer to becoming a book, my greatest support and most valuable reader has been my wife, Nina Gilden Seavey.

Textual Note

Where Franklin's *Autobiography* is cited in the text, the edition used is *The Autobiography of Benjamin Franklin*, edited by Leonard W. Labaree, Ralph L. Ketcham, Helen C. Boatfield, and Helene H. Fineman (New Haven: Yale University Press, 1964), designated in parentheses as (A) followed by a page number. In the case of Franklin's other writings or writings to him, I cite where possible the yet uncompleted *Papers of Benjamin Franklin*, edited by Leonard W. Labaree, William B. Willcox et al. (New Haven: Yale University Press, 1959–). Past the year 1778 I cite the most complete earlier edition, *The Writings of Benjamin Franklin*, edited by Albert H. Smyth (New York: Doubleday, 1905–7).

PART ONE
The *Autobiography*

1 Introduction

We know Franklin most of all through his *Autobiography*. It is difficult to conceive of him outside the terms which that book dictates, so persuasive is the image offered there. As a result, our responses to Franklin are in large measure responses to a text. We know him not so much as we know Lincoln but more as we know Gatsby; he is a character in a book. He was determined that he should endure in that way, as the protagonist of his own text, and this is probably the first thing to understand about him.

Autobiographies are quite often a somewhat accidental comment or a momentary reordering of their authors' lives. In Franklin's case his life story was a natural and necessary culmination of a lifetime of preoccupations with self-creating. Henry Adams leaves out almost his entire career as a historian, and Gibbon treats his memoirs as an indulgence to which he is entitled after completing *The Decline and Fall*. But Franklin wrote nothing else so long and complex as his *Autobiography*, and he spent the final months of his life trying to pack in as much more material as he possibly could. That he wrote such a book explains both his distinctiveness and his representativeness in eighteenth-century America.

Franklin's preoccupation with controlling and preserving his own story stands out in particular when he is compared to his associates among the Founding Fathers, the leaders of the Revolution, and the early Republic. Washington, Adams, Jefferson, Madison, and Hamilton made no comparable effort to characterize their own personalities for the benefit of posterity. They saw themselves as contributors to a history of thought and action; they were satisfied to be known for military campaigns, legislative enactments, diplomatic negotiations, and state papers. Where they preserved autobiographical records of themselves, they located their lives in a narrative of public events, not in a comprehensive pattern of experiences centering around themselves. They had played their parts in a large drama that lacked a central character or a clear plot line.[1]

Like his associates in the Revolution, Franklin was committed to a life of action, but his *Autobiography* shows that for him events continually became occasions for self-discovery and self-expression. He describes his quarrels with his older brother as a foreshadowing of his later opposition to arbitrary tyranny. He represents his civic and political accomplishments as manifestations of a particular kind of self. The Franklin who helps to found the Pennsylvania Hospital is the canny negotiator for the public good; the Franklin who serves as unofficial quartermaster for the army of General Braddock is the helpful and sensible American confronting the obtuse and imperious Britisher. Ideology was less important for him than it was for the other Founding Fathers because he always subordinated ideology to the demands of experience—not simply for the sake of being more pragmatic and *doing* more but also so as to allow himself the greatest field of self-expression. It might be said that Franklin was drawn to public life for reasons similar to those which drew Whitman to poetry (and away, incidentally, from the politics of the 1850s): public life and poetry offered them occasions to play to the largest possible audiences, to exhibit themselves as embodiments of national traits. Whitman achieved this end by opening himself up to the varied human possibilities he saw in the country; Franklin displayed himself to the nation by engineering a set of reflections of his own qualities. The lightning rod showed his practical inventiveness and his love of gadgets; the Library Company of Philadelphia became for thousands an access to a self-directed education like his own; the French alliance set the seal of international approval on an America whose highly visible embodiment was Franklin himself.

As the *Autobiography* reveals, Franklin's personality was not just an element in his success. It was the success itself. That image of a self had to be carefully preserved for posterity. Jefferson left his personality for the biographers to describe, but Franklin was determined to forestall any possibility that his historical image might get out of his control. As a careful student of character and a master at manipulating audiences, he had worked all his life at the creation of himself and at the presentation of that self—not as ordinarily vain people do, with continual but discontinuous displays of themselves, but more as an artist, who must think continually about the comprehensive effect of his work as a whole. Both in his actions and in his writings, Franklin was aiming at a certain large effect, of which the *Autobiography* was to be the fullest realization.

In other words, Franklin saw himself as an exemplar of a particular mode of consciousness, which the *Autobiography* makes available for imitation. On the first page of his text he makes his intentions quite clear. "Having emerg'd from the Poverty and Obscurity in which I was born and bred, to a State of Affluence and some Degree of Reputation in the World, and having gone so far thro' Life with a considerable Share of Felicity, the conducing Means I made use of, which, with the Blessing of God, so well succeeded, my Posterity may like to know, as they may find some of them suitable to their own Situations, and therefore fit to be imitated" (A, 43). The "conducing Means" entail something more subtle than a collection of directly imitable activities, like pushing his wheelbarrow through the streets of Philadelphia or being careful to repay borrowed money. A mode of consciousness has generated those activities, and it is that consciousness which his "posterity" is invited to adopt.

By "mode of consciousness" I am referring to a self-consistent assemblage of beliefs, attitudes, and mental reflexes, distinguishable from "personality type" in that its style and signature reflect some engendering cultural situation. D. H. Lawrence in particular saw Franklin as the advocate of such a mode of consciousness, and whatever might be said about the tone of his well-known essay in *Studies in Classic American Literature*, that central perception about Franklin is correct. (Lawrence himself, it has often been pointed out, saw himself as the representative of a certain mode of consciousness.) The concept of the mode of consciousness is useful in describing certain recurring patterns of cultural behavior. When Perry Miller refers to "the Augustinian strain of piety" at the beginning of his great exposition of American Puritanism in *The New England Mind*, he is noting the kinship between the inner lives of the Puritans and the mode of consciousness set forth in Augustine's *Confessions*. Emerson describes Montaigne as the exemplar of a particular response to the varying appeals of ultimate reality and immediate experience; that response can be somewhat unsatisfactorily labeled "skepticism," but its fullest articulation appears in Montaigne's own renditions of the world in the *Essais*. Though the figures who originate or exemplify modes of consciousness are highly

aware of the distinctiveness and dimensions of their casts of mind—
and aware as well of the possibility that others might imitate them—
they are also responding to their own deeper or unconscious impulses,
in ways that link their thought and expression to certain emotional
states. Thus, for example, a restlessness with transient earthly pleasures is symptomatic of Augustine and his inheritors; a contented dis-
orderliness exemplifies the disciples of Montaigne. Each style can be
related to a pattern of inner life. Franklin's own mode of consciousness, in turn, arose from a set of unconscious energies which are partially discernible in the *Autobiography*.[2]

Franklin also insists that his own consciousness has connected him
with a certain body of people. It has been an *American* consciousness.
In the words of Benjamin Vaughan, his English editor, "All that has
happened to you is also connected with the detail of the manners and
situation of *a rising people*" (A, 135). The *Autobiography* records both
his own consciousness and his sense of identity—a second term in
need of definition here. The term "identity" obviously implies a relationship of resemblance, in this case between self and group, but this
recognition of connection also involves the self's own most basic
awareness of its own distinctiveness. The two processes are reciprocal
and mutual: as one discovers affective ties to a human community, one
discovers who one is. The particular nature of the identification with a
group is a further aspect of identity. In orthodox psychoanalytic terms
identification means the absorption of something into the subject,
whether that something be a role, a loved one, or a group association.
Identification is thus distinguishable from object-choice: in object-
choice one *has* something; in identification one *is* something. Naturally in the case of group identity the stronger the incorporation of the
group into the ego ideal, the less accessible that incorporation is to
conscious direction by the ego.[3]

In the case of Franklin, the question of group identity included the
problems he faced as a writer addressing an audience. His first audiences were small, the reading publics of Boston and then Philadelphia,
and the group identities available to him were similarly circumscribed.
Eventually it became possible to be an American and to address an
American audience, but neither that identity nor that audience had
much meaning while he was first writing and coming into maturity in
the 1720s. Creating the audience and the possibility for identity as
something more than a colonist (the inhabitant of a single colony, itself
by definition a society of marginal people) required a sequence of political events, the most important being the American Revolution. But
those events were brought about to a great extent by writing, by pieces

in newspapers and resolutions of committees and legislatures, by correspondence among men and factions that were widely scattered. All his life Franklin was engaged in this sort of writing. His own identity as a writer demanded an audience proportioned to his sense of himself; he could not think of his early successes as a ballad writer or author of clever periodical letters in Boston as substantial or satisfying for long, because he knew how few people were reading his work and how slight an impact he was having. The *Autobiography* represents the culmination of his efforts to create an audience, a "posterity" to which he could be attached, in the deliberate, mastering ways by which writers connect themselves to their readers.

If the *Autobiography* remains our principal access to Franklin's life, it also serves as an obstacle that must be removed or neutralized before we can gain any closer access to him. It is an elaborate fabrication, truthful in its details yet subtly misleading in its overall plan. As a literary creation, the *Autobiography* must be examined in terms of its genre, its structure, and its rhetoric, which together impose certain alterations in the record of his experience.

The basic distortions in the *Autobiography* derive from the very act of organizing the materials of his experience and giving them shape and direction. The *Autobiography* asserts that Franklin's life was in marvelously good order, certainly beyond what his readers could ever have experienced. At the beginning of his narrative he compares his life to a book which he has written himself. What another might have called faults, sins, or mistakes he refers to as "*errata*"—mistakes in type, errors of presentation. The Philadelphia that he describes as the backdrop to his activities appears as the perfect complement to his own notion of himself; it honors the appearance of industriousness, it forms itself into committees and organizations to do good, it responds generously to appeals to its good will. The city appears as an extension of Franklin himself, a field on which he could display his own personality. He lacks the sense, common to others who have recorded their own lives extensively and persuasively, that the world is frustrating and mysterious, that their lives have only intermittently been under their own control. Writers as different as Augustine and John Stuart Mill have attested to such a feeling. Franklin, by contrast, insists on his capacity to adjust to his surroundings and to resolve the apparent dilemmas of his experience.

Franklin considered setting forth his ideas about the way life should be led in a straightforward expository form. He was accustomed to that sort of writing, and in various shorter versions he had set down what he called "Hints to Those Who Would Be Rich" or "Advice to a Young Tradesman"; he even had a title in mind for his projected work: *The Art of Virtue.* But he ended up incorporating that project in his *Autobiography*, so that the whole record of his experience might stand as proof of the soundness of his teaching.

All autobiographies, even the most honest, distort the lives they describe, in the same way that depictive art distorts the material depicted. Many of the distortions are introduced by the implied presence of a reader in the text, because readers necessarily impose certain expectations. Any reader will require that the narrative should hold together, based around a single figure whose perceptions will determine what is presented. That central figure must be recognizable as a personality, not so much for consistency of perspective as for a believable pattern of inconsistencies. The Franklin who advocates planning out one's life also confesses several times to his own tendencies for disorder; the confessions serve to make his personality, and even his message, more believable. Readers also expect the described events to be true, by an inner if not a literal standard; autobiographies fail more from the author lying to the reader than from the author lying to himself. Franklin professes to understand himself thoroughly; the work would founder if the reader felt any real acknowledgment from him of the limits of that understanding or any palpable concealment of the inner truth about himself. Finally, the reader cannot be satisfied with the fact that all lives are different and lived on their own terms; readers wonder what general category of life this will be—the confessions of a saint, for example, or the memoir of a politician or soldier, or the adventures of a scoundrel. Even unsophisticated writers respond to these expectations by projecting a pattern on their recollections; Franklin was in no way unsophisticated, and he had a comprehensive design for the description of his life that operates from the first page.[4]

The consistency of Franklin's purpose in the *Autobiography* is somewhat masked by the rather casual and offhand way he appears to treat the project. The book may seem at first glance to have problems of unity and coherence. He wrote it in several installments, probably of concentrated effort in each case, in between long interruptions; Franklin began the work in 1771, purportedly as a letter to his son, and was still working on it almost nineteen years later. In the meantime he had broken with his son, the American Revolution had taken place, and his fame had grown to immense proportions. The disruptions are indicated in the text of the life: in 1771 he is on vacation at Twyford, the estate of the Bishop of St. Asaph, while in 1784 he is at Passy in the suburbs of Paris, moved to continue, he says, by the advice of friends.

These disjunctions give the *Autobiography* its appearance of artlessness, as if the project were one pottered around with in spare moments.[5] As he puts it himself, "I shall indulge the inclination so natural in old Men, to be talking of themselves and their own past Actions, and I shall indulge it, without being troublesome to others who thro' respect to Age might think themselves oblig'd to give me a Hearing, since this may be read or not as any one pleases" (*A*, 44).

It would be foolish to accept this good-humored description of his motives or to believe that the sporadic surges of writing in the *Autobiography* led to a mixed presentation. Franklin understands that the reader's attention is best engaged by casual and subtle means, and he is determined to secure that attention. Unlike old men who talk about themselves out loud, Franklin says he will indulge that inclination by writing. He juxtaposes hearing and reading as if the reader is in some way freer, less under obligation to be attentive than the hearer. The reader can easily put the book down, whereas the hearer cannot graciously walk away from an interminable story. But the reader once engaged can be exposed to the writer for much longer, and the written word can be more deeply coercive. Franklin is not, after all, telling a story so much as he is setting forth a mode of consciousness; he does not want to be in front of his audience talking but rather inside their heads.

Despite its artless appearance the *Autobiography* makes large, uncompromising claims for its own importance. Franklin's rhetorical strategy is to assume rather than to demonstrate his basic claims; the reader is not offered this consciousness to accept or reject it but is instead invited inside to see how everything works. Rather than asserting overtly that his life has been the exemplary American life, Franklin introduces letters into the text from two friends who say more than he could have dared to, and he permits those letters to stand as the explanation for why he resumed writing. The consistency of his perspective through large changes of condition is a given, just as it is a given that his life is susceptible to being imitated by others. The *Autobiography* leads its readers to believe that it is perfectly natural to be Benjamin Franklin; anyone else, at any later date, can do it too. He says that his motive for writing is an old man's self-indulgence, to which he then adds the motive of vanity. But self-indulgence and vanity are quickly transformed from their usual meanings; self-indulgence turns out to be an aspect of self-direction, and vanity operates for the benefit of the public as a whole. What he appears at first to be excusing in himself he is in fact advocating. Confession is converted to assertion without any change in the inflection of presentation.

The force of Franklin's rhetoric of self-presentation depends upon the reader's impression that he is not alone, that he has been a representative or exemplary figure. As David Levin and Daniel Shea have noted, the *Autobiography* is oddly reminiscent of the tradition of spiritual autobiography, with its tendency to identify the authorial self as sinner or saint rather than as someone to be known primarily on his or her own terms.[6] In Franklin's case, saint and sinner are replaced by the category of man in general. He arrives at a creed that he claims to share with every other believer anywhere. He bequeaths his project for the advancement of virtue to the world as a whole. Always he is careful not to locate himself in any limiting pattern of unreproducible events and circumstances, and that stance is intended to associate him with all of humanity. Though the reader sees him throughout as a somewhat detached observer of his surroundings, that detachment is shared by all the other recognizable figures of his story except his parents; everybody else picks up and moves on to another place or changes jobs or spouses. Franklin maintains a balance between alienation and full identification in his relationship with others, and that balance seems related to his successes. He is continually introducing himself—to governors, employers, merchants of Philadelphia, the readers of Boston—rather than coping with circumstances where he has long been known; he manages to escape the limitations of his own past circumstances and define the terms under which he will live. When he needs an outlet for his sexuality, he gets married to someone he had discarded earlier; when he is stranded in London, he finds work as a printer and soon convinces some of his fellow employees to adopt his own diet. Throughout he presents his accomplishments not just as the product of one particular personality but as the natural human response to his circumstances.

The belief in the existence of natural human responses—those of the reasonable man, who is also the sentimental man—was an article of faith in the eighteenth century, and Franklin found in that belief another means of translating his own particular experience into a sort of universal language. The *Autobiography* will appear to be only a charming story of material success if its deep connection with the Enlightenment is not understood. However much he may have remained detached from his social surroundings, Franklin readily adjusted to the climate of opinion in the Enlightenment. His own version of the age, to be sure, left a good deal out; it was not the same Enlightenment as Voltaire's or Hume's or even Jefferson's. The problems of epistemology that concerned his contemporaries never bothered him. Intrigued as he was with natural science, it was a sort of game for him, though for others like Diderot or d'Alembert it provided a philosophical foundation. Franklin was never seriously involved in the *philosophes'* campaigns against religious fanaticism; believers were around him everywhere in America, and he sought nothing more than to get along with them all. Franklin never allowed those differences of emphasis to develop into differences of theory because he was determined to embrace all the positive possibilities of his age. The *Autobiography* registers little awareness that the eighteenth century was a domain with its own constraining peculiarities; instead he calls it "the Age of Experiments" (*A*, 257), a field of possibilities, and those experiments he could not undertake himself he felt sure would be undertaken by others.

The Enlightenment collaborated in the portrait of Franklin in the *Autobiography*, and its part in the process of recreating Franklin will need to be described further. Certain Enlightenment assumptions about the self seemed to explain or validate his life. It promised, above all, that one could know oneself better—and that there was, perhaps, more of the self that was worth knowing than one could have known in previous ages and that one's relationship to society was newly comprehensible and subject to conscious adjustments. These, of course, are the premises upon which the *Autobiography* was written.

2 *"Expecting a Weeks Uninterrupted Leisure"*

Franklin's *Autobiography* begins like a letter, with a superscription indicating the time and place of composition: "Twyford, at the Bishop of St. Asaph's, 1771." Franklin was on holiday in the country when he began writing; he evidently thought he could write his life story during his spare time while visiting friends. As he puts it in the opening remarks, "expecting a Weeks uninterrupted Leisure in my present Country Retirement" he starts out (A, 43). The holiday actually lasted about two weeks in early August, and Franklin almost certainly wrote only part of that first section at Twyford. As he was writing the first words of his great life, he truly did not know what he was getting into.[1]

The setting and circumstances leading to this sudden burst of writing—even in itself the longest single thing he had ever written—suggest the character of the recorded life. Twyford, where he was visiting, was a pleasant and restful village located just south of Winchester, a scene of rolling chalk hills with the little river Itchen flowing south toward Southhampton and the sea, about ten miles away. In his letters to his host, Franklin comments on "the sweet air of Twyford," so different from the smoke and dust of London. The gracious English comforts of Franklin's holiday residence and the hospitality of a bishop must have served to highlight a contrast between that present and Franklin's past, growing up obscurely and poorly in raw America.[2]

His host was Jonathan Shipley, the fifty-seven-year-old Bishop of St.

Asaph, who had inherited his stately and substantial house from his mother's family. Franklin had met Shipley not long before and had visited earlier in the same summer for about a week; the visit during which the writing started was prolonged by a day so that the Shipleys could celebrate the second birthday of Franklin's grandson, back in Philadelphia. There were five Shipley daughters at home, ages twenty-three to eleven; Franklin, who was always becoming an adoptive uncle for the daughters of his friends, made himself immediately at home. It was the Shipley family who served as his most immediate audience at the beginning. Family tradition says he read parts of the *Autobiography* to the family as he was working on it; whether or not he did, he was surrounded with people who would accept him at his own value. Shipley was a staunch Whig, a protégé early in his life of Bishop Hoadley, the Whig theorist: he advocated reconciliation with America and toleration of dissenters. His daughters were sprightly and independent-minded: Anna Maria Shipley later married the great linguist Sir William Jones; Georgiana Shipley became an artist and wife to Francis Hare-Naylor, an author; two of the daughters remained single. On his way back to London from Twyford, Franklin shared a coach with eleven-year-old Catherine Shipley and drew her gradually into conversation about what sort of person each of the girls should marry. Franklin then reported in detail on this conversation in a delightful letter to the girls' mother (P, 18: 199–202). All the great events of maturation—growing in and through adolescence, choosing a mate, having children—were present around Franklin as he began writing his own life, and he took an interest in them that was both engaged and also humorous. The happy moments at Twyford and on his return to London left him with a feeling of privileged intimacy that was to be both shared and protected; in the letter to his wife about his grandson's special birthday and in his letter to the bishop's wife he cautions the recipients against showing the letter around.

Franklin had already been thinking about his own childhood in the weeks before the visit to Twyford. A chance occurrence helped to trigger his interest: about three weeks before the August vacation in Twyford, a book dealer had offered to sell him a set of political pamphlets from the period 1688 to 1715. Franklin looked them over and thought they were the collection his uncle Benjamin had left behind in England before emigrating to America. He bought the whole set and wrote immediately to his uncle's grandson, his second cousin Samuel Franklin in Boston. The memory of his industriously collecting uncle prompted Franklin to write a long letter to his sister Jane Mecom in Boston; the letter reminisces about the difficulties his father and uncle had experienced living under the same roof. Franklin knew the difficulties of living in a family and had worried earlier over possible tensions between his wife and his sister on his sister's recent visit to Philadelphia. Franklin goes on to offer some information about the Franklin family that he had gathered in England, including a rudimentary family tree diagram going back to the sixteenth century. Several phrases from the letter would later be repeated in the genealogical section at the beginning of the *Autobiography*. Franklin liked to surround himself with relatives, including quite distant cousins, and to look after his extended family in his capacity as its most distinguished member. As the first sentence of the *Autobiography* states, "I have ever had a Pleasure in obtaining any little Anecdotes of my Ancestors" (A, 43). With that modest and beguiling beginning he starts the project moving.

Franklin could afford to think about such personal matters because the political demands on him in the spring and summer of 1771 had been slack. At the beginning of the year he had had a nasty confrontation with Lord Hillsborough, the Colonial Secretary, but by late summer the difficulties had been put aside, and Hillsborough insisted on having Franklin visit his Irish country estate. In the colonies the controversies over the Townshend duties had been eased by their partial repeal; the colonial boycott of English imports was now restricted, where it had any effect, to tea. In tumultuous Massachusetts the House of Representatives continued to spar with the governor and to issue heated instructions to Franklin, their colonial agent, but Parliament was not in session and the ministry was quiescent for the time being. Franklin's comments to his American correspondents had been baleful in their assessment of Anglo-American relations earlier in the year, but now he was outside of those conflicts, disposed to travel and reminisce. He had time to return to his scientific theorizing, a pleasant game for him; the imaginary husband Franklin and Kitty Shipley chose for her older sister Georgiana was a country gentleman who enjoyed traveling and "lov'd to see an Experiment now and then" (P, 18: 200). Franklin was at peace with himself, a peace based on his understanding of human limitations. In the July letter to his sister Jane he wrote that though he considered human beings in general a race of devils, the greatest harm they inflicted was upon themselves. "Upon the whole I am much disposed to like the World as I find it, and to doubt my own Judgment as to what would mend it" (P, 18: 185).

Franklin's acceptance of the world was made significantly easier by an awareness of his own growing prominence in it. As a present to fifteen-year-old Georgiana Shipley he was able to send a copy of the fourth edition of his *Experiments and Observations on Electricity*, a major scientific treatise. Through his membership in the Royal Society he was in touch with all the other English experimenters, and in the next year he was named *associé étranger* to the French *Académie royale des sciences*, one of eight people so honored in all Europe (P, 19: 259-60). In 1773 a two-volume edition of assorted Franklin writings would be published in France, edited by a young French disciple. While on his later journey to Scotland, he enjoyed the hospitality of David Hume, who, in a letter nine years earlier, had called Franklin the first man of letters America had given to the world. In August of 1772 he would describe the state of his international reputation in a letter to his son. He felt finally impervious to the assaults of his political enemies, he says, because of his established name. "Learned and ingenious foreigners that come to England, almost all make a point of visiting me, for my reputation is still higher abroad than here; several of the foreign ambassadors have assiduously cultivated my acquaintance, treating me as one of their *corps*" (P, 19: 259). In a postscript Franklin remembers to congratulate his son for his election two years earlier to membership in the Society for the Propagation of the Gospel in Foreign Parts, an Anglican missionary organization.

It is to this same son, William Franklin, that the *Autobiography* is ostensibly addressed. William Franklin was at that time the forty-year-old Royal Governor of New Jersey, a patronage job acquired nine years earlier when his father's relation to the ministry was more comfortable and the ministry hoped to inspire the father's gratitude. The salutation to the *Autobiography* is like the typical salutation to Franklin's letters to William—"Dear Son." Franklin corresponded frequently with his son and relied on William to keep him abreast of political matters in Pennsylvania; William was also charged with looking after family problems at home, particularly his stepmother, Franklin's ailing wife. But, after the salutation, the *Autobiography* does not read quite like a letter. Franklin's genuine letters are typically responses to previous letters or are otherwise addressed to particular problems or occasions; his letters nearly all begin with a sentence referring to the previous correspondence: "I received your kind Letter of the 2d inst., and am glad to hear that you increase in Strength," or "I received duly your letter of May 2, 1777, including a copy of one you had sent me the year before, which never came to hand," or "I received and read the Letter from my dear and much respected Friend with infinite Pleasure."[3] Instead Franklin begins abruptly by describing his fondness for family anecdotes. It is almost as if he is explaining to William why this piece should be particularly addressed to him. He reminds William of the visit they had paid together to the home parish of his English ancestors, evoking the memories of a shared genealogical jaunt. "Now imagining it may be equally agreeable to you to know the Circumstances of my Life, many of which you are yet unacquainted with," Franklin sits down to write (A, 43).

In the next few sentences, the apparent audience, his son, is turned into a kind of literary fiction. Franklin declares that he intends to provide something more than "little Anecdotes of my Ancestors"; the piece he is writing is to be a continuous narration with a moral, his rise to affluence and public reputation. It is his "Posterity," a term evocatively vague in the eighteenth century, that will profit from reading the story; William is a kind of stand-in for Posterity. Addressing oneself to a titular audience as an excuse for an air of greater intimacy has long been a literary device for the writer of epistles: Piso and Arbuthnot are not the primary recipients of the epistles from Horace and Pope. In light of Franklin's relations with his son, it is not surprising that William should serve as an authorial convenience. Franklin was in general highly alert to the distinct personalities of the people who received his letters. But the letters written to his son during the period of his colonial agency in England have a different quality. They are more self-absorbed, not so much concerned with convincing his son to see his position as simply assuming that his son shared his perspective. In those letters he appears to be talking to a detached part of himself.

The circumstances in which the *Autobiography* was begun—a casual holiday, an ostensible audience who would never read it—may suggest a project casually and unwittingly undertaken. How long would the work be? Who is its audience? Is it to be a collection of anecdotes or a connected narration? It is understandable that at the very beginning these problems should exist; Franklin was suddenly writing with no immediate purpose in mind, no measures to be enacted, no specific person to be informed or entertained. This was in some sense to be an imaginative work, an effort of selection and memory, the reconstruction of character. What could have readied Franklin to put his life together on paper?

Yet within the first two or three paragraphs the work's structure and intentions are made clear, and Franklin would remain with those intentions throughout the complicated and disrupted genesis of the text. In part the sense of sure control and rapid, easy narrative movement comes out of Franklin's experience as a writer; he had always had to write fast and well and gave himself credit for being "a tolerable English writer" (A, 62). But his skills of expression had always before been exercised in small writings—essays or letters of little more than a few pages. Here he was obliged to deal with much more subtle problems; personal anecdotes such as he often told might easily carry their own limited point, but to find a point to one's whole life would require a drastic subordination of materials to the demands of consistency. The *Autobiography*, particularly the first part, reads as if Franklin had been preparing to write it all his life. And in fact he had.

In the first few pages Franklin shows that he is aware of the reader's expectations about autobiography as those expectations had developed by his time. A number of significant autobiographies were available at the time he started writing, several of them published quite recently. The year before, Franklin's friend Horace Walpole had published the first public edition of the autobiography of Lord Herbert of Cherbury, one of the first full-dress autobiographies in English. In the same year that Franklin started writing, Benvenuto Cellini's autobiography was first published in English, translated by Thomas Nugent, the translator also of Montesquieu and Condillac. The coincidence of these two publishing events with Franklin's beginnings is interesting, if inconclusive. They would not have been the only examples of the genre Franklin would have known about, though. The first collection of books he ever bought as a young apprentice was John Bunyan's *Works*, in which he would have found *Grace Abounding to the Chief of Sinners*. As a printer, publisher, and bookseller he knew of the American tradition of spiritual autobiography; his neighbors the Quakers were especially prolific in recording their experiences of the inner light. In England, Colley Cibber's *Apology for the Life of Colley Cibber* (1740) was well known, partly because its author had been a celebrity, actor, and poet laureate, as well as a principal butt for satiric abuse from Pope and Fielding. Franklin had seen Cibber on stage in London in the 1720s and thought enough of the experience to note it in the outline for the *Autobiography*. The great autobiographies of the century were not yet available. Hume's brief "Story of My Life" was written in 1776, shortly before his death. Gibbon did not begin until 1789. Rousseau's *Confessions*, completed in 1765, did not appear until 1781.[4]

By 1771 a repertory of autobiographical motifs and expectations had developed. The act of self-revelation posed the author in a more unmediated relation to his reader than exists in other works, so various problems of tone had to be confronted directly; who is the reader assumed to be, and what is the character of his interest? It was customary for the autobiographer to offer some explanation for writing—if only to deal with the palpable vanity of devoting numerous sheets to the recording of his own life. The writer almost invariably devotes some time to discussing his own ancestry. The parallel rise of the novel induced autobiographers to use various kinds of novelistic tactics in the descriptions of their lives.[5] The autobiography led to a direct realization of Locke's distinction between sensation and reflection. The autobiographer was simultaneously the author who reflected and the character who experienced directly. An interplay necessarily exists between the sensing and the reflecting selves. Even more than in the novel, the autobiography celebrates a kind of incarnation, of personality manifesting itself in the world of action.

In autobiography one is called upon to reveal oneself as one really is. But to whom? The situation is not directly comparable to fiction or poetry, where tradition had guaranteed and defined a special status for the author. Nor is autobiography simply a branch of history or biography. The most influential of autobiographies in the past had taken God as the audience. Augustine made the sacrament of confession into the working metaphor for the depiction of his own life. When secular autobiography became a significant mode, in the eighteenth century, various other audiences had to be found who could listen with comparable sympathy and understanding. Colley Cibber addresses himself to his noble patron, Henry Pelham, so that his life can be insinuated as a presentation piece. Gibbon begins his autobiography by apologizing for his tone, a public voice now addressing private matters. "Truth—naked, unblushing truth, the first virtue of more serious history—must be the sole recommendation of this personal narrative. The style shall be simple and familiar. But style is the image of character, and the habits of correct writing may produce, without labor, or design, the appearance of art and study."[6] Franklin's object, which he shares with Cibber and Gibbon, is not to strip his soul bare but to present a clothed self-portrait. Franklin could not think of his son as the particular ear into which the details of his life were to be told, but neither could he tell his story to an indifferent hearer. As a purported audience, the son serves as a mediator between Franklin and his wider audience.[7]

Even more troublesome than tone and the definition of audience for the eighteenth-century writer of autobiography was the question of why he should be writing in the first place. What could be the value of this account to its designated audience, especially in relation to a conception of self that treated each person's experience as comprising a private system of significances? Herbert of Cherbury in the seventeenth century had voiced a traditional sort of justification for his account: to know the behavior of one's own biological ancestors is to understand one's own self better. "[A]nd certainly it will be found much better for men to guide themselves by such observations as their father, grandfather, and great grandfather might have delivered to them, than by those vulgar rules and examples, which cannot in all points exactly agree unto them."[8] But Franklin was not thus bound by a sense of family traits, and he had been a great giver of "vulgar rules and examples" already in his almanac. An autobiography might be written as self-justification, like Rousseau's *Confessions*, or conversely as an object lesson to others.[9] Functions secondary to self-revelation could be offered as justification for autobiography. Cibber's *Apology* is to serve as "an historical view of the stage in his own time"; Gibbon's autobiography will be a convenience to other historians, interested in the author of *The Decline and Fall*.

Franklin launches into a justification for the writing, and reading, of his work in the first paragraph. "Having emerg'd from the Poverty and Obscurity in which I was born and bred, to a State of Affluence and some Degree of Reputation in the World, and having gone so far thro' Life with a considerable Share of Felicity, the conducing Means I made use of, which, with the Blessing of God, so well succeeded, my Posterity may like to know, as they may find some of them suitable to their own Situations, and therefore fit to be imitated" (A, 43). This is a more public motive for writing than a mere penchant for family anecdotes. Franklin differs from his origins in two ways. His life had been a success story, going from private to public life, from obscurity to reputation. Franklin's readers have tended to see only the success story and to neglect the central importance for Franklin of personal reputation and fame. It was, after all, not Franklin's modest fortune itself which brought him his renown. He is sure of his affluence, but he speaks of "some Degree of Reputation in the World," which the qualifying expression suggests an unwillingness to assert.[10] It is not modesty that holds Franklin back, but rather, as he makes clear, a principle of self-restraint from certain kinds of ego assertion. And also, Franklin was not so prominent in 1771 as he would be ten years later. Vacationing with his friend the bishop, addressing himself to his son the governor, he could enjoy a sense of having emerged, but he was in England, where this confession of his humble origins which he was now writing could only confirm his status as an upstart tradesman in a society run by gentlemen. Franklin's reputation had not yet overcome that handicap.

Despite Franklin's claims to a settled perspective and a completed state, we look back and see this moment as no more than a temporary pause in a continuing process that would soon catapult him beyond the status of an aspiring country gentleman. Yet whatever psychological truth his perspective might have, or lack, it is a perspective perhaps necessary to his writing at all. Certainly writers of autobiography had felt some responsibility to show that the stories they told were in some way complete and unified, not just the unintelligible fragments of a continuing action. Augustine records a life culminating in conversion; John Bunyan, a life that prepared him to preach the divine word. Gibbon turns to his own story after his great history is finished, and the story of that life is also the story behind that history. Hume's autobiography is written as he prepares for death, when he has all his life at his disposal. In 1771 Franklin was still in the midst of major political projects. Yet he had achieved by then a capacity for detachment from his own life that allowed him to treat it as something complete and intact, like an artifact. "That Felicity [which he has enjoyed in his life], when I reflected on it, has enduc'd me sometimes to say, that were it offer'd to my Choice, I should have no Objection to a Repetition of the same Life from its Beginning, only asking the Advantage Authors have in a second Edition to correct some Faults of the first" (A, 43). Of course writing is much easier if one can believe that the book already exists intact before even being physically recorded.

The metaphor of life as a book becomes thereafter the controlling metaphor for the first section of the *Autobiography*. It would have been a metaphor natural to Franklin, a printer and bookseller by trade. What to another would be considered faults or sins are for Franklin *errata*, errors in the setting of type. His broken apprenticeship, his desertion of Deborah Read, his advocacy of irreligious opinions are all *errata*, and he specifies what efforts he took to correct them, as far as he could. According to the implications of the metaphor, Franklin is not so much the author of his own life as the agent by which that life is published, made public in the world. He had coined the metaphor long before, in about 1728, in a bagatelle circulated among his friends. It purports to be his epitaph:

> The Body of
> B. Franklin,
> Printer;
> Like the Cover of an old Book,
> Its Contents torn out,
> And stript of its Lettering and Gilding,
> Lies here, Food for Worms.
> But the Work shall not be wholly lost:
> For it will, as he believ'd, appear once more,
> In a new & more perfect Edition,
> Corrected and amended
> By the Author.

(P, 1: 111)

In the epitaph explicitly, the Author of his life is God—the most compelling possible authentication for his actions.

Vanity must necessarily seem the true motivation for secular autobiography, in the eyes of the author as well as of the reader. Out of his own quite self-conscious and idiosyncratic vanity, Benvenuto Cellini had asserted that it is "a duty incumbent on upright and credible men of all ranks, who have performed any thing noble or praiseworthy, to record, in their own writing the events of their lives."[11] In a later age the problem of vanity could not be thus brushed aside; the self-knowledge necessary for autobiography may well be at odds with the vanity which impels the autobiographer to write. Colley Cibber promises "as true a Picture of myself as natural Vanity will permit me to draw: For, to promise you that I shall never be vain, were a Promise that, like a Looking-glass too large, might break itself in the making: Nor am I sure I ought wholly to avoid that Imputation, because if Vanity be one of my natural Features, the Portrait wou'd not be like me without it."[12] Cibber's tactic is frank confession—perhaps necessarily, since his vanity was, by the time he wrote, a national joke.

Franklin makes a similar admission, after saying that he is indulging in an old man's natural inclination to talk about himself.

> And lastly, (I may as well confess it, since my Denial of it will be believ'd by no body) perhaps I shall a good deal gratify my own *Vanity*. Indeed I scarce ever heard or saw the introductory Words, *Without Vanity* I may say, &c. but some vain thing immediately follow'd. Most People dislike Vanity in others whatever Share they have of it themselves, but I give it fair Quarter wherever I meet with it, being persuaded that it is often productive of Good to the Possessor and to others that are within his Sphere of Action: And therefore in many Cases it would not be quite absurd if a Man were to thank God for his Vanity among the other Comforts of Life. (A, 44)

Here at the beginning Franklin establishes the mixed perspectives and elusive tone of the work as a whole. It is obviously a mixture of seriousness and self-mockery, yet the mixture itself is so integrated that the two seem to serve as complementary sides of a fuller intention. Vanity is not just a motive for the *Autobiography*; it is a principal subject. Cibber had been willing to display his own vanity, just as an actor who has always played a certain kind of role is happy to play it again. Franklin is never vain in Cibber's obvious, trivial way. He carefully frames his own accomplishments with qualifications. When he was only fifteen his series of periodical letters was published in the *New-England Courant*, but he notes that his judges were perhaps not so good as he thought they were. He describes himself as an inept poet, inferior to his friend James Ralph. The vanity he confesses to is not a mere personality defect but a principle of action.

Franklin adopts his usage of the term *vanity* not from social convention but from the Bible as interpreted by the Puritans. Vanity or pride for them meant the love of self; it is the human condition. Humility is its opposite, the last of Franklin's list of virtues and the only one which he added to the list at the urging of another. A Quaker friend "kindly inform'd me that I was generally thought proud; that my Pride show'd itself frequently in Conversation; that I was not content with being in the right when discussing any Point, but was overbearing and rather insolent; of which he convinc'd me by mentioning several Instances" (A, 158–59). Franklin admits that he never achieves humility, just as his Puritan forebears might have predicted. "In reality there is perhaps no one of our natural Passions so hard to subdue as *Pride*. Disguise it, struggle with it, beat it down, stifle it, mortify it as much as one pleases, it is still alive, and will every now and then peep out and show itself. You will see it perhaps often in this History. For even if I could conceive that I had completely overcome it, I should probably by [be] proud of my Humility" (A, 160). The note of comic resignation in this passage suggests how far Franklin is in spirit from his Quaker friend or from his Puritan upbringing. Though the Puritan conception of vanity survives, the attitude is reversed. Self-love is not only natural but desirable and necessary to the public good. What Franklin forecasts in the mock encomium to vanity at the beginning of the *Autobiography* is his eventual depiction of an American society based on the Enlightenment ideal of mutually compatible self-interest.

But Franklin makes no frontal attack on the piety of his ancestors. In the next paragraph he expresses his thanks to Providence for the happiness of his life, and he hopes, "tho' I must not *presume*," that the same happiness will be continued. He knows however that his future is known "to him only: and in whose Power it is to bless to us even our Afflictions" (A, 45). Franklin was not indulging in the rhetoric of the Puritans merely as a platitude. In a sense, the security of his identity as an independent self made that older rhetoric comfortable and unproblematic. It was a kind of half-forgotten first language to him, one still necessary for the most profoundly felt assertions. Franklin's sense of his own personal history demanded that he should not reject but rather go beyond the faith of his fathers. Still, the reader is inclined to pass quickly by a paragraph full of such conventional pieties, however genuinely offered. Providence is a kind of absent guest of honor in the Enlightenment. Flattering things are said, but the guest is unavailable either to act in his own right or to acknowledge the compliments.

Directly following the paragraphs of introduction and self-justification is Franklin's description of his own ancestry, traced back to the reign of Queen Mary. Franklin indulges in these pages in his fondness for family anecdotes, relying both on notes provided him by his Uncle Benjamin and on his own research into parish records. Ancestors filled a particular function in Enlightenment autobiography. They could not dominate the action, yet they had existed, and the established biographical tradition demanded some treatment of them. So they become prefigurations of the autobiographer's personality and accomplishments—not the cause or source, but an early anticipation. "We seem to have lived in the persons of our forefathers," writes Gibbon; "it is the labor and reward of vanity to extend the term of this ideal longevity."[13] Gibbon's description well matches Franklin's use for his ancestors. We read that he is the youngest son of the youngest son for five generations—underlining Franklin's awareness of what it means to be a youngest son. He suggests, erroneously but revealingly, that the name Franklin implies that in the Middle Ages his ancestors were freemen, members of a sort of sub-gentry class. His Uncle Thomas was a smith by profession but rose through his learning to become "a considerable Man in the Country Affairs . . . a chief Mover of all publick Spirited Undertakings, for the Country, or Town of Northampton and his own Village" (A, 47). Like the raw materials of his own life, his forefathers are deployed according to his own design.

For the first several manuscript pages Franklin wrote without any definite outline. In those pages he records various traditional family anecdotes, a few stories about his early childhood, and a characterization of his father. (Of his mother, he writes only that she had an excellent constitution and suckled all her ten children.) The experiences he preserves in the childhood passage are not all relevant to the predicated direction of the book. There is his Uncle Benjamin, who lived with the family, collected pamphlets, took down sermons in shorthand, and wrote bad poetry, which Franklin illustrates by quoting. His schooling took several erratic turns, as his father changed his mind about the son's career. As a child young Benjamin longed to run off to sea, an understandable impulse for a boy growing up in a seaport town but hardly conducive to affluence and reputation. Even the incident in which Franklin describes leading a band of other boys in building a wharf of stones stolen from a construction site is only by a strained reading an instance of "an early projecting public Spirit" (A, 54). The events in this passage are not in chronological sequence, necessarily, since the events of childhood will tend to fall into patterns of their own in the memory. But Franklin was not wholly satisfied with his narration. "By my rambling Digressions I perceive my self to be grown old," he writes. "I us'd to write more methodically. But one does not dress for private Company as for a publick Ball. 'Tis perhaps only Negligence" (A, 56–57). This remark is addressed to himself; even at this point he seems to have some remaining question about whether this is to be a private or a public work.

To counteract what he feared was a tendency to ramble, Franklin drew up an outline. The "Notes" then served as an abstract for the rest of his narrative. They consist of brief phrases which refer to experiences, writings, people met, characterizations to be drawn, and lessons to be deduced. The "Notes" underline nothing. They suggest a continuous narration, without any events that alter the character of Franklin's life, dividing it into distinct parts. But certain experiences, such as the journey from Boston to Philadelphia, are given greater concentration of details in the "Notes." In several instances events are grouped together in conjunction with a moral lesson.

> Marry. Library erected. Manner of conducting the Project. Its plan and Utility. Children. Almanack. the Use I made of it. Great Industry. Constant Study. Fathers Remark and Advice upon Diligence.... (A, 269)

Franklin followed the outline fairly closely, which suggests that his sense of the values and emphases on his life remained steady through the perhaps nineteen years during which he intermittently worked on it.

The first item listed in the "Notes" is "My Writing." It is a revealing beginning. In the text he describes in considerable detail how he learned to write. At first he wrote a sort of poetry, ballad narratives about public occurrences. Then he found an odd volume of Addison's *Spectator* and proceeded to imitate its style through a careful process of exercises in which he competed with his model. The process of learning to write culminated in the publication of a series of periodical essays that he submitted secretly to his brother's newspaper. Writing was basic to Franklin's sense of his own identity, as the metaphor of the book-in-life suggests. Learning to write was, in a sense, his real birth, the necessary first item in his "Notes," the beginning of the possibility of recording himself on paper.

Along with this account of his writing career, Franklin records in some detail the books he read as a youth. He describes himself as a "Bookish Lad," and indeed books seem to have created his real intellectual context. Never in the *Autobiography* does he attribute any of his ideas to contact with a particular person whom he knows. He learns lessons of character but not ways of thinking. His taste for argumentation he attributes to the Puritan sermons and tracts in his father's library. He buys as his first set of books the complete works of John Bunyan, and he attributes to Bunyan his sense of narrative and dialogue. From Cotton Mather's *Bonifacius* (or *Essays to do Good*) and Defoe's *Essay on Projects* he learns the concept and tactics of mobilized benevolence. After reading Xenophon's *Memorabilia*, he decides to suppress his tendency toward argumentation in favor of the Socratic method. "I was charm'd with it, adopted it, dropt my abrupt Contradiction and positive Argumentation, and put on the humble Enquirer and Doubter" (*A*, 64). Ideas, modes of belief, and rhetorical stances are for Franklin poses that can be tried out, attire for a self which has no required dress. And, like his contemporary Jonathan Edwards, he remembers reading Locke's *Essay Concerning Human Understanding*. Just as Franklin saw a special importance in writing and the learning of writing, he remembered books, not people, as his real teachers.

His precocious writing talents and his independent disposition led him into conflicts with his brother James, who was also his master. The printer and his apprentice brother had trouble first about their eating arrangements; Benjamin had decided, from a book he had read, to become a vegetarian and refused to eat the food served to him.[14] He had become an important writer for his brother's newspaper, and when James got in trouble with the authorities, Benjamin was nominally promoted to the title of publisher. It became impossible to treat the younger brother as an apprentice. Disputes between the two were arbitrated by their father, where Benjamin's adeptness at persuasion often gave him the upper hand. In frustration James would sometimes hit his apprentice brother. Eventually Benjamin broke with his brother, left the print shop, and took off for Philadelphia. In the *Autobiography* he seems to be trying to be fair about this fifty-year-old quarrel. His breaking of the apprenticeship bonds with his brother he counts among his *errata*. "But the Unfairness of it weigh'd little with me, when under the Impressions of Resentment, for the Blows his Passion too often urg'd him to bestow upon me. Tho' he was otherwise not an ill-natur'd Man: Perhaps I was too saucy and provoking" (*A*, 70). "But," "Tho'," "Perhaps"—Franklin's connectives reveal a still mixed and unsettled attitude toward the episode. By suggesting that he was too saucy and provoking, he can assert a sort of control over the experience, since candor implies a settled self-knowledge, but the unresolved note at the end of this paragraph points to the limits of such control and self-knowledge. In a footnote to the episode Franklin draws a lesson of experience: "I fancy his harsh and tyrannical Treatment of me, might be a means of impressing me with that Aversion to arbitrary Power that has stuck to me thro' my whole Life" (A, 69). James Franklin thus prefigures the royal governors, Proprietaries, and British ministers whom Franklin was to confront later. If so, the younger brother's uncertainty about whether he, too, was not at fault forecasts an attitude of greater ambiguity toward arbitrary power than he explicitly admits. But the *Autobiography* was not written to explore such ambiguities.

In the "Notes" a fair amount of space is reserved for his confrontation with his brother, but in the draft itself Franklin treats the episode quite succinctly. Unlisted in the "Notes" but given considerable emphasis in the draft are various extended comments about the dangers of excessive assertiveness and love of disputation. Lessons take precedence over events in Franklin's recollections. It is useful for his Posterity to learn the value of cautious and judicious expressions in place of expressions that insist or demand. It is less useful to bring up old quarrels that have no clear instruction in them.

In the description of his childhood Franklin avoids appearing unusual or specially gifted. His early poetry was only hack work; his prose was applauded by judges he concludes to have been undiscriminating. It may seem to require some effort to downplay his own early prominence: a published prose writer at sixteen, the publisher at seventeen of a newspaper in which he could attack the colonial government. Yet Franklin does not indulge in similitudes; he characteristically avoids describing himself as either like or unlike the people around him. He also avoids describing surroundings or circumstances that might be seen as impinging upon him, defining or limiting him in some way. There is no characterization of Boston in the 1720s, or of the interaction in his large family. One thing he learned from his father, he says, was an indifference to the food he ate, a readiness to eat whatever was there. With such frame of mind he could readily leave the table, his family, Boston, and his father's Puritan beliefs without a sense of something lost or left behind. Still, he rejected nothing of his experience.

The *Autobiography* is a continuous narration, without any breaks for chapters or headings. Naturally Franklin's usual kinds of writings were too short to require division or subordination of parts, but the continuous character of his account, projected also by the "Notes," reflects his unwillingness to admit of breaks in the continuity and consistency of his life. It had not broken down into discrete chapters, with scenes that constitute smaller dramas within the larger movement of the life. He had been thinking about his life recently, in the July letter to his sister and in the August visit to the Shipley family. Despite the disparity between his past and his present, the gaps and disruptions in his experience, he chose to affirm the continuity and wholeness of his life. His Uncle Benjamin's pamphlets, the family recipe for crown soap that he asked Jane Mecom for, the charming Shipley girls who were growing up in the world—all of this was in the background as he began to write.

3 The Self-Made Man in the Enlightenment

U nable to find other employment as a printer and conscious of hostility toward him in Boston, Franklin arranges passage by boat to New York, and from there to Philadelphia. This is the decisive episode in the *Autobiography*. No incident is given so much close attention, and probably none is better remembered by his readers. The puffy rolls Franklin carried under his arms and ate as he first walked the streets of Philadelphia have become symbolic accoutrements of his, like his kite. It was a story Franklin told his friends from time to time, and one such account got into print in a London newspaper in 1778; at one point, Franklin even tried to calculate the actual date of his arrival. The interest of the story extends beyond the bounds of Franklin's own experiences, as he himself realized. Franklin was not alone in setting out to establish a new identity elsewhere; the scene he described was enacted repeatedly in life and in fiction during the eighteenth century. That desperate and exhilarating break with the past served to authenticate a mode of selfhood that was especially valued by the Enlightenment.[1]

The narration of his journey is dense with detail. He describes his harrowing voyage from New York to Perth Amboy, the difficulties he had while on foot from Amboy to Burlington, and the amusing company of Dr. Brown, the ingenious unbeliever. When he arrives in Philadelphia, he reports his first wanderings in the town so particularly that the reader could retrace every step. We know how he was dressed and how much money he had. All this detail is assembled in service of his thematic point; the one usable episode along his way that serves a different theme is deliberately withheld, put in parentheses in his "Notes," and included later at an appropriate point. The concentration of details in the passage is deliberate. "I have been the more particular in this Description of my Journey, and shall be so of my first Entry into that City, that you may in your Mind compare such unlikely Beginnings with the Figure I have since made there" (A, 75).

Why should this episode have been crucial for him? Other experiences from adolescence might have formed or defined him as readily—the break with his brother and father, for example. Or he might have denied to any experience the special attention he gives to this one; certainly his general instinct was to include materials without overt subordination, so that many small episodes, such as those in London, can characterize him as observer. Other adolescent experiences afford him that contrast between past and present that he seeks—his status in London as a duped provincial in the 1720s, as compared with his current standing there, for example. One might easily have seen the trip from Boston to Philadelphia as merely the description of a young journeyman traveling to seek another job which he could be reasonably sure of finding. Trained journeyman printers were not easy to find, as one can see later on from Franklin's description of the motley assortment of workers in Keimer's print shop. But all the events of his journey reported in such detail—the lack of any work for him in New York, his fever at Amboy, the confusion in the night about whether his boat had passed Philadelphia—belie any such reasonable probabilities. The story combines rupture with continuity, separation from his own family with the continual presence of other people. Something about the experience confirmed his later perception of what he was, a person capable of leaving to seek his fortune elsewhere, able to live by his wits and to rely on what he knew and had read, a close observer of everything that happened.

Franklin is in fact deliberately novelistic in his attention to detail through this episode in order to impress the reader with the heightened state of consciousness with which he made the journey. His self-consciousness as a narrator is revealed in particular by one incident along the way. Sailing from New York in a small boat, Franklin rescues a passenger who has fallen into New York harbor in squally weather. The passenger is a drunken Dutchman who asks Franklin to dry out a book he had in his pocket. The book proves to be a translation of *Pilgrim's Progress*; Franklin the young printer particularly admires the edition. Franklin the narrator then notes the importance of Bunyan as a literary innovator. "Honest John was the first that I know of who mix'd Narration and Dialogue, a Method of Writing very engaging to the Reader, who in the most interesting Parts finds himself as it were brought into the Company, and present at the Discourse. Defoe in his Crusoe, his Moll Flanders, Religious Courtship, Family Instructor, and other Pieces, has imitated it with Success. And Richardson has done the same in his Pamela, &c" (A, 72).

By the mixture of narration and dialogue Franklin seems to mean something different from the mere incorporation of conversations in the midst of narrated action. Conversations appear in the course of narrated action long before Bunyan; the Bible, after all, is full of this mixture of narration and dialogue. Franklin is referring to something closer to a narrative voice representing a distinctly identifiable personality which is addressing the reader. It is this mixture of narration and dialogue, one of the distinguishing features of the novel, that Franklin had observed in Bunyan, Defoe, and Richardson. Franklin was aware of the development of the novel; he published Pamela in 1744, only shortly after its first English edition, the first edition published in America. Here in this passage he hints at how he himself is employing the narrative technique of the novel. He is bringing the reader into his company so the reader will compare his unlikely beginnings in Philadelphia with the figure he has made there since.

Franklin is in two places at once throughout the first section of the Autobiography because he is both teller and actor. Correspondingly, the readers are in both places as well, "brought into the Company, and present at the Discourse" as they accompany the actor and the teller. These two perspectives, which establish a tension between two distinct persons, give structure to the first section of the Autobiography. Franklin the narrator has universal knowledge, while Franklin the character has only limited knowledge. The narrator looks back at the success of his first Dogood paper among the wits of the New-England Courant. "I suppose now that I was rather lucky in my Judges: And that perhaps they were not really so very good ones as I then esteem'd them" (A, 68). The break with his brother is weighed according to both perspectives. He now reckons it one of his first errata, yet the resentment he then felt at his brother's blows overcame any sense of his own unfairness. Once he is on his own in Philadelphia, Franklin the character begins having numerous experiences that Franklin the narrator must reinterpret. The resulting dialectic reveals the psychological complexities of Franklin's situation. The reasonings of the character are given a fair chance to be heard. Franklin the character explains why he was taken in by the empty promises of Governor Keith, who sent Franklin to England on the pretext of buying the equipment for a print shop. "Had it been known that I depended on the Governor, probably some Friend that knew him better would have advis'd me not to rely on him, as I afterwards heard it as his known Character to be liberal of Promises which he never meant to keep. Yet unsolicited as he was by me, how could I think his generous Offers insincere? I believ'd him one of the best Men in the World" (A, 86–87).

What distinguishes the two Franklins in the first section is their relative knowledge. Old Franklin the narrator really understands the direction and significance of the life he has led and is still leading; young Franklin can anticipate that final significance, but his view is undeveloped. Unlike John Stuart Mill or Henry Adams, Franklin is not reporting merely whatever momentary stage of understanding or confusion he has achieved at the time of his writing. The perspective from which Franklin writes is one of professed total self-knowledge. And once the perspectives of character and narrator converge, even the world itself becomes knowable in the same way as the self has first been known.

The doubleness of perspective subordinates the actions of the character Franklin to the mature perceptions of the author Franklin. Young Franklin walks up Market Street eating his puffy roll, and his future wife "thought I made as I certainly did a most awkward ridiculous Appearance" (A, 76). His later evaluation—"as I certainly did"—is necessary to authenticate the evaluations of the time. Old Franklin is something of a bemused and affectionate onlooker at his younger incarnation, though even the young Franklin described in the *Autobiography* tended to be an onlooker at himself as he made his way in the world. He admires the handsome Dutch edition of *Pilgrim's Progress*; he stands by and watches old William Bradford pump Samuel Keimer about his business strategies. Franklin's pose as the dispassionate observer prompted Carl Becker, his most perceptive biographer, to see that response as his basic way of dealing with the world. "In all of Franklin's dealing with men and affairs, genuine, sincere, loyal as he surely was, one feels that he is nevertheless not wholly committed; some thought remains uncommunicated; some penetrating observation is held in reserve. In spite of his ready attention to the business at hand, there is something casual about his efficient dispatch of it; he manages somehow to remain aloof, a spectator still, with amiable curiosity watching himself functioning effectively in the world."[2] Becker's formulation is elegant and seductive. Certainly Franklin wished to be seen in those terms and contrived his self-portrait to make himself appear as a spectator, aloof and curious but never fully involved.

He was not alone in his attachment to that role. His contemporaries in the Enlightenment found new possibilities in the role of the detached and observing spectator, a figure who is aloof but not alienated and who is outside the emotional bonds of the community. The spectator was Addison's *persona* in his influential periodical essays; Franklin, who consciously modeled his writing style on the *Spectator*, would have learned there how one might be an outsider even while living in society. The spectator's pose of ironic but interested detachment became so attractive in the eighteenth century because individual selves now looked separable from society, no longer necessarily a part of it as a tissue is part of an organism. The spectator enjoyed a heightened consciousness; he was able to see society for what it is. Thus, in 1721 Montesquieu could invent in *The Persian Letters* a group of Persian travelers whose foreignness enabled them to see Regency France in a revealing and unexpected light. Or Voltaire, himself a traveler and exile, could delineate English culture in his *Philosophical Letters*. These literary observers were not lost or disoriented or endangered or lonely, as newly arrived observers frequently are; their spectator status has somehow given them access to a superior vantage point, whether that be called the state of nature or the disinterested search for truth or a fund of ironic wit. Ultimately one might even become so much of a spectator as to detach oneself from the vicissitudes of one's own feelings. Along the way from Boston to Philadelphia, in circumstances that might have brought discouragement or confusion, Franklin reports only the details of what he sees.

But he did not travel all that way to observe. He was looking for work. Cash on hand, the cost of things, and the possibilities for employment or business are always carefully noted. He sold some of his books in Boston to pay for his passage to New York; to the boatsmen who rowed with him into Philadelphia he gave a shilling; leaving himself only a Dutch dollar. There had been no work for him in New York, and there would be delays before he could work steadily in Philadelphia; he mentions his former desire to go to sea, a boyish *wanderlust*, as a kind of work that he now rejected in favor of his acquired competence as a journeyman printer. Money and food are closely related to each other, particularly in this account. He notes where he ate and the food eaten: a bottle of filthy rum on the thirty-hour boat trip to Amboy, gingerbread in Burlington and later a dinner of oxcheek, paid for by a pot of ale, the puffy rolls in Philadelphia and the next day a breakfast provided by Andrew Bradford the printer.

As he walked along the Philadelphia streets, he noticed numerous signs indicating that buildings were for sale, "which made me then think the Inhabitants of the City were one after another deserting it" (A, 124). The problem, he decided later, was actually a business slump created by a shortage of currency; an issue of paper currency the following year revived the local economy. Money for Franklin was not a fixed measure of wealth or well-being, but instead something to be manipulated for personal or the public interest. It was potentially under Franklin's control, as were its equivalents. "Remember that TIME is money," he writes in 1748 in his "Advice to a Young Tradesman" (P, 3: 306). Like money, time could be brought under control and put to human use. Franklin shows no diffidence in his treatment of money in the *Autobiography*. When he returns to Boston from Philadelphia and shows up in his brother's print shop, he spreads out five pounds sterling for his brother's journeymen, "which was a kind of Raree-Show they had not been us'd to, Paper being the Money of Boston" (A, 82). He describes the details of his financial transactions and partnerships. When he describes his marriage, he says that his wife "assisted me much by attending the Shop, we throve together, and have ever mutually endeavour'd to make each other happy" (A, 129). In London he describes in detail the circumstances of an old Roman Catholic lady, a fellow lodger of his, who lived a life of great self-abnegation. She is for him "another Instance on how small an Income Life and Health may be supported" (A, 103). Franklin's reaction to his marriage and to the old Catholic lady may seem callous unless one recognizes the expanded sense he has of money and commerce. Money, he wrote in the 1748 essay, "is of the prolific, generating nature." It can expand in quantity in ways almost mystical; he compares it to a breeding sow, fertile with generations of offspring.

Franklin's contemporaries did not find such a fascination with commerce demeaning. When the eighteenth century sought for images to describe society, it talked about the marketplace. The State of Nature itself, Locke asserted, was essentially a marketplace, where men assembled voluntarily to barter their goods and their labor. "To understand Political Power right, and derive it from its Original, we must consider what State all Men are naturally in, and that is, a *State of perfect Freedom* to order their Actions, and dispose of their Possessions, and Persons as they think fit, within the bounds of the Law of Nature, with out asking leave, or depending upon the Will of any other Man."[3] For Adam Smith, man is distinguishable from the animals by his "propensity to truck, barter, and exchange one thing for another."[4] Man enters into relationships with other men not out of some herd instinct, nor for the sake of self-protection alone, nor out of some inner principle of controlled aggression. All these possibilities would suggest that a limitation on independence was built into the nature of society. Rather man deals with other people because he voluntarily chooses to, for certain specifiable returns. For Locke and the Enlightenment, social instinct could be reduced ultimately to the economic instinct, the propensity to truck and barter.

Nor was this a dismal perception. The marketplace was peaceable and free of ideology. Out of its wonderful operations seemed to come great increases in the wealth of individuals and communities. "Commerce is a cure for the most destructive prejudices," Montesquieu writes in *The Spirit of the Laws*, "for it is almost a general rule, that wherever we find agreeable manners, there commerce flourishes; and that wherever there is commerce, there we meet with agreeable manners."[5] The market somehow reconciles the individual welfare and the collective welfare. "The riches of the several members of a community contribute to encrease my riches, whatever profession I may follow," writes Hume.[6] Addison's Mr. Spectator found a patriotic thrill in contemplating the market. "There is no Place in the Town which I so much love to frequent as the *Royal Exchange*. It gives me a secret Satisfaction, and, in some measure, gratifies my Vanity, as I am an *Englishman*, to see so rich an Assembly of Country-men and Foreigners consulting together upon the private Business of Mankind, and making this Metropolis a kind of *Emporium* for the whole Earth."[7] To be a merchant, dealing with this welter of differing people, is to have the sensation of being a citizen of the world. Addison gets uncharacteristically emotional at this scene, his heart overflowing with pleasure at the sight of the prosperous and happy multitude. "Go into the Exchange in London," writes Voltaire, "that place more venerable than many a court, and you will see representatives of all the nations assembled there for the profit of mankind. There the Jew, the Mahometan, and the Christian deal with one another as if they were of the same religion, and reserve the name of infidel for those who go bankrupt."[8] In George Lillo's bourgeois tragedy *The London Merchant*, Thorowgood the merchant descants to his attentive employee Trueman on the principles of trade:

> Methinks I would not have you only learn the method of merchandise and practice it hereafter, merely as a means of getting wealth; 'twill be well worth your pains to study it as a science, to see how it is founded in reason and the nature of things; how it promotes humanity, as it has opened and yet keeps up an intercourse between nations far remote from one another in situation, customs and religion; promoting arts, industry, peace and plenty; by mutual benefits diffusing mutual love from pole to pole.[9]

The traditional criticisms of avarice and of the sordidness of trade were muted in the eighteenth century as never before or since. Trucking and bartering were not merely inevitable but laudable.[10]

Franklin thought of himself as a trucker and barterer on his way from one market to another, from Boston to Philadelphia, except for those moments of discouragement trudging on foot through a cold rain across New Jersey. To others along his route, however, he looked like a runaway indentured servant; twice he mentions suspicious looks and questions asked of him, to the point where he felt in danger of being apprehended. And indeed he was running away; he left Boston on the sly with some fear that his brother or his family might take measures to stop him. The desperateness of his situation along the way is given its due, yet that desperateness was somehow consistent with his status as an economic man. He was an *adventurer* in the older sense—one who invests at risk, hoping for great returns.

Franklin's sudden departure for a new city was part of a noticeable pattern in the eighteenth century, both in life and in fiction. Samuel Johnson gave up schoolteaching in disgust and rode to London with the young David Garrick, taking turns riding a single horse. Young Rousseau broke his apprenticeship and set off through Savoy, where he would eventually be taken in by Mme. de Warens. Tom Jones leaves the Allworthy estate in search of his fortune and his identity. The possibility of self-discovery attends these drastic departures; for Franklin it was the beginning of being on his own, the first contact with his real city Philadelphia, his first acquaintance with his future wife. It was not a rebirth or spiritual awakening in the Puritan sense: the new identity did not come through a renunciation of his past life, and it was achieved by his own efforts alone. When he arrived in Philadelphia, he joined a crowd of people going to Quaker meeting, and there he fell asleep until the meeting broke up. What was awakening in him was not an awareness of the Spirit but a consciousness of himself as a separate, independent being.

Franklin's delighted narcissism was widely shared in his time. The *philosophes* of the Enlightenment took a special interest in describing the imagined state of consciousness whereby a person first discovers his own existence and the existence of the physical universe. Whether as child or as Adam, the first man, such a being goes about recreating the world through the operations of his senses. In his *Histoire Naturelle* the naturalist Buffon proposed to examine "a man in the same situation with him who first received existence; a man whose organs were perfectly formed, but who was equally new to himself and to every external object which surrounded him." To evoke this situation Buffon offered a discourse of several pages, in the midst of the multi-volume scientific treatise, in which this imagined first man describes his sensations:

> I remember the moment when my existence commenced: it was a moment replete with joy, amazement, and anxiety. I neither knew what I was, where I was, nor from whence I came. I opened my eyes; what an increase of sensation! The light, the celestial vault, the verdure of the earth, the transparency of the waters, gave animation to my spirits, and conveyed pleasures, which exceeded the powers of expression.[11]

Gradually the new being discovers the use of his senses and the existence of external objects; reason, it is clear, accompanies and orders each step in perception. Similarly, Condillac in his *Traité des Sensations* imagines a statue which is in sequence endowed with each of the five senses. Simply from the knowledge provided by the five senses and the impulse to satisfy hunger and curiosity, solitary man can, according to Condillac, achieve the condition of a rational being. Condillac's enlivened statue "has, then, by the help of the senses alone cognitions of every kind."[12] In all these examples, to derive all learning from collected sense impressions involved descriptions which leave out that learning which is inspired by society.[13]

The process of self-recognition, expressed sometimes as if it were a process of self-creation, had a necessary complement, an inevitable sequel. This independent and self-conscious being then chooses voluntarily to associate himself to a society. This decision was not simply an event in pre-history. The *philosophes* tended to speak of it as a decision made as part of one's earliest experiences of the world. In the *Preliminary Discourse* to the *Encyclopedia*, d'Alembert describes the sequence of experiences of one whose senses have just opened to the world. "The fact of our existence is the first thing taught us by our sensations and, indeed, is inseparable from them." We next discover external objects, and conclude them to be real. Among those objects are beings like ourselves, perceiving the world as we do and sharing our needs. "Whence we conclude that we should find it advantageous to join with them in finding out what can be beneficial to us and what can be detrimental to us in Nature."[14] Thus every infant acts out the first event in universal history. The motive for joining society is to better satisfy human needs. One joins society as a deliberate economic transaction.

Franklin's awareness of the favored modes of selfhood in the Enlightenment served almost as a collaborator with his recollections in the depiction of his life. As it happened, he had made those character traits his own, partly because he was generally disposed to conform his appearance to the expectations of others and partly because those traits served him well. On the trip to Philadelphia and later in that city he was a spectator, interested but not wholly engaged. He was following his own healthy self-interest, trucking and bartering. He had broken away from a constricting personal past. That these features should carry a large cultural significance in the eighteenth century is not incidental to the emphasis they receive in the *Autobiography*.

But the rhetoric of the *Autobiography* is subtle. The book is not set up to be a self-portrait of the ultimate man of the Enlightenment, the fulfillment of his age's highest expectations. Franklin was too shrewd to deck himself out even in flattering ways as a cultural stereotype: the *errata* and the mischances of his life are part of the picture too, and they make him recognizable as part of the blundering, ill-starred human condition, of all places and times. One must allow a few faults in order to keep one's friends in countenance, Franklin says.

A certain ingenuousness colors his recollections, particularly in the first part, and screens him from concerns about the large historical context. Naturally the young Franklin was ingenuous, trusting, a little out of it, but the old Franklin who writes seems to participate in some of young Franklin's illusions, even as he suggests their shortcomings. The pleasures of playing the role of the humble inquirer and doubter, however much it may appear a nifty adolescent pose, are still present for him. The spectator role, as it was played in the Enlightenment, often entailed ingenuousness: the Persian observers of Montesquieu are naive but perceptive, as is Voltaire's Huron Indian who is appropriately called *Ingenu* in the philosophical tale of the same name. Franklin was perhaps prudent not to avail himself of too sharp a sense of the large world, since his aim was to cut the world down to his own size. Continual small improvements, "little Advantages that occur every Day" (A, 207), will have an eventual grand effect, he believes. When he thinks in the *Autobiography* of large historical patterns, he is determined to avoid those inevitabilities; to counteract the spirit of party interest, he proposes a United Party of Virtue (though he himself is too preoccupied with his own business to get tied up in the organization of such a party).

Other writers of autobiography have been overtly aware of the character of their times as they wrote—Gibbon, Wordsworth, and Henry Adams, for example. For Franklin the age is almost entirely excluded from consideration. He was not disposed in the *Autobiography* to treat the eighteenth century as a distinctive period, burdened with its own limitations and proclivities. He was conscious all along of addressing posterity; he would be read not by his contemporaries but by the unforeseeable future. So he was unwilling to suggest that there have been large differences from one historical period to another, for fear of being trapped in a period himself.

Nowhere in the *Autobiography* does Franklin appear to be a mystery to himself. Others are self-deceived or unaware of their real interest, like his friend James Ralph, who fancied himself a poet, or the Quakers, who could not square the need for colonial defenses with their doctrinal prohibitions. Franklin is only deceived by others, never by himself. He seems always to have figured out something that his neighbors fail to understand: he discovers that all his disputatious acquaintances can be stymied by the pose of Socratic questioning; both in Boston and in London he follows a special abstemious diet that enables him to work better in the afternoon. This pose as the discoverer of the simple truth was a special favorite in the Enlightenment. Voltaire's ultimate compliment about Locke in the *Philosophical Letters* is paid not to Locke's complexity of mind but to the simplicity of his vision. "After so many deep thinkers had fashioned the romance of the soul, there came a wise man who modestly recounted its true history."[15] What Voltaire attributes to Locke, what Franklin claims for himself, is nothing less than total understanding of the self's inner workings. If Franklin has not been capable of exercising perfect control over his own behavior, he at least feels he has an adequate grasp of his intentions and his self-interest.

It was perhaps in this belief that Franklin represented most perfectly the aspiration of his time. Certainly his contemporaries applauded him for his self-mastery. The letters from Abel James and Benjamin Vaughan inserted in the text of the *Autobiography* describe him as a model of virtuous conduct. Jefferson, in a letter to his grandson, offers Franklin as a perfect model of sociability. The duc de La Rochefoucauld, who had read the manuscript of the *Autobiography*, in a eulogy to Franklin in 1790, said, "He speaks of himself as if he were speaking of another person." Such total detachment was a sort of ideal.[16]

These claims to self-mastery are worth examining more extensively as a way of understanding the background of Franklin's self-portrait. Just as Franklin felt he understood himself better than his associates understood themselves, the Enlightenment claimed to have made a breakthrough in the ancient effort to know ourselves. A useful distinction among modes of self-consciousness has been formulated by Georges Gusdorf, who distinguishes between *conscience de soi* and *connaissance de soi.* The two might be translated as self-awareness and self-knowledge. Self-awareness takes place in a special moment of perception: Montaigne notes his passing reflections over the course of his unpredictable life; Hamlet soliloquizes over the significance of an instant in the dramatic action. It involves no extended recognition of one's relation to others or to one's own past. Because self-awareness must be momentary and fleeting, it is akin to a religious experience; indeed, religious experiences often present themselves as moments of self-awareness. By contrast, self-knowledge, as it appears in the eighteenth century, implies both a self greatly more knowable and also a more sustained period of knowing. Franklin's nature or fate is never suddenly revealed to him; his personality is known continuously over the uninterrupted course of his life. No moment of transcendent insight is ever called upon to clarify what has always been out in the open.[17]

The two modes of self-consciousness differ importantly in the way they assess the differences that can be observed in the self over time. Personality as revealed by self-awareness is continually changing, but it could not be said to be developing and evolving in a series of stages. When Montaigne wrote of his own self-perceptions he reported no continuity. "I do not portray being," he declared, "I portray passing. Not the passing from one age to another, or, as the people say, from seven years to seven years, but from day to day, from minute to minute. My history needs to be adapted to the moment. I may presently change, not only by chance, but also by intention. This is a record of various and changeable occurrences, and of irresolute and, when it so befalls, contradictory ideas: whether I am different myself, or whether I take hold of my subjects in different circumstances and aspects."[18] The changes revealed no pattern.

Self-awareness readily accompanied an older theory of personality formation, according to which character is understandable in terms of certain ideal modes of behavior. In the Middle Ages and the Renaissance, qualities like courtesy, chastity, and courage manifested themselves, in life as in allegory, as personalities. Character was achieved through a process of imitation, by which a man conformed to a fixed and preexisting standard of conduct. In Mark Antony's eulogy to Brutus:

> His life was gentle; and the elements
> So mix'd in him, that Nature might stand up
> And say to all the world, 'This was a man,'[19]

the words ring so strongly because that ideal of a man beggars all reality. In *Pilgrim's Progress* a man's journey through life is described as a narrative of confrontation with people who embody ideals, both good and bad. Such a conception of personality gives the excited moment of self-awareness real poignancy: all at once one sees what one really is. A fearful tension may exist between one's unformed state of mind and the ideal of character which beckons: when Hamlet sees Fortinbras acting as the proper prince, he is in anguish. Traditional tragedy and comedy in fact required the assumption that what has happened before the action of the play revealed less to the protagonists than what would be revealed on stage. In the Christian versions of these dramas such peak experiences served to rescue one from selfhood and reveal one's preexisting sanctified status, just as the Red Cross Knight in *The Faerie Queene* discovers in the House of Holiness his true identity as Saint George.

It might be said that self-awareness is appropriate to souls, while self-knowledge applies to selves. The words are used in quite different contexts: a soul is given to one; a self is what one becomes. Unlike souls, selves are the products of their accumulated experiences. Franklin is not on the way to recognizing and accepting some preexisting identity; his identity is with him all along, and the act of writing the *Autobiography* affirms the continuity of his attitudes and responses. Self-knowledge involves embracing childhood as the first origins of the self; it assumes that personality is formed by development. In place of the dramatic possibilities made available by self-awareness, self-knowledge organized life narratively, in the manner of novels or autobiographies. The two modes, seemingly akin, are actually the reverse of each other. The instant of self-awareness separates one from society. One feels different from others, incomprehensible except to oneself. Self-consciousness, though, associates one with others in patterns of relationship consciously arrived at or recognized. The two processes also relate to different stages of maturity. Self-awareness is the mark of freedom from adolescence, from the anxieties of dependence upon acceptance by others. Self-consciousness comes with the acceptance of ties with others, the acknowledgement that one can be simultaneously aware of oneself and of the social world. Along with its described evolution from poverty to affluence, Franklin's *Autobiography* depicts a progress from the isolated, self-assertive, doctrinaire young Franklin to an older Franklin who thrived on voluntary ties with others. The progression is like that described in Wordsworth's *Tintern Abbey*, from the period of utter absorption in the sensations inspired by nature to the time when "the still, sad music of humanity" colors one's perceptions of the world.

The Enlightenment tended to believe that the self was not confused and disordered but complex and, finally, comprehensible. The *philosophes* prided themselves on grasping the nature of those complexities for the first time. "A mighty maze, but not without a plan," Pope pronounced about the nature of man. When Diderot refers to Montaigne in the article "Pyrrhonism" in the *Encyclopedia*, he praises Montaigne for precisely the quality that Montaigne would have denied, the underlying consistency of his perceptions. "There is a necessary relationship between the two most disparate ideas; and this relationship is either in the senses or in words or in the memory, either inside or outside man. It is a rule to which even the insane are subject in their greatest derangement of reason. If we had the complete history of everything that takes place inside us, we would see that everything is related there, just as it is in the wisest and most sensible man."[20] Where the man of the Renaissance had seen inner confusion, the man of the Enlightenment saw an ordered complex not yet fully understood. The novel was credited as a breakthrough in depicting personal character. In his enthusiastic *Éloge de Richardson* Diderot asserts that no one had ever explored the human heart as deeply as Richardson.[21] When Franklin indicates his awareness of novelistic technique in the description of his Philadelphia journey, he is registering his awareness of how fully selves were known in his time.

Where greater self-knowledge seemed possible, it might also be possible to bring the recalcitrant self under firmer control. Franklin perceived his own life as a successful exercise in self-mastery, and he wrote the *Autobiography* in part as a sort of textbook example. Further along he seems to have conceived of his life story as an adjunct to a practical treatise on the achievement of virtue, to be called the *Art of Virtue*. Self-mastery, as Franklin and his contemporaries saw it, required adaptation and flexibility; it was a matter of precept rather than rule, and his own successful instances of self-mastery were meant to be adapted by his readers to suit their own circumstances. The modern reader may see Franklin's recollected life as an adventure, in particular the journey from Boston to Philadelphia, but Franklin is clear that it was also part of a plan, a design for his life which he became gradually more successful at recognizing and implementing. The modern reader may enjoy the moments of confusion and wonderment in Franklin's experience. His contemporaries saw in such episodes a further and more subtle level of self-mastery, a readiness to submit all his experiences to his own detached analysis to make it all, his whole life, public.

The *Autobiography* deliberately fabricates an identity, purporting to be that of Franklin as a boy and man. Creating a role for oneself, with all the theatrical associations that such a notion implies, represented the furthest reach of self-mastery. The fabrication of identities and the adoption of masquerades were great preoccupations of the eighteenth century; Lemuel Gulliver, Isaac Bickerstaff, Martin Scriblerus, the Spectator, the Rambler, Junius, Poor Richard, Voltaire—the list of pseudonyms and *personae* is endless. Franklin candidly admits the pleasure he took continually in the concealment of identity, as when he submitted his first contribution to his brother's newspaper. A certain playfulness was involved in this manipulation of identities, but there was also a recognized purpose. Lord Chesterfield advised his son that the donning of a mask in society was both a pleasure and a necessity for the continuance of civil harmony.[22] Franklin, who like Chesterfield was writing to his illegitimate son, came to see society and the concealments of identity it required as the real guarantor of the independence he exemplified.

Franklin and his contemporaries valued this disposition toward self-mastery for more than the pleasure of self-consciousness that it afforded. One mastered oneself for the sake of engagement with society. Where self-awareness tended to detach one from social bonds, self-knowledge required the active awareness of others, including not just one's friends but society at large. Pure narcissism, the eighteenth century believed, could never be the source of anything but delusions. The astronomer in Johnson's *Rasselas* who believes he causes the heavens to move, the abstract speculators with their eyes turned inward or heavenward whom Gulliver meets in Laputa, Dr. Pangloss with his grotesque philosophical babble—all of these characters have denied their real nature as social beings. Franklin was not going off into the wilderness when he left Boston, and he chooses not to describe his experiences of solitariness. He seems to be continually among people, and he judges them in large part for their capacity to adapt to and serve society. Dr. Brown, despite his hospitality, later wrote a burlesque of the Bible that would have "hurt weak minds," so Franklin refused to publish it. In Philadelphia, Samuel Keimer, Franklin's employer, became the perfect negative example of self-centered, religiously fanatical unsociability—an unsociability directly linked in Franklin's mind to his lack of self-control.

Society as Franklin conceived of it was comprised of varied individuals bound by no predetermined pattern. It was not, as the older models of social organization would have suggested, an organism or any other systematic arrangement of human functions. In the market place it is every man for himself. Franklin does not conform his life to a traditional function, nor does he expect others to. There is thus an unavoidable uniqueness in the lives that surround him, and his readers are expected to be similarly distinctive. The eighteenth century valued uniqueness of personality. Boswell cultivated and even amplified Dr. Johnson's singularity as a deliberate part of his biographical technique. But distinctiveness and singularity were supposed to be reconcilable with a disposition to participate fully in society, and society was supposed to be the richer for the harmonious variety of which it was comprised. A Bostonian in Philadelphia, an American in England, Franklin never describes himself as deeply accepting or accepted in the societies in which he took part, but he insists regardless that he had found a place.

Despite the uniqueness of these eighteenth-century lives, it was supposed to be possible for such lives to have meaning and coherence as a whole. Since character represented a summation of gradually accumulated experience, the autobiographies of the eighteenth century tended to insist that all experiences counted. They tried to reject nothing. Franklin's impulse to include all that he remembered made his narrative run slower and slower by the time he wrote the last sections, but no principle of exclusion permitted him to abridge. Plump and bookish, Edward Gibbon made an unlikely militiaman, yet he records the incongruous episode of his service. "The discipline and evolutions of a modern battalion gave me a clearer notion of the phalanx and the legions, and the captain of the Hampshire grenadiers (the reader may smile) has not been useless to the historian of the Roman Empire."[23] The officer and the historian are roles Gibbon has played, but he has imposed a pattern and a purpose on those roles. Rousseau includes sordid passages about his own callousness in the *Confessions* not to show how he has since been transformed but to preserve the whole record of his life.

This, then, is the cultural ideal available to Franklin as he was assembling his own self-portrait. It is a being without unconscious or uncontrollable desires. The emotions of such a self are exercised but kept in check. His relations to others and to the state are a series of limited transactions calculated to secure mutual benefit to all parties. He is what he is because of his development from childhood, and he is developing eventually toward some final, completed stage of maturity. He is a model of self-regulation and social responsibility. Though Franklin did not meet this description, he measures himself and expects to be judged by that standard.

The immediate events that prompted Franklin to begin the *Autobiography* at the time and place where he did have already been described. A more basic question remains. In some important sense Franklin wrote in response to the needs of his time. If he began the project in a moment of special well-being, he pursued it out of a sense that posterity and his contemporaries needed it. And he was not alone in feeling that the autobiography of such a person as he had been would be required. The Enlightenment called upon the exemplars of its preferred modes of consciousness to testify on their own behalf, to demonstrate that such lives were possible and efficacious in the world. New sorts of autobiography appeared in the eighteenth century in response to the new self-consciousness. This body of self-referential writing was expected to show that life was now more fully understood.

Certainly self-expression became more important in the eighteenth century than it had been before. The feeling that one must write, that a record of one's experiences would be of use to others, and even that others need one's writing became a significant cultural phenomenon. For Pope the world was filled with people frantic to write or obsessed with the effects of writing. The observation seems to have been more than just an obsessed poet's perception. Even Franklin, surely no strong candidate for the muse's garland, had to be warned away from poetry by his father, and he records in his *Autobiography* a significant number of characters driven by the desire to write and publish. The urge to express oneself began early in life. Pope lisped in numbers, he claims in the *Epistle to Dr. Arbuthnot*—that is, his earliest childhood speech took the form of heroic couplets—and though he was at pains to show himself a person as well as a poet, his life was given over utterly to writing. The chance for self-expression could utterly transform one's life, as it did for Rousseau. His life had been without direction until he chanced to read the Dijon Academy prize question. "The moment I read this, I beheld a new universe and became another man."[24] Finding a fit occasion for writing, he was reborn. In a sense, the eighteenth century believed, writing *creates* the self. Certainly Boswell thought so. His fragmented energies found both a corrective and a display in his journal. He would fret on days when nothing exciting could be found for it, as if it led a surrogate existence more valuable than his own.[25] So important did the act of writing become in the Enlightenment that it seemed to take a logical priority over life itself, so that Swift could describe the aftermath of his own death in *Verses on the Death of Dr. Swift*.

"Knowing oneself" for the writers of the eighteenth century no longer meant the recognition of one's limitations in a world incomprehensibly better ordered than one can grasp. Self-knowledge had become a complex and exacting study, leading to knowledge as genuine as any that one could have about the physical world. Self-study was necessary in a situation where the self had cut itself loose from a belief in an assured place in a divine plan and floated in society guided only by its own navigation. Such a self must be sure that, in some way, its inner life counts in the world. Autobiography, in this broadened sense, thus enacts a kind of miraculous incarnation: a person's thoughts, feelings, and ambitions can be seen to interact with the large world of action.

Self-expression in the Enlightenment did not serve merely the function of revealing the author's inner state. One's own writings, and not just those that were overtly self-descriptive, served as a mirror, revealing oneself and one's surroundings. But the mirror image could be subtly altered. The writer's relationship to it was not the stunned fascination of Narcissus but the considered appraisal of the self-portraitist. In the case of Franklin a long series of pseudonyms and poses could serve the ultimate purpose of revealing himself to the world. In the case of Boswell the act of recording his experiences daily gave some coherence and continuity to a life otherwise chaotic. Johnson encouraged Boswell's plan of keeping a journal. "I told Mr. Johnson," Boswell records, "that I put down all sorts of little incidents in it. 'Sir,' said he, 'there is nothing too little for so little a creature as man. It is by studying little things that we attain the great knowledge of having as little misery and as much happiness as possible.'"[26] People in the eighteenth century showed an unprecedented concern for the preservation of the details of their own and others' lives. To hold such details in consciousness was in some way a means of control.

The Enlightenment took an increased interest in the writer himself and in writing as a manifestation of personality. There is something fairly new about this interest; in an earlier age the survival of a writer's works was not supposed to depend upon his own limited character and circumstances. Though he was an intimate friend of Shakespeare, Ben Jonson says nothing of personality in his dedicatory poem in the First Folio. A little later in the seventeenth century, John Aubry and Izaak Walton produced some short biographies of English writers, evidence of a new interest. By the later eighteenth century, literary biography would be important enough to command the talents of Dr. Johnson, the period's most important man of letters. The fame of authorship could even lure a young provincial like James Ralph from so distant a place as Philadelphia; Franklin recalls with dismay the effect of this mania on his friend. (He himself found more subtle and effective means to that end.) Gibbon could assert that Fielding's *Tom Jones* would outlast the Hapsburg dynasty. Together with the claims to a greater factual and psychological authenticity for the writings of their time came a greater emphasis on the validating stamp of the author's personal identity. Literary fame meant both the reputation of one's own work and the lingering echo therein of one's own personality.[27]

It would be a mistake to assume that the new emphasis on self-study and self-expression emerged simply out of the race's growing wisdom. The satisfactions of self-consciousness were considerable, but certain severe cultural problems emerged simultaneously. Young Franklin on his way to Philadelphia had cut himself loose from family, place, and religion, but he was therefore adrift and, as he later felt, in danger of capsizing in the sea of open possibilities. Under the older paradigm of selfhood that he was leaving behind, no one was truly intelligible by himself, but everyone could feel secure in his place in universal history and the cosmos. Above were the angels; below, the animals. Before was the Fall; later would be the Last Judgment. Within those large coordinates was one's place, whoever one was. And if one could not find one's own place, still one could be sure that a place had been assigned, because all places were assigned. But Franklin the free-thinking runaway apprentice had no divine gyroscope orienting him to the cosmos; knowing oneself does not supply one with knowledge of the largest frame of reference.

This dissociation between the self and the universe affected relations with history as well. The *philosophes* sought to replace God as the principle regulating history with a system of social laws by which societies operate, just as they had replaced God with Newtonian mechanics in the physical management of the universe. Hume explicitly compared the historian's task to the physicist's. "These records of wars, intrigues, factions, and revolutions, are so many collections of experiments, by which the politician or moral philosopher fixes the principles of his science; in the same manner as the physician or natural philosopher, becomes acquainted with the nature of plants, minerals, and other external objects, by the experiments, which he forms concerning them."[28]

But in the process of this revision of history, the self's capacity for independence was in danger of being lost. If the significant occurrences of history resemble the predictable movements of mechanical bodies, what room is left for individual action or agency? What room, for that matter, for specific histories, if one learns only the invariant principles of human nature? Hume and Gibbon sensed this problem and tried to make room for the depiction of personal character in their histories.[29] But the scale of Enlightenment history was too vast to serve as a plausible stage for effectual individual endeavor.

Consequently, the central persisting problem of the Enlightenment was the relationship between the individual and the collective spheres of life. On one hand were the stars and planets, admirably moving according to the laws of gravity, and the immense movements of universal history, which followed yet undiscovered laws of their own. On the other hand was the self, proceeding about its business, trucking and bartering, examining and organizing its own life quite without regard to the larger order of things. Neither sphere seemed to relate to the other. At the level of personal experience the self appeared to be free, or at least rightfully free. The claims to personal distinctiveness made so forcefully by Franklin and others depended upon the sense of being free. But the universe was clearly oblivious to the efforts of such individual wills; it was in general perceived to be ordered and utterly stable. Both order and freedom offer considerable satisfactions, but the two are apparently contradictory as modes of describing how the parts of the universe relate to the whole.

The Enlightenment tried continually to reconcile the personal and individual spheres of action. Leibniz and others after him tried to say that there was no contradiction between the two spheres: at the individual level we are all aware of a capacity for spontaneity and choice, but God also somehow converts the discordant results of individual freedom into the components of his overall system. As Pope expresses it,

> All Nature is but Art, unknown to thee;
> All Chance, Direction, which thou canst not see;
> All Discord, Harmony not understood;
> All partial Evil, universal Good...[30]

Mandeville, whom Franklin met and no doubt read in London, turned this formula into a rationale for unrestrained selfishness: "private vices, public benefits" was his paradoxical equation. Adam Smith later on justified the freedom to truck and barter by arguing the existence of a hidden hand, which turned everything out for the best. There is something subtly unsatisfying about these discussions. According to Leibniz and his successors, the self is free in some sense but powerless except within its tiny reference frame. The self's effects on the larger frame have no necessary relation to its intentions. Franklin himself discovered early the frustrations that come from thinking about such things. As a bumptious journeyman printer in London, he wrote and printed a treatise on the subject, *A Dissertation on Liberty and Necessity, Pleasure and Pain.* "How exact and regular is every Thing in the *natural* World!" he exclaims. "How wisely in every Part contriv'd! We cannot here find the least Defect! Those who have study'd the mere animal and vegetable Creation, demonstrate that nothing can be more harmonious and beautiful! All the heavenly Bodies, the Stars and Planets, are regulated with the utmost Wisdom! And can we suppose less Care to be taken in the Order of the *moral* than in the *natural* System?"[31] And it followed inevitably that in a universe so perfectly planned man had no such thing as free will, and the term *evil* became meaningless. Recalling the writing of this pamphlet later, Franklin "doubted whether some Error had not insinuated itself unperceiv'd, into my Argument, so as to infect all that follow'd, as is common in metaphysical Reasonings" (A, 114). He turned instead to more useful lines of inquiry.

From the perspective of the universe and universal history, individual selves must look powerless and insignificant. History turns out to have no people in it, only vast forces and patterns. Historians themselves seemed to be leery of their own work's value. As a historian Voltaire had produced thick volumes, but in *L'Ingenu* he says, "Indeed history is only the picture of crimes and misfortunes. The crowd of innocent and peaceful men always disappears on these vast stages."[32] Those who persisted in thinking on the universal level often found themselves driven to inhuman conclusions. Thus, a kind of history had to be defined in which individual selves could be found to be efficacious. Otherwise the only alternatives were a public world apparently inaccessible and immovable and a private world of free and virtuous impotence. Of what use was the new self-knowledge, to what point the expanded self-expression, if the self was imprisoned within the limits of private life?

Consequently, the most satisfying form of history was biography. It was biography that linked the great world and the small, public and private, historical and intimate. History, it was argued, would have to be the field for interminable and unresolvable debates; since its material was, ultimately, an invariable human nature, it had to view its subject from too great a height to see anything well. "The stratagems of war, and the intrigues of courts," wrote Dr. Johnson, "are read by far the greater part of mankind with the same indifference as the adventures of fabled heroes, or the revolutions of a fairy region. Between falsehood and useless truth there is little difference."[33] Histories and romances offered alternative defects; the one had no recognizable selves, and the other no believable societies. As Fielding argued in *Joseph Andrews*, "it is most certain that truth is to be found only in the works of those who celebrate the lives of great men, and are commonly called biographers."[34] Johnson, the great apologist for biography, asserted that no life could be uninteresting. A proper sense of the details of a life would have to show its kinship with other lives.[35]

So there was a great vogue for biography in the eighteenth century.

In France the eulogy became an important genre, particularly in the hands of Fontenelle and Condorcet. Voltaire wrote to Condorcet that "the public wishes that an academician might die every week so that you might have the opportunity of writing about him."[36] In England the biographical impulse expressed itself both in Grubstreet biographies of celebrated criminals and in immense and self-conscious literary biographies like Mason's *Life of Gray* and Boswell's *Life of Johnson*. Johnson's *Lives of the Poets* offered a way of reading both lives and works in relation to each other; his *Life of Savage* is a more extended portrait in which events and psychological observations are coordinated in an effort to account for Savage's tortured existence.

Since biography aimed at revealing character in the world, the subject of biography should speak, if possible, for himself. Thus, letters and passages of conversation were extensively incorporated into biographies. Biographers sought to be in reality what novelists like Richardson had pretended to be—the editors of papers and memorabilia entrusted to them. The inherent difficulty of biography was that its most basic subject, personality, was not really fully knowable by the biographer. Boswell began the *Life of Johnson* by lamenting, a little insincerely, that Johnson had not written his own life, and he offers as the defense for his own work the fact that it includes so great a quantity of Johnson's letters and conversation. The *Life of Johnson*, Boswell suggested, approached as closely as possible to being an autobiography of Johnson.[37]

Autobiography might then be seen as the highest form of biography. Johnson himself had argued as much in *Idler* 84. "The writer of his own life," Johnson stated, "has at least the first qualification of an historian, the knowledge of the truth."[38] As for the supposed impartiality of the biographer, Johnson suggested that he was no more likely to be without prejudice than the subject himself. "I must be conscious that no one is so well qualified as myself to describe the series of my thoughts and actions," wrote Gibbon at the beginning of his autobiography.[39] The two friends of Franklin who wrote encouraging him to continue his autobiography both use the same argument. "Considering your great age, the caution of your character, and your peculiar style of thinking," Benjamin Vaughan wrote, in a letter incorporated in the text of the *Autobiography*, "it is not likely that any one besides yourself can be sufficiently master of the facts of your life, or the intentions of your mind" (A, 139). The biographer might record accidental details about his subject's life; what the autobiographer sets down is the very essence of his experiences.

The eighteenth century assumed that a man might know himself in

all his own essential features and tendencies.   The sense that the
mind's natural operations are an unintelligible jumble, as in Montaigne or Pascal, was no longer current. The feeling that one's inner life
is too buried to be fully understood would emerge later. Self-doubt existed in the eighteenth century as at any other time, but the age also offered a material number of significant figures who firmly claimed to
know themselves. When Rousseau set out in his *Confessions* "to display to my kind a portrait in every way true to nature," he had no doubt
of his perfect adequacy as portraitist.[40] In the last days of his life Hume
wrote an autobiographical sketch, concluding with a summary assessment of his own personality. "I am, or rather was (for that is the style I
must now use in speaking of myself, which emboldens me the more to
speak my sentiments); I was, I say, a man of mild dispositions, of command of temper, of an open, social, and cheerful humour, capable of
attachment, but little susceptible of enmity, and of great moderation in
all my passions."[41] The characterization goes on for a paragraph, detail-
ing his sense of his own general relations to his friends, his work, and
the literary public. In the present age of anxiety there is something
rather breathtaking in this passage of Hume's, in the critical detachment that can put one's whole life into the past tense. It was in such a
spirit of confident self-knowledge that Franklin went about the writing
of his own autobiography.

4 *"Thro' This Dangerous Time of Youth"*

The *Autobiography* becomes more dense with details as Franklin gets further into the writing. His early life in Boston he treats briefly and quite economically, providing only the necessary outlines of his education, his apprenticeship, and his quarrel with his brother, except for details concerning his reading and the beginning of his career as a writer. The move to Philadelphia is deliberately more detailed, as he indicates, so as to emphasize that episode and its meaning for his life. But once in Philadelphia he does not resume the succinct treatment of the Boston years. Anecdotes are more frequent; characters appear who must be described. The interlude in London is even more filled with material that he could not summarize, and there the reader sees for the first time a young Franklin who is the interested and careful observer, not just the figure on his way to affluence and reputation. This first section of the *Autobiography* closes with Franklin in his early twenties, established in Philadelphia. By this time the project of writing his life had drawn him into a considerable commitment of effort, and even of ambition.

In the last months of his life, Franklin went to considerable efforts to assure that his *Autobiography* would be published as he had left it. He had copies of the parts so far completed sent to two friends, his British editor Benjamin Vaughan and his former landlord in Paris, Louis Gillaume Le Veillard. In his will he designated his grandson William Temple Franklin as his literary executor, leaving him the task of publishing his memoirs. The result of Franklin's care has been that all the copies representing his final intentions were lost, his grandson dawdled twenty-seven years before publishing the *Autobiography*, and the text that was then published was so tampered with as to make the reconstruction of Franklin's own revisions impossible.[1]

Literary scholars are supposed to fret over the imperfections of texts, and a good deal of fretting has gone on during the past 190 years, as well as much careful reconstruction of the history of the text. What we have to go on is a manuscript version, in Franklin's hand, recovered after seventy-five years by John Bigelow, a gentleman scholar, and published in 1867 for the first time. It is likely that Franklin reworked this version somewhat, changing expressions and revising awkward sections, and that the lost copies mailed to Vaughan and Le Veillard represent his final intentions. In the manuscript that has survived he provided space for revisions; he divided his folio sheets in half, wrote on only one side, and left the other side blank to allow for changes. (Even in the first few pages of this supposed letter to his son, there are instructions to the printer included in parentheses.)

Despite Franklin's later efforts to revise and polish the first section of the *Autobiography*, the most commonly accepted editions of his life preserve the responses and wording of 1771.[2] Though there may have been many cosmetic revisions, it is significant that fifteen or seventeen years after beginning the task Franklin saw no need to make basic structural changes. Gibbon at about the same time was making continual false starts on his own memoirs, six in all, and was never able to put them together. Rousseau found it necessary to supplement his *Confessions* with two more volumes of largely autobiographical writing. Franklin was never a finicky writer, but his basic satisfaction with the earlier account suggests a settled response. He was beyond the point of revising his childhood and youth to suit a changing sense of himself.

The older Franklin was a man of leisure, holder of honorary degrees and memberships in learned societies, but as an author he insists on the reality of his early identity as journeyman printer in Philadelphia and London. He records the kind of work he did for Samuel Keimer and at Watts's and Palmer's, setting type and carrying forms. It is the continuity of his identity that he insists on most strongly. Where there seem to be differences between past and present selves, the continuous narrative movement toward the present operates to disintegrate those apparent differences. Autobiographies often make the assertion that the writer is no longer what he once was, whether for better (as Augustine would claim) or for worse (as Rousseau mournfully insists). Not so in Franklin's case, where even the earliest recollection recorded—the waterfront construction project in Boston—is offered as a foreshadowing of his later disposition toward public improvements.

It is perhaps a generic characteristic of autobiography that no other selves can take on a reality so vivid as the author's. A single figure, whose thoughts are known and recollected in detail, fills the frame. The bodies around that central figure can easily look pallid in the light of this self-examination. Eighteenth-century autobiography in particular tended to treat its subjects as selves on their own rather than as group members, enmeshed in a social context. Gibbon gives little sense of an intellectual context which defines his perspectives. Rousseau denies the influence of other *philosophes* on his thought. In the nineteenth century Mill will describe himself as one of the philosophical radicals and Newman documents his membership in the Oxford Movement and the Catholic Church, but the autobiographers of the Enlightenment, whatever their genuine affiliations, tend to be lone agents in their reconstructed lives. Franklin's *Autobiography* has few subordinate characters. Samuel Keimer, the fat religious fanatic for whom Franklin worked at first in Philadelphia, is the most recognizable of these secondary figures. His associates in Philadelphia who worked with him on his many projects—Syng, Breintnall, Kinnersley—are only names. One must look outside the *Autobiography* to discover their importance.

As a result of this exclusive focus on Franklin, the reader comes to feel that Franklin has created himself, out of a sequence of acts of will. The accidental and meaningless character of most human experiences is implicitly denied; all the odd changes of direction and shifts of emotion in his early years have combined to make him into Benjamin Franklin. He describes the fruitless voyage to London in order to purchase equipment for a print shop; when he arrives, he discovers that Governor Keith, who had promised to finance the print shop, had casually betrayed him, leaving him stranded. So Franklin stays on in London for two years. But what might have been seen as a disruption in his plans to establish himself in business proves to be an occasion to display his adaptability and gain experience of the world. He has included already the opinions expressed by his father and his future mother-in-law, that he was younger and more unready than he had thought. And Denham, the merchant who befriends him on board ship, advises him to improve his skills as a printer in London so that he can set himself up at greater advantage when he returns to Philadelphia. Even the *errata* do not affect the design of his life. In each case—his desertion of his brother and of Deborah Read, the long delay in repaying a debt—he is able to rectify his mistake in some fashion. Our common experience would suggest that the world breaks in upon us continually and disrupts our designs, but the disrupting world appears to be held in check in Franklin's *Autobiography*.

The social world of the *Autobiography* seems not to impinge upon young Franklin, constraining or subtly directing him. Individuals may hamper or betray him, and many do, but Franklin's rise is never affected, in the *Autobiography*, by the presence of society as a whole. Instead, that world appears to be passive and at his disposal. He does not report experiences of being ignored, snubbed, or treated as a plebeian. In America he notes all the prominent people who took favorable notice of him, including two governors and several members of the New Jersey legislature. When he turns his hand to a pamphlet on paper currency, the pamphlet proves immediately successful and brings his print shop more business, "another Advantage gain'd by my being able to write" (A, 124). Franklin does not admit to suffering feelings of frustration on his way to affluence and reputation. There are people around him with overly ambitious plans who suffer for their presumptuousness: Samuel Keimer the would-be religious leader, James Ralph the would-be actor and poet, Hugh Meredith the would-be printer. It is always suggested, though, that Franklin's ambitions are proportioned to his means, and a chorus of background figures chimes in with predictions of future success for him. In his case there is always a neat fit between the work expended and the success achieved. As he expresses it, in a phrase suggestive of how fluid and buoying his surroundings could be for him, "I went on swimmingly" (A, 126).

Though he has a story to tell, Franklin arranges his material to emphasize certain points, even disrupting the chronology if his theme demands a concentration of separate episodes. Before beginning the description of his career as a printer, he pauses to summarize the history thus far of his religious opinions, "that you may see how far those influenc'd the future Events of my Life" (A, 113). The conjunction of religion and business may seem odd to the modern reader, but Franklin finds an intimate connection. He describes how he had abandoned the religion of his parents and become, on the basis of his reading, "a thorough Deist." It is freethinking, he has concluded by the time he has reached his early twenties, that had caused many of his difficulties, both his own beliefs and the beliefs of others who have behaved irresponsibly toward him. The very activity of metaphysical speculation had come to seem futile and frustrating. "I grew convinc'd that *Truth, Sincerity and Integrity* in Dealings between Man and Man, were of the utmost Importance to the Felicity of Life, and I form'd written Resolutions, (which still remain in my Journal Book) to practice them ever while I lived" (A, 114).[3] He has reached a sort of independent concurrence with the moral teachings of revealed religion, concluding that it is prudent to obey them without regard to the question of moral rightness. This accommodation with religion has made his career in business possible, because it has solidified his trustworthiness. "I had therefore," he writes, concluding the discussion of religion and morality, "a tolerable Character to begin the World with, I valued it properly, and determin'd to preserve it" (A, 115).

A more striking example where the narrative sequence is altered involves an incident that took place in the original journey from Boston to Philadelphia. Describing his plans to leave Philadelphia for London, Franklin interjects that he had neglected to include the story of how he had abandoned his vegetarian principles. Diet is a continuing theme in the *Autobiography*, and many of the references to diet involve the relations of employers and employees. There are also religious and moral dimensions to diet; in the episode immediately following, when Franklin and Keimer pool their religious convictions, Franklin agrees to observe the Sabbath on Saturday and not to cut his beard if Keimer will join him in vegetarianism. Franklin's vegetarianism proves to be a convenience for him, he says, but he had also taken it up on moral grounds, on the assumption that the world is fairly and reasonably ordered. Where diet is an issue, Franklin generally emerges as superior in his capacity for self-restraint, as he does in London as a nondrinker among the beer-guzzling workers at Watts's printing house. But on the boat from Boston, his self-restraint breaks down. While becalmed, the crew catches fish and fries them on deck. Franklin balances a while between principle and inclination, as he puts it, "till I recollected, that when the Fish were opened, I saw smaller Fish taken out of their Stomachs: Then thought I, if you eat one another, I don't see why we mayn't eat you" (A, 87–88). So he eats heartily. It is a victory not merely for inclination but for a different view of the world from that upon which his vegetarianism had been based—that the world consists of big and little fish who swim about consuming one another.[4]

The episode does not fit thematically with the story of his journey from Boston to Philadelphia. But it does apply to Franklin's situation at this point in the narrative, swimming about with larger and quite amoral fish like Keimer (who is later described as "an odd Fish" [A, 112] and as a great eater) and Governor Keith. Franklin's circumstances were teaching him about the difference between moral theory and a brutal world. He draws the lesson clearly. "So convenient a thing it is to be a *reasonable Creature*, since it enables one to find or make a Reason for every thing one has a mind to do" (A, 88).

A lesson that might have carried bitter associations is here put to the service of humor. Franklin's humor is his signature. Like a signature, it is distinguishable from anyone else's; like a signature, it is employed to mark things as his own. The eighteenth century produced a literature of wit, and Franklin's capacity for irony had formidable predecessors. His wit is milder than that of Swift or Pope, and in various ways it is more subtle and elusive. The naiveté of the anecdote about fish and vegetarianism, the disposition there and elsewhere to make himself the object of the humor—these qualities separate him from the great Augustan satirists. Swift's satire in particular always carries with it a demanding ideal of human behavior to which human failings are compared; Franklin's story, by contrast, subverts all pretense to ideals of conduct. His humor is also distinguishable from the sometimes facile benignity of Addison, his model as a prose stylist and in other ways a figure with a kindred outlook. John Lynen has pointed to the bases of Franklin's characteristic irony in *The Design of the Present*.

> Franklin's irony is not of a random kind but arises from the essentially comic nature of the self's situation, a situation within which reason and experience never quite match. A man must live by rules, general concepts, formulas, and the like, yet his understanding is so imperfect that he cannot get his principles straight or even understand what they mean. There is always some discrepancy between the universal truth and the human formula for it, and between what we think we mean by a given statement and the meaning our statement would have if we could see all its implications, yet man's rules would not be rules if they did not pretend to universal validity; they mean to be the actual principles of reality, though in fact they are but inferences from a partial view of things.[5]

As Lynen points out, Franklin's irony is not incidental or ornamental: it is integral to the perception of the world which he sought to sustain. I would offer one qualification to this cogent formulation. In the *Autobiography* experience continually takes precedence over reason or principle; in the pulling and tugging between universal values and the claims of the self, the self always emerges superior. To be a reasonable creature means finding reasons for doing what one wants to do anyway.

The reader who is taken in by Franklin's pose as a garrulous old man will miss his irony. It is not a public irony, where the contrasted elements are forced on the reader for his judgment. Franklin never confronts his readers with the awful choices that Swift presents; the reader of the *Autobiography* is drawn into a world where all values derive from Franklin's own experience. The dilemma young Franklin faces off Block Island is not presented as a universal moral problem but as a personal choice entirely his own.

The danger, then, is that the irony of the *Autobiography* may appear to be no more than an extended private joke. What keeps this tendency under control is Franklin's sense of himself as a representative figure, one who continually undergoes experiences that are like those of everyone else. When he dines on fresh-cooked cod, he does not claim to discover something particular about his own unique self; he discovers what it means to be "a *reasonable Creature*," the very definition of man. Franklin never seems to assume that anything happening to him could be uninteresting or without instructive lessons, and the engagement he assumes in the reader is designed to dissolve the distance between them. Somehow the very extent of his self-absorption has qualified him to project his life in the broadest public terms, like the vanity which redounds to the common good.

The first part of the *Autobiography* is devoted to the problem of growing up and getting settled into work. He breaks off writing when that process has been fully described. As he of course knew, Franklin was dealing with a universal human problem, how to get out of adolescence and into the stage of productive mature life. The rhetoric of the *Autobiography* demands that those problems seem considerable and yet that the protagonist rely only on widely accessible gifts—in this case, industry, frugality, and an ability to express himself tolerably well in English prose. It is important that Franklin not seem a youthful prodigy. The evidence of an extraordinary character is available in the *Autobiography*, ready to be used if Franklin were as vain as he promised he would be. His father recognizes him as the brightest of his sons; his writing, both prose and poetry, attracts much attention in Boston by the time he is sixteen years old; without benefit of formal education he writes and publishes a philosophical pamphlet at nineteen; he has his own press at twenty-two. But he discounts all this: his earliest writing was only impressive in the eyes of the unsophisticated readership of Boston; his pamphlet was a mistake and probably infected with unintended inconsistencies; his competitors in Philadelphia were lazy and inept. He even tells a story about a writing contest with his two friends Ralph and Osborne in which Ralph's verses were substituted as Franklin's to fool Osborne, who was prejudiced against Ralph's work. Osborne is taken in and remarks at how surprised he is to see such talent in Franklin. "But who wou'd have imagin'd, says he, that Franklin had been capable of such a Performance; such Painting, such Force! such Fire! he has even improv'd the Original! In his common Conversation, he seems to have no Choice of Words: he hesitates and blunders: and yet, good God, how he writes!" (A, 91). The story at the most obvious level describes a practical joke played by Ralph on Osborne, but it also operates to inform the reader that Franklin was not the most impressive figure among his earliest of friends in Philadelphia.

As a story about how to grow up, the *Autobiography* must satisfy certain psychological requirements. The earliest version of Franklin that we can discern is an argumentative show-off with a demonstrated inability to get along with friends and work associates. The mature Franklin who recalls the story must not, however, repudiate the younger version; all of the younger Franklin's experiences, even his *errata*, have contributed to form the ultimate Franklin, and that early version is supposed to be as appealing to the reader as it is to Franklin himself. Franklin the narrator always appears to be thoroughly detached and amused by the behavior of Franklin the protagonist, yet the narrator is also thoroughly involved in the telling of the story. He does not get distracted into his own present, and he does not belittle or deny the significance of the struggling young printer's experiences. The evolution from adolescence is gradual, involving both Franklin's own resolve and the help and advice of others, like his father or Mr. Denham. Franklin describes no moments of transforming insight, but rather a series of accumulating perceptions: the wisdom of a nondogmatic style of conversation, the realization that he had best stick to his trade, the discovery that friends may be untrustworthy, the necessity of being able to pay debts, the preferability of a reliable wife over the excitements of loose women. Despite the lack of anything like a grand conversion experience, Franklin seeks to convey his belief that there had been something marvelous, even providential, about his growing up. In the passage where he describes his religious attitudes, he expresses the relief he feels at having passed through adolescence so unscathed. "And this Persuasion [that it is best to abstain from certain forbidden actions], with the kind hand of Providence, or some guardian Angel, or accidental favourable Circumstances and Situations, or all together, preserved me (thro' this dangerous Time of Youth and the hazardous Situations I was sometimes in among Strangers, remote from the Eye and Advice of my Father) without any *wilful* gross Immorality or Injustice that might have been expected from my Want of Religion" (A, 115). Providence, a guardian angel, luck—whatever it was, Franklin had made it through.

Franklin's emergence from adolescence into stable adult life seems the more marvelous against the background of plotting and knavery he describes in London and Philadelphia. He had had to connive in order to leave Boston, offering one dubious reason for sneaking out (that he was responsible for a girl's pregnancy) instead of another. The range of sharp practices in the ensuing narrative is very rich. As soon as he arrives in Philadelphia he witnesses one business competitor, Andrew Bradford, prying business secrets from another, Keimer. He himself manipulates Keimer for his own interests both before and after the sojourn in London, biding his time until he can set up shop independently. Keimer in turn tries to use him to train a shop full of inexperienced workers well enough so that he, the teacher, could be dispensed with. There is the casual, seemingly motiveless manipulation of Governor Keith, who seems to have been associated at one time with another schemer named Riddlesden, who in turn had bilked Deborah Read's father. Identities are concealed, as when Ralph takes Franklin's name in his schoolteaching phase. There are attempted seductions and abrupt desertions of women. Debts are defaulted or in danger of default. During this period, Franklin seems always to be narrowly escaping from some act of knavery. On the way back to Philadelphia with his friend Collins after a visit to his family in Boston, the two youths strike up a shipboard acquaintance with two enticing young women. But a Quaker matron takes Franklin aside, noticing, as she says, that he " 'has no Friend with thee, and seems not to know much of the World, or of the Snares Youth is expos'd to' " (A, 84). She warns Franklin against the two women, and indeed they are caught with stolen goods in New York. "So tho' we had escap'd a sunken Rock which we scrap'd upon in the Passage, I thought this Escape of rather more Importance to me" (A, 84). In such a world it is not easy to get ahead honestly.

The backdrop of knavery and manipulation that Franklin reconstructs imposes some subtle rhetorical problems for this tale of success and maturation. He might have described himself as an innocent throughout, as the adolescent Gibbon and Henry Adams do in their autobiographies. At least in relation to Governor Keith, Franklin emphasizes his own naive trust. "But what shall we think of a Governor's playing such pitiful Tricks, and imposing so grossly on a poor ignorant Boy!" he exclaims (A, 95). Nowhere in the Autobiography does Franklin speak with such passion as in this outburst, yet one notices that the victim is "a poor ignorant Boy." His detachment from the younger Franklin has also reached its height. Having asked his question, of us, the world at large who are called to witness, he backs away into a dispassionate analysis of Keith's character, allowing him his virtues and his small achievements. Despite the occasions where Franklin behaves naively, the narrator is unwilling to let him be merely the victim of the machinations that surround him. He does not get ahead by denying the reality of knavery or by being incapable of coping with it. In fact, the record of his *errata* shows that he was involved in some of it himself. As he emerges into adult life he discovers the importance of a show of fair dealing with the world. It is not enough to have estimable qualities; people need to see them. Virtue alone, unrecognized by others, is insufficient to succeed in the fallen, knave-infested world of Franklin's Philadelphia.

Franklin's success must appear to be the result of his independence. He must be seen to have gained control over his dealings with others, whether his superiors or his inferiors. In the "Notes" the final lesson toward which his entire narrative is moving is the lesson of how to maintain the best relation to others: "Costs me nothing to be civil to inferiors, a good deal to be submissive to superiors &c. &c." (A, 271). Young Franklin was always disposed to cultivate friends in high places, but with Governor Keith that disposition failed him. In London he found that defiance of his fellow workers led him into problems; once he paid the price of admission into their "chapel," he could make himself a leader and convince some of them to leave off beer drinking. The sacrifice of what he considered to be his rights gained him independence of action—and the opportunity to change the behavior of others.

It is the *cost* of civility to inferiors and submissiveness to superiors that he notes—again the economic metaphor. Independence of the sort he values involves control over one's expenditures, whether in money, affection, ambition, or self-display. His longstanding debt to Vernon impedes him. He has squandered friendship on Collins and Ralph and is thereby enmeshed with them. In Boston he discovers that his prominence is getting in his way: in Philadelphia, with the Junto and in other activities, he cultivates secrecy. The latter section of the first part of the *Autobiography* reads like a series of accounts successively settled. Independence does not mean that he is utterly self-sufficient. He acknowledges his debt to William Coleman and Robert Grace, who invested in his print shop, and to others who counseled him well, like Andrew Hamilton. But he stipulates in each instance that he was not encumbered by those debts and that he was able to repay each fully; all of those arrangements prove to serve the mutual advantage of all parties.

His success, as described in the *Autobiography*, is due to the conscious and calculated display of diligence and independence. "In order to secure my Credit and Character as a Tradesman, I took care not only to be in *Reality* Industrious and frugal, but to avoid all *Appearances* of the Contrary" (A, 125). He is even able to cite evidence of the way this appearance of diligence operates in the business community; one of the few unqualified compliments to Franklin that is allowed into the text comes from a Dr. Baird, who was heard to speak of Franklin's industriousness as "superior to any thing I ever saw of the kind" (A, 119). Dr. Baird's commendation is one of the few superlatives Franklin allows to refer to himself in the course of the first part of the *Autobiography*; it is paid to what Franklin considers to be his most readily imitable trait, the capacity for hard work. Dr. Baird's remark was addressed to a gathering of merchants who thereupon were prompted to bring their business to Franklin. Franklin is quite candid that the display of hard work is important in itself. He made sure to dress plainly, stay out of taverns, and avoid fishing and hunting. "[A] Book, indeed, sometimes debauch'd me from my Work; but that was seldom, snug, and gave no Scandal" (A, 126). Reading, for the enterprising young Franklin, was like illicit sex, as his metaphor suggests; Franklin is passive and enticed by books, just as he suggests elsewhere that he was enticed by loose women, but he succeeds in keeping those secret pleasures out of the public view. To underline the causes of his success, he cites the story of a competitor, Keimer's successor David Harry, who "was very proud, dress'd like a Gentleman, liv'd expensively, took much Diversion and Pleasure abroad, ran in debt, and neglected his Business, upon which all Business left him" (A, 126). Harry's career is in each respect the perfect opposite of Franklin's formula for success.

Even his most intimate relationships can be conducted in order to increase his independence. The friendships with Collins and Ralph serve as a negative example; Franklin became too mixed up with each man for his own good. In the case of Collins, the final episode of their friendship features the two of them in the same boat, going nowhere, until Franklin throws Collins overboard. Both Collins and Ralph, like Franklin, have left cities and creeds behind them; both of them end up owing Franklin significant sums of money. When Franklin returns to Philadelphia, he is more careful in his friendships; the young men of his Junto band together to help each other out. His marriage in turn is supposed to further his independence and his success. "We have an English Proverb that says,

> He that would thrive
> Must ask his Wife,"

he writes early in the second section of the *Autobiography* (A, 144). Industry and frugality have recommended Deborah Read to him, as well as a lingering feeling of guilt at having dumped her. Without embarrassment he reports the negotiations with young Miss Godfrey that fell through because of her parents' stinginess; he does not consider it discreditable to Miss Read that she was an afterthought. She proved to be "a good and faithful Helpmate, assisted me much by attending the Shop, we throve together, and have ever mutually endeavour'd to make each other happy" (A, 129). It was a successful partnership, with mutual benefits.

Franklin's independent stance and the emotional detachment he acquires enable him to appraise the characters of the people he must encounter. Though he makes no special point about this capacity, he clearly considers it one of the powers he has acquired during this period in his life. Twice he entered into arrangements to set himself up in a printing shop of his own; in the first he was duped by Governor Keith, but in the second he formed a prudent partnership with Hugh Meredith, whose weaknesses he knew and was able in part to bring under control. Nine times in the outline for the *Autobiography* Franklin notes "His [or Her or Their] Character." Of this rather considerable number of people scheduled to be characterized, there are few whose characters are better than ambiguous in his eyes. James Ralph, Thomas Godfrey the nitpicking mathematician, Governor Morris the lover of unnecessary disputation, Lord Hillsborough—the figures he chooses to depict tend to be people who have opposed or frustrated him. Friends like Watson, Breintnall, and William Strahan are merely listed, without indication that they are to be characterized. Though he is generous in acknowledging the assistance he has received and the useful friendships he has formed, he leaves the positive figures undepicted. It is best to be wary, the *Autobiography* emphasizes, and the patterns of characterization support that emphasis.

No one besides Franklin himself receives more vivid attention than Samuel Keimer, and it is worth pausing to note his character in the *Autobiography*. To some extent he fits into the instructive pattern that Franklin seeks continually to discover in his experiences; Keimer is the most prominent negative example. Franklin is quite terse in describing his appearance in the world, specifically among the prominent men of New Jersey. "In truth he was an odd Fish, ignorant of common Life, fond of rudely opposing receiv'd Opinions, slovenly to extream dirtiness, enthusiastic on some Points of Religion, and a little Knavish withal" (A, 112–13). Each trait in the catalogue is one Franklin actively sought to avoid: he cultivated an appearance of normality and piqued

himself on his awareness of common life; he came to avoid disputations and left religion alone; he was tidy and fair-dealing. Yet Keimer
proves to be too big a figure to fit merely into the rhetoric of success;
the pleasure of making a fool of his boss, so irresistible to the young
Franklin, has not left the older narrator. Keimer is really a minor mas-
terpiece of characterization. When the governor and another finely
dressed gentleman come to the door of Keimer's shop, he hurries his
fat frame downstairs to greet them. But the visit is to young Franklin,
who is invited to a nearby tavern to taste some excellent madeira. "I
was not a little surpriz'd, and Keimer star'd like a Pig poison'd" (A, 80)
Later on, Keimer, who had been duped into a vegetarian diet by his
crafty young employee, gives up on the diet, orders a roast pig, and eats
the whole thing before Franklin and his companions can join him for
dinner. All of Keimer's schemes are transparent; all his religious notions absurd. Where he appears in the narrative, the reader enters the
realm of comedy, where fat employers and their rascally employees
perform their timeless roles.

The passages featuring Keimer best exemplify the narrative verve
that keeps the story moving through eighty-three manuscript pages.
Why, then, did Franklin stop? The absence of chapters and the continuous character of the "Notes" indicate that he was not writing within
discrete units. He was not distracted by some sudden press of business,
if we assume that he worked over it for a longer period than just the
visit to Twyford. Moreover, he left the manuscript alone for several
years in England, during which time he might have returned to it; he
brought it to America along with the rest of his papers, and then left it
there when he departed for France—as if he had no expectation of re-
suming it. Did he consider the story finished?

Franklin was an inveterate and skillful story teller, as his own shorter
pieces and the reminiscences of his contemporaries can attest. He
would not have left off telling a story in the middle. The first section describes what he has reconstructed as a coherent and distinct unit of his
life's experience. The directionless quality of his early life, his financial
anxieties, his unmarried and unsettled state, all his errata—all this is resolved or reconciled. He was settled as a printer; he had assembled his
group of associates in the Junto; the first public project, the subscription library, had been carried out successfully. (It is interesting to note
that he did not end this section with his marriage.) He concludes with
a sudden shift toward the present, connecting the library with its successors throughout the colonies. "These Libraries have improv'd the
general Conversation of the Americans, made the common Tradesmen
and Farmers as intelligent as most Gentlemen from other Countries,

and perhaps have contributed in some degree to the Stand so generally made throughout the Colonies in Defence of their Privileges" (A, 131). The gap between past and present, so carefully preserved this far in the narrative, is suddenly bridged in a single sentence, and Franklin has no more to say.

Yet Franklin had not finished the story in the way he had first meant to, as promised by the introductory paragraphs and outlined in the "Notes." He had described an extended period of gradual accommodation to the exigencies of work and life in society; the identity thus far achieved was that of a promising young tradesman, someone with a canny eye to what was possible (and impossible) for a person in his condition. The continuation of the story would involve almost a reversal in the direction thus far established, for he found it impossible to leave work and to alter the character of social life in Philadelphia. But it seems as if he could manage no transition into the next stage. He had written himself into a premature conclusion, so he put the eighty-three pages and the outline away. He did not send the so-called letter to his son or, so far as we know, show it to anyone—evidence that he considered it still unfinished.

When he resumed again, he did not have the manuscript of the first part available, but he knew almost exactly where he had left off.[6] He overlaps one item; the second part retells the story of the founding of the Library Company of Philadelphia. As a concluding episode the founding of the Library is treated as an instance of successful collaboration with friends, in contrast to his competitive and frustrating relationships with those other bookish friends, Collins and Ralph. The episode reads like a kind of coda, distinct from the previous stage but self-contained. The reference to the colonies' defense of their privileges lets in suddenly the jarring political realities that Franklin was temporarily protected from. The tone of mellow recollection had been sustained as long as it could be.

5 "Bettering the Whole Race of Men"

W ho was supposed to read the record of his life that Franklin composed in 1771? All the extensive writing he had done up to this point was meant to be read at once, so it was published immediately after it was written. This piece was stowed away for thirteen years, during which Franklin seems to have wholly ignored the project. All the rest of his writings had audiences that could be rather readily identified. But the first part of the *Autobiography*, despite its ostensible recipient, develops for itself an implied audience different from any that Franklin had so far addressed. One reason he stopped writing in 1771 may have been his feeling that this audience had disappeared. He resumed writing, in turn, when he felt a renewed sense that the audience could exist.[1]

No other colonial American writer had Franklin's opportunities for noting the audiences different sorts of writing had—or for creating an audience of his own. He was a printer and bookseller; even if he had no more than an economic motive, he would have had to concern himself with what the public, or rather various publics, would buy. And Franklin always had more than economic motives for his writing and printing. After his first periodical letters, submitted surreptitiously to his brother's newspaper, he appeared in print as the publisher of the *Pennsylvania Gazette*, *Poor Richard's Almanack*, and a variety of pamphlets written for particular occasions. In those writings he found a variety of ways to mediate between himself and the reader: the *Gazette* was speaking, or Richard Saunders the astrologer, or an anonymous friend of the public good. After his active printing career was over, his most common mode of publication took the form of letters to friends who would arrange for the letters to circulate and eventually be published. His writings on electricity, for example, were first of all a series of letters to Peter Collinson, a correspondent of his who was a Fellow of the Royal Society. The initial recipient of the letter thus took the initiative of publishing it; Franklin's formal standing as a private person was not impaired. Eventually those letters would be collected in editions of his papers; by 1771 four editions of his *Experiments and Observations on Electricity* had appeared, and in the later editions several letters and treatises having nothing to do with electricity were included in the volume. Franklin's published writings at this point already had a miscellaneous but interlinked quality; his most important writings had found their way into the editions thus far published of his *Experiments and Observations*, and a more extensive selection was in the process of being assembled in his first French edition, the *Oeuvres de Franklin*, edited by Barbeu Dubourg and published in 1773.

In editions of collected papers published in the eighteenth century, the author often included some notice of his own life. Even Pope's *Moral Essays* appeared with the *Epistle to Doctor Arbuthnot* as an autobiographical preface that in some sense authenticates the moral perspective represented in the *Essays*. A memoir of Voltaire appeared in the Kehl edition of his papers, and Hume's brief autobiography seems to have been intended to appear in his collected works.[2] For all of these writers the autobiography was not to be seen as an independent text; it appeared in conjunction with other writings and served as an adjunct to them. (Even Gibbon's autobiography is supposed to memorialize the author of the *Decline and Fall*.) Jefferson's autobiography, left uncompleted, deliberately avoids reference to matters that were already adequately covered elsewhere in his public papers. If Franklin thought in 1771 that his memoir was similarly to be part of his collected writings, then the implicit audience would be the same audience who would read his papers. (In fact, the *Autobiography* first appeared more or less fully as part of his grandson's 1817 collected edition of Franklin's papers.) Collected editions of a writer were not in those times intended only for specialists or for libraries. Every educated person's collection of books included such editions; the first books Franklin describes owning were Bunyan's works "in separate little Volumes" (A, 57), a collection no doubt including Bunyan's autobiography.

Yet by the time he put aside the first part of his life, the *Autobiography* had become something that could hardly fit snugly into any collection of his writings. Instead, as the *Autobiography* grew, it came to absorb his other writings, revealing them as subordinate revelations of a self now more fully exposed to the world. To frame the circumstances, for example, behind his London philosophical pamphlet serves to convert that piece from an effort in philosophy to a gesture for public attention; it was one of his *errata*. Thus in turn the audiences for his earlier works are absorbed into the more comprehensive audience for his life as a whole.

William Franklin the son provides some vestige of the mediation between himself and his readers that Franklin was accustomed to, but even within the first paragraph of the manuscript the father had shifted from singular to plural in describing his audience. Writing of the impulse in old men to talk about themselves and their past actions, he notes that he will indulge that impulse "without being troublesome to others who thro' respect to Age might think themselves oblig'd to give me a Hearing, since this may be read or not as any one pleases" (A, 44). The distance Franklin professes to establish between author and reader is thus in part a protection for the reader. The distinction between written and oral discourse is central for Franklin; oral discourse is characteristically described as disputatious, unchecked, and self-indulgent, while written discourse serves to unite and instruct its readers. Describing the process by which he learned to write, Franklin digresses about the habits of argumentation he fell into as a result, he says, of reading the sermons and tracts in his father's library (A, 60). In the Junto the club members were required to bring in written essays and to avoid all disputative and dogmatic statements (A, 116–17). His closest friends are identified as lovers of reading. And since his own life is by the act of writing made into a text, his reader may examine it as he himself had examined the water-logged copy of Bunyan, with the bookman's love of a well-presented text. Significantly this section ends with the forecast of the great increase of libraries and reading in America, which has "improv'd the general Conversation of the Americans" (A, 130–31).

The freedom Franklin grants in the first paragraph, to put the book down, carries with it certain requirements for those who are willing to become his readers. Moreover, the express grant of freedom is one in a series of strategies of inclusion, by which all possible readers may be enrolled in his audience. Those who might read on are provided all kinds of assistance in recapturing the social contexts of Franklin's life (though, to be sure, Franklin needs less detail for such social contexts because they impinge on him less, he implies, than on other people). All the characters of his story are identified for us; one need know little more than a very general sense of American geography to locate the action; he reports about his calling, but not as if talking to a fellow printer. (Since virtually nothing of what he wrote in 1771 still lingered in the public memory, he could make his selection of details without fear of correction.) He asks only that readers accept his own evaluation of himself as a success. This is not an ambiguous or problematic claim; he has arrived at prosperity and reputation and can point to that as an outward and visible manifestation of a corresponding inner state. Appearances for Franklin are not a contrast to reality; they are part of reality. He makes sure to appear busy; he safeguards his character before the world. The reader is continually asked to see Franklin's life in terms of promise and fulfillment, so that reality and appearance—the appearance of Philadelphia in the 1720s or the reality of Franklin's risky venture into printing—are like contrasting plot elements in a story that must be continued until it is at last completed in Franklin the author's present.

The basic strategy of inclusion practiced by Franklin in this first part of the *Autobiography* is his pervasive insinuation that his reader is in every significant way like him. In part his humor operates toward this end. He is never jolting or divisive in his laughter; the audience is invited to laugh at the famished Keimer eating a pork roast by himself, but it had also been amused by Franklin's awkward naiveté as he walked about the streets of Philadelphia with puffy rolls in his pocket. He is careful to dissociate himself from any theological position; he was, at one time, a "thorough Deist," but he evolves from that to a set of ethical presuppositions that are shared with the believers in revelation. After reversing the orthodox evaluation of vanity in the first paragraph of the manuscript, he turns around in the next paragraph and ascribes all the happiness of his life to God. The prudent skepticism which he seems to settle on by the end of this section is a widely adoptable mental habit, not part of a body of beliefs.

Though he is an American, he does not play to an American audience. Later, in the third part, he describes how he devised a method to clean London streets that was adapted from the practice he initiated in Philadelphia, and he mentions in passing that Philadelphia street lamps are better designed than those in London (A, 202–8). However different they might have been, Philadelphia and London are presented in the *Autobiography* as cities with dirt and light problems. He was able to make himself at home in all countries, so his readers are endowed with a similar adaptability. He makes no special point about his own adaptability, treating it as in every way what anyone else would do, and he is continually surrounded by people whose lives are divided between one side of the Atlantic and the other: Ralph, who has returned to England after a stay in Philadelphia; Mr. Denham, who visits Bristol to repay his creditors; Dr. Baird, who had praised young Franklin's industriousness and was visited by Franklin and his son at St. Andrew's—the list could be extended. Franklin's America in 1771 is British, and his England is filled with people who have American connections. His repeated references to those interconnections serve to extend the bounds of his audience.

This audience was, however, a particularly fragile construct while Franklin was writing. Franklin ignores political considerations in Part I, except for a note connecting his opposition to his brother with the current disputes between the colonies and England. In avoiding those considerations he was trying to appeal to the enlightened perspective as opposed to the party perspective; whatever the current disputes might be, Franklin was both fully English—at home with the bishop— and fully American—the "water American" whose drinking habits had seemed so outlandish to his fellow workmen in London in 1725. But an audience whose political and national ties could be subordinated to a genial cosmopolitanism was already impossible by 1771, despite Franklin's efforts to the contrary. It would take thirteen years, as well as some unexpected prodding from friends, before he could try to reconstitute or redesign the audience to which he was presenting his life.

In the meantime the manuscript joined the disorderly mass of papers that was accumulating at Franklin's Craven Street residence in London. When he left England in March 1775, his papers went with him; when he left America for France in October 1777, his papers were stored with his friend and political ally Joseph Galloway at Trevose, Galloway's country residence north of Philadelphia. Galloway, who joined the Loyalists, left the city; his wife remained, dying in 1782. That year Abel James, an executor of her estate and a friend of Franklin, wrote him in Paris that the manuscript and its outline had turned up in the trunk of Franklin's papers. James sent along with his letter a copy of the outline.[3]

Franklin in turn forwarded James's letter and the notes to his English friend Benjamin Vaughan, who had produced three years earlier an English edition of Franklin's works. Upon receiving that volume, Franklin had written that the papers he had left behind in America (including, of course, the first part of the *Autobiography*) would provide material enough for three more such volumes, "of which a great part would be more interesting" (*W*, 7:411). Now Franklin was asking Vaughan's opinion of a continuation of the first part. Vaughan wrote back vigorously encouraging the project, joining James in urging Franklin, who was by this time seventy-seven, to resume writing immediately. It was over a year, though, before Franklin went back to it.

The continuation is prefaced by a note, apparently meant to be printed, explaining the reasons for the interruption in narration.

> Memo.
> Thus far was written with the Intention express'd in the beginning and therefore contains several little family Anecdotes of no Importance to others. What follows was written many Years after in compliance with the Advice contain'd in these Letters, and accordingly intended for the Publick. The Affairs of the Revolution occasion'd the Interruption. (A, 133)

As we have already seen, the address to a family audience had been an authorial device; hereafter, however, he dispensed with that device. (His son had sided with the King during the war, a fact not mentioned here but sufficient to disqualify him from serving as an apparent audience.) Franklin links the change in audience to "the Affairs of the Revolution"; the Revolution had alienated him from that transatlantic English audience that he had first addressed, so he had to find another. The letters from James and Vaughan, which Franklin offers as his incentive for continuing, provide him also with a revised version of an audience.

Thus, the history of the *Autobiography* manuscript significantly affects the meaning of the work as a whole. The Revolution is not part of the action narrated, but it took place between the two sections. Instead of going on without pause, as his recovered outline would have enabled him pretty much to do, he brings the reader's attention to the break, reminding the reader that there is a narrator who exists in a changing reality different from that of the character.

Situated in the middle of the *Autobiography*, the letters of James and Vaughan become the first critical interpretation of the work. They are all the more important because they carry the implicit endorsement of Franklin himself. The use of dedicatory letters both to advertise and to suggest interpretations was not new with Franklin; in early editions of *Pamela*, Samuel Richardson included numerous letters that instructed the readers how to understand the novel.[4] The letters of James and Vaughan define the purpose and true audience for the *Autobiography*; they appear to force upon Franklin the meanings to his work which his own native diffidence will not allow him to admit. James does not assume that the manuscript was intended only as a family document. A tradesman himself, James has been acquainted at first hand with Franklin's business reputation, so we may believe him when he says, "I know of no Character living nor many of them put together, who has so much in his Power as Thyself to promote a greater Spirit of Industry and early Attention to Business, Frugality and Temperance with the American Youth" (A, 134). By the 1780s there was no question that Franklin's biography would be written. "Your history is so remarkable," writes Benjamin Vaughan, "that if you do not give it, somebody else will certainly give it; and perhaps so as nearly to do as much harm, as your own management of the thing might do good" (A, 135). Franklin's life is not merely a sequence of events important only to himself. His life has a public meaning that must be interpreted correctly.

Vaughan suggests that Franklin's *Autobiography* will be superior to past examples of the genre. "This style of writing seems a little gone out of vogue, and yet it is a very useful one; and your specimen of it may be particularly serviceable, as it will make a subject of comparison with the lives of various public cutthroats and intriguers, and with absurd monastic self-tormentors, or vain literary triflers" (A, 138). Vaughan's statement describes the extant autobiographical tradition. The pamphlet lives of condemned criminals, like the notorious Jonathan Wild, were hawked on the London streets during the eighteenth century. Saint Augustine's *Confessions* had inspired imitators among what the enlightened Vaughan considered "absurd monastic self-tormentors." Colley Cibber's *Apology* is almost a conscious self-portrait as "vain literary trifler." Surely Franklin's *Autobiography* would generate imitations more useful than its predecessors. If so, "it will be worth all Plutarch's Lives put together" (A, 139). In an age that consciously modeled itself after Greek and Roman patterns, Vaughan could hardly have made a more drastic assertion.

Vaughan's letter is filled with contrasting images of blind confusion and ordered awareness. The source of disorder in the lives of men is the preoccupation with the present. "Our sensations being very much fixed to the moment, we are apt to forget that more moments are to follow the first, and consequently that man should arrange his conduct so as to suit the *whole* of a life" (A, 137). The source of Franklin's wisdom is his escape from the limiting perspective of the present. He had waited and prepared for his time to appear on the stage of the world, subordinating the present to the effect of the whole. Until now the tyrannous present moment has blinded men, leaving them "blundering on in the dark...from the farthest trace of time" (A, 136). Franklin's wisdom has enabled him to establish a pervasive order in his life, so that "the passing moments...have been enlivened with content and enjoyment, instead of being tormented with foolish impatience or regrets" (A, 138).

"For the furtherance of human happiness," Vaughan writes, "I have always maintained that it is necessary to prove that man is not even at present a vicious and detestable animal; and still more to prove that good management may greatly amend him" (A, 139). Franklin offers a final response to a whole tradition of interpreting human character that culminated in Swift. His *Autobiography* is to be empirical proof of human perfectibility. Since at least the 1760s Franklin had been planning a treatise to be entitled the *Art of Virtue*, which he had described in letters to Lord Kames and to Vaughan. In the *Autobiography* letter, Vaughan mentions the *Art of Virtue* as another reason for continuing the *Autobiography*. The two would accompany each other as theory and practice and in turn would be complemented by Franklin's other writings. Franklin's writings as a whole would demonstrate that virtuous principles can be displayed in a man's conduct.

This proof of Franklin's virtue in action would also justify the American Revolution, of which Franklin had been the author. "[A]s your own character will be the principal one to receive a scrutiny, it is proper (even for its effects upon your vast and rising country, as well as upon England and upon Europe), that it should stand respectable and eternal" (A, 139). Vaughan compares the *Autobiography* to Caesar and Tacitus, Roman authors who had described the simple and noble societies of the Gauls and Germans. Franklin's personal experience is actually an epitome of American experience. "All that has happened to you is also connected with the detail of the manners and situation of a *rising* people" (A, 135). The *Autobiography* will reconcile Englishmen to Americans, since Englishmen will come to respect and love him through reading his life. Ultimately the *Autobiography* will address an even wider audience. "Extend your views even further; do not stop at those who speak the English tongue, but after having settled so many points in nature and politics, think of bettering the whole race of men" (A, 140). Here was an audience to compensate for the one Franklin had lost with the Revolution. By becoming the representative American self, he could convert his experience into a model for mankind as a whole.

Franklin indicates in the opening of the new section begun in France that the inserted letters had arrived some time before he started writing again. His experiences this time are different from those he had entertained at Twyford. Here at Passy, in the house rented from his friend Le Veillard, he was also writing because of "having now a little Leisure" (A, 141), but he remarks the absence of his papers and proposes to write what he can, figuring to resume in America when his papers would be available. He seems a bit hesitant to resume the project without the materials he had been able to work from in the first part, but he was seventy-eight years old and he knew that it was uncertain whether he would ever see those papers again.

Though he did not have the manuscript available in France when he resumed writing, Franklin recalled almost exactly where he had left off. (A vertical line is drawn though the Notes to the point where he had stopped, though it is hard to say when that line was drawn [A, 269].) The two sections overlap only in the description of how the Philadelphia Library company was founded. The overlap is consequently of some interest because it provides a measure of the continuities and modulations of his intentions from the first to the second parts. In both versions Franklin attributes to the libraries the high level of intelligence and public awareness among the common people of America. As he does in other cases, he uses much the same phrasing for the two versions of the same event. In 1771 he had written, "This was the Mother of all the N American Subscription Libraries now so numerous. It is become a great thing itself, and continually increasing" (A, 130). In 1784 he speaks of the library, "which from a small Beginning is now become so considerable" (A, 141). But the focus in the first version had been on Franklin and his friends, the Junto, and their club meetings; the first collection of books had been aimed at serving their needs. In the later version Franklin emphasizes the general lack, in the colonies south of Boston, of books and booksellers. The Library Company was thus a gesture in the direction of intellectual self-help and self-sufficiency for the colonies as a whole. Also, he goes into some detail about the means he used to raise subscriptions for the Library and describes how best to advance public projects.

Beginning with the second part, the *Autobiography* is no longer a record of *errata* and their correction. It has become a book of practical suggestions for those who would wish to imitate Franklin. Franklin's original outline had provided, or at least left room, for such a shift of emphasis; following the mention of the Library his notes read "Manner of conducting the Project. Its plan and Utility" (A, 269). Still, he had not proposed his practice as a model for future imitation in the first part.

The second part in general is less easygoing and anecdotal than the first part had been. Several items in his Notes are left out of the sequence he had first established: "Children. Almanack....Carolina Partnership. Learn French and German. Journey to Boston after 10 years. Affection of my Brother. His Death and leaving me his Son" (A,

269). All these items appear in the third section; Franklin omits them here so he can include more public and theoretical concerns: "Great Industry. Constant Study. Fathers Remark and Advice upon Diligence. Art of Virtue" (A, 269), to which should be added his comments on religious dogma and private worship, unlisted in the Notes. The humor is drier and cooler than in the first section, where he himself had been the principal source of his amusement.

In part his changes of emphasis from the first part and from the initial outline seem to arise from the work's increased importance for him. Before, he had been freed from direct confrontation with his ultimate readers by the editorial convenience of an implied audience. Now he was not only deprived of the mediation, but he was also clearly addressing a far larger audience than he could have imagined in 1771. He had been a prominent, but somewhat anomalous, figure in London in 1771—an American tradesman and scientist in the London of Pitt and Burke and Johnson. By 1784 he had attained far more than what he had once guardedly described as "some Degree of Reputation in the World." His fame in France was extraordinary; six years later a period of national mourning would be declared by the National Assembly at the news of his death. Even his touchy rival John Adams testified that the commonest people of Europe saw him as a benefactor of mankind. He was writing in France, far from an audience who would readily comprehend the details of a small business in Philadelphia fifty years earlier. Besides, Benjamin Vaughan had exhorted him to address all mankind.

In the second section the distinction between author and actor, so carefully preserved thus far, disappears. Franklin the character is hereafter linked to Franklin the narrator. As a result, the sharp discrimination between the past and the authorial present begins to blur. A chance remark Franklin records signals this development; as he is retelling the Library Company story, he reports the scrivener Brockden's remark that none of them signing the fifty-year contract would likely survive the period. But several did, he notes, including himself. In the first section Franklin had generally avoided the opportunities to connect his action to the present: he had drawn no contrasts between the London of the 1720s and the London where he then lived; even in the case of the "croaker" Samuel Mickle, who had discouraged Franklin in his first days as an independent entrepreneur, he does not bring up the city's present flourishing state for contrast. In the second part, connections are continually drawn between young Franklin and old Franklin. He mentions the importance to him of his father's saying, from Proverbs, "*Seest thou a Man diligent in his Calling, he shall stand before*

Kings, he shall not stand before mean Men," and he adds that in time he stood before five kings and that one invited him to sit down (A, 144). He offers further discussion of his religious opinions; here the opinions he cites are those which he acquired in his twenties and still holds (A, 145–48). And he gives an abbreviated account of what he calls the Art of Virtue. In each case, a principle of life is set forth which Franklin has permanently put into effect in his life. As a result, the chronological sequence in this section gives place to concerns that the eighteenth century would have considered broadly philosophical.

The mention of dining with a king leads Franklin naturally to a key transitional motif. His wife greatly furthered his rise to wealth, he says, through her household economies and her assistance in running the print shop. The Franklins lived simply, without expensive furniture, elaborate food, or elegant kitchenware. Franklin ate his regular breakfast of bread and milk with a pewter spoon from an earthenware porringer.

> But mark how Luxury will enter Families, and make a Progress, in Spite of Principle. Being call'd one Morning to Breakfast, I found it in a China Bowl with a Spoon of Silver. They had been bought for me without my Knowledge by my wife, and had cost her the enormous Sum of three and twenty Shillings, for which she had no other Excuse or Apology to make, but that she thought her Husband deserv'd a Silver Spoon and China Bowl as well as any of his Neighbours. This was the first Appearance of Plate and China in our House, which afterwards in a Course of Years as our Wealth encreas'd augmented gradually to several Hundred Pounds in Value. (A, 145)

The plate and china in the Franklin household proliferates to hundreds of pounds in value within a single sentence. The acquisition of wealth does not come as a slow and uncertain process; indeed he says that "My Circumstances ... grew daily easier: my original Habits of Frugality continuing" (A, 144). The completed Benjamin Franklin does not emerge slowly out of a complex experience. Instead he bursts into affluence; the china cabinet fills suddenly as if by itself.

The second section concludes with an abbreviated version of something that Franklin had for some time been planning as a longer work. "It was about this time," he writes, "that I conceiv'd the bold and arduous Project of arriving at moral Perfection" (A, 148). Of all Franklin's models of self-improvement, this was the most elaborate and ambitious; it was this passage in particular that prompted the rage D. H.

Lawrence expressed in his essay on Franklin in *Studies in Classic American Literature*. He had written about this projected treatise to friends years earlier, and Benjamin Vaughan's appended letter alludes to it as a companion piece for the *Autobiography*. As the editors of the Yale edition of his *Papers* point out, by 1784 Franklin "probably realized he would never write such a separate work, so he compromised by introducing the main outlines of his plan into the autobiography here" (*A*, 148n). The name he used for this treatise is the *Art of Virtue*. It is not a speculative discussion on the nature and kinds of virtue, but rather a kind of psychological experiment, or what the eighteenth century called a "project."

At the beginning Franklin drew up a catalogue of virtues that appear to be "necessary or desirable." Each week he would work on one virtue. The virtues were organized so as to make mastery of the later ones contingent on those previously acquired; all other virtues, for example, depended on the first, Temperance, which would give Franklin a cool head to watch out for violations. Silence was next, a high priority for Franklin, who wished "to break a Habit I was getting into of Prattling, Punning, and Joking, which only made me acceptable to trifling Company" (*A*, 151). He even made up a little book for keeping his records of moral perfection, inscribed with quotations in praise of wisdom and virtue from Proverbs, Cicero, and Addison's *Cato*.

Part of the book was devoted to a daily schedule, in accordance with the third virtue, Order. At five o'clock he would "Rise, wash, and address *Powerful Goodness*; Contrive Day's business and take the Resolution of the Day; prosecute the present Study" (*A*, 154). With all his resolutions thus organized, he set forth on the bold and arduous Project. "I enter'd upon the Execution of this Plan for Self Examination, and continu'd it with occasional Intermissions for some time. I was surpriz'd to find myself so much fuller of Faults than I had imagined, but I had the Satisfaction of seeing them diminish" (*A*, 155). In time the little book wore out, full of holes from the erasures made each time he began the thirteen-week sequence again. Order always eluded him. His time refused to pass according to the established schedule. Humility, the last virtue, was also a problem. A Quaker friend had had to point out Franklin's need for it, so he added it to his list, "giving an extensive Meaning to the Word. I cannot boast of much Success in acquiring the *Reality* of this Virtue; but I had a good deal with regard to the *Appearance* of it" (*A*, 159). Eventually Franklin abandoned the thirteen-week course because of the press of public affairs, leaving Order and Humility imperfectly attained.

Yet his difficulties with Order did not distress him. "For something that pretended to be Reason was every now and then suggesting to me that such extream Nicety as I exacted of my self might be a kind of Foppery in Morals, which if it were known would make me ridiculous; that a perfect Character might be attended with the Inconvenience of being envied and hated; and that a benevolent Man should allow a few Faults in himself, to keep his Friends in Countenance" (A, 156). "Foppery in Morals" betrays Franklin's attitude toward the project. The moral perfection he sought is not like the Puritan's justification, the attainment of a state of grace, nor even sanctification, the outward appearance of that state. Morality is a style of dress which the self must put on to make its way in the world. In this abbreviated Art of Virtue a Franklin consciousness is offered to us—not the sort of consciousness D. H. Lawrence, for example, would have insisted on, a skin-grown into unconsciously over time, but consciousness as a suit of clothes worn over the natural self.

If we ask what Franklin's attitude is toward this scheme, we find no simple answer. His whole life is, in some sense, offered as an advertisement for the bold and arduous project. He cites the advantages accruing to him from such mastery as he has achieved, listing the virtues and their separate benefits and commending the program to his posterity for its service in providing him "the constant Felicity of his Life down to his 79th Year" (A, 157). Yet he also describes the project as an elaborate and obsessive game, an experiment like his experiments in electricity.[5] And he implies that the attempt to achieve moral perfection is somewhat ridiculous. He pauses after describing his problems with Order to tell the story of a man who wanted an axe ground to make its face bright. Eventually the effort of turning the grindstone made the man decide that a speckled axe was best. Franklin is determined to maintain differing and contradictory perspectives toward the project simultaneously.

Thus, the bold and arduous project is both commendable to Franklin's posterity and a foppery in morals. The two perspectives are linked by his characteristic irony, an irony that is both controlled and elusive. We see two Franklins: one who would live according to his highest ideal of himself and another who jokes too much, argues rashly, sleeps late, and leaves his papers in disarray. These two Franklins serve as opposed and coordinated principles within the same self. There are other opposing Franklins as well in the Autobiography: Franklin the actor and Franklin the evaluator, old Franklin and young Franklin, Franklin the solitary experimenter with himself and Franklin the published life spread before the world. Supervising each of these oppositions is the conscious ego, represented in the Autobiography by the narrator. The bold and arduous project is not an effort of the superego. It resembles a game rather than a spiritual exercise because the superego has been so completely directed by consciousness.

The *Art of Virtue* concludes the second section. Here, as in the first section, he had arrived at a natural stopping place, and the emphasis on principles of life made it difficult to resume the narrative of events which he had, for the most part, set aside.[6] The last of the virtues he tried to acquire was humility; he goes into an extended discussion of his difficulties with it. He has achieved at least the appearance of humility, he claims, by avoiding direct contradiction of others. But pride cannot be subdued completely. "Disguise it, struggle with it, beat it down, stifle it, mortify it as much as one pleases, it is still alive, and will every now and then peep out and show itself. You will see it perhaps often in this History. For even if I could conceive that I had compleatly overcome it, I should probably by [be] proud of my Humility" (A, 160). Franklin reverts here to addressing his audience directly as he had at the very beginning. A little earlier he had referred rather formally to his posterity, addressing them in the third person. But here he returns to the self-delighted, often self-mocking tone so characteristic of the first section, and of many of his letters, and he recovers the old sense of audience he had at the beginning.

6 Writing to the End

A ll the separate parts of Franklin's *Autobiography* were written while his active political life appeared to be in abeyance or at an end. They represent periods when his whole life seemed behind him. At Twyford he was able to envision a conclusion in his Notes that would present his character and a few summary lessons of his experience. At Passy he had completed the wartime negotiations with the French and the peace negotiations with the British; he had petitioned Congress to be relieved of his post. (Probably at around this time he added a few items to the Notes, taking him from 1771 to the treaty of 1783.) And in 1788 when he took up the writing for the third time, he was finished with the Constitutional Convention and looked forward to the imminent end of his term as President of the Supreme Executive Council of Pennsylvania.

Now Franklin was at home in Philadelphia, among the papers he had missed while writing in France. Though he continued the account on the same page where he left off, he had delayed the resumption of the project by three years despite the exhortations of European friends to finish it.[1] In certain ways Franklin was responding in this last section to his present moment in America: he enters a lengthy cautionary note against malice and altercation in the newspapers, a theme in his other writings of this period as well; in the midst of the factional struggles about the Constitution he puts forward a proposal, formulated fifty-seven years earlier, for a united party for virtue, composed of men free from partisan concerns. But his own immediate present is not at all Franklin's greatest concern in the summer of 1788; for him time was by no means divided so clearly into past and present as it had once been. He had put off writing into the end of his life until he could no longer end it.

A sense of projects uncompleted pervades that last section of the *Autobiography*. He begins by noting that he could not have the help from his papers that he had hoped for, since many were lost in the war (A, 161). He had mentioned toward the end of the previous section "*a great and extensive Project*" related to the program for achieving moral perfection; so he picks up the narrative by describing this project. This was his idea for a party of virtue or, as he called it, the Society of the Free and Easy, a secret organization of young men trained in virtue and obedient to Franklin's all-purpose creed. "But my then narrow Circumstances, and the Necessity I was under of sticking close to my Business, occasion'd my postponing the farther Prosecution of it at that time, and my multifarious Occupations public and private induc'd me to continue postponing, so that it has been omitted till I have no longer Strength or Activity left sufficient for such an Enterprize" (A, 163). One detects a certain nostalgia for this unfulfillable ambition, so much more grandiose even than Franklin's real accomplishments. Other projects as well had to be abandoned before fruition, like the Albany Plan of Union or his plan for keeping the streets of London clean. Even in the case of his experiments on electricity he reports that he left his papers undefended against the attacks of his rival, Abbé Nollet, letting them "shift for themselves; believing it was better to spend what time I could spare from public Business in making new Experiments, than in Disputing about those already made" (A, 243–44). Franklin frequently notes the lack of time available for significant projects—a comment applicable no doubt to the *Autobiography* itself. He was eighty-two years old and in considerable pain much of the time from a bladder stone that had bothered him for ten years. As he wrote further, the end of his narration seems to have receded from him.

Still, he turns the theme of incompletion into an opportunity and sets up a kind of collaboration; the reader is continually invited to finish or amend what Franklin has begun. In the case of the Society of the Free and Easy, Franklin does not dismiss it as a visionary scheme or fret over his inability to make it work. Though it would be a great undertaking, "I have always thought that one Man of tolerable Abilities may work great Changes, and accomplish great Affairs among Mankind, if he first forms a good Plan, and, cutting off all Amusements or other Employments that would divert his Attention, makes the Execution of that same Plan his sole Study and Business" (A, 163). One would not need genius, but rather tolerable abilities, a good plan, and a total concentration of effort. The transformation from his son to posterity as the putative audience is complete in this last section; Franklin is now addressing a general audience who can fulfill his multifarious designs. His scheme for cleaning the streets is, through the *Autobiography*, made public and thereby available for adoption. When he describes crossing the Atlantic in 1757, he reflects on the experimentation that might be done on the lading of ships. "I am therefore persuaded that ere long some ingenious Philosopher will undertake it: to whom I wish Success" (A, 257).

Of course the Franklin who recommends concentration dispersed his own energies widely. To his friend Le Veillard he had promised he would complete the manuscript of the *Autobiography* on his voyage to Philadelphia in 1785; instead he wrote short essays on the Gulf Stream, on fixing smoky chimneys, and on a new design for a stove (W, 9:497; also W, 9:371). Once arrived in Philadelphia, he was elected to the office as the President of the Supreme Executive Council of Pennsylvania, an office he held for three straight years. His letters indicate that these responsibilities, the disorder of his papers, the Constitutional Convention of 1787, and the frequent visitors he saw all conspired to keep him from starting again (W, 9:559, 637, 645). Le Veillard in particular pressed him to resume writing, and Franklin in return kept promising, like many another writer, to start soon, the next day even. Several of Franklin's correspondents, including a significant share of his close acquaintances in England and France, knew about the *Autobiography*, so references to the work are frequent in his letters of the late 1780s.

Like the other parts of the *Autobiography*, the major portion of the third part was written in a spurt of concentrated effort, stretching from August to October 1788. During that period he wrote 103 manuscript pages, taking him to his fiftieth year and to the time when he was to leave for England. Both his letters and the evidence of the manuscript indicate that he paused at that point. Earlier he had tended to refer to the work as a "little history" that could be easily turned out with a bit of concerted application. By October 1788, though, the *Autobiography* no longer seemed like another of those neat self-limited projects he had been doing all his life. To Edward Bancroft, his former associate in the Paris mission, he wrote that the work "may be useful to the rising Generation," adopting the very phraseology Vaughan had used in spurring him on to complete it (W, 9:550). When he was finally ready to begin the American continuation, in the summer of 1788, he wrote to Le Veillard jokingly accusing him of being "a hard taskmaster" for enquiring about Franklin's possible role in the new government. "You insist on his writing *his life*, already a long work, and at the same time would have him continually employed in augmenting the subject, while the time shortens in which the work is to be executed" (W, 9:665). The metaphoric confusion between book and life that Franklin had played with in the first section was still on his mind as he began the last. Rereading what he had written thus far, when he reached his fiftieth year in the narrative, Franklin remarked in a letter to Vaughan that he was pleased with it. "If a writer can judge properly of his own work, I fancy, on reading over what is already done, that the book will be found entertaining, interesting, and useful, more so than I expected when I began it" (W, 9:676).

The last section is characterized by a strong interest in events. The reader does not see Franklin as a character as in the first section; here he is the recorder of occurrences—the death of his little son, his political offices, his projects for Philadelphia. He does not carry over the novelistic tendency of the first section or the broadly philosophical concerns of the second; perhaps the availability of some of his papers and the effect of his old Philadelphia surroundings influenced him toward a greater emphasis on the public substance of his life. So far as he can be, he is rigorously chronological, prefacing most episodes with the date. He departs from this annalistic mode only by accident, as in the entries on the Franklin stove and his experiments on electricity. On the other hand, in the continuation he was following his Notes, which were themselves largely chronological in sequence. (Several of the items omitted from the Notes while he was writing in Paris are picked up here: "Children. Almanack. the Use I made of it. . . .Carolina Partnership. Learn French and German" [A, 269].) Moreover, in the first section Franklin had been making public his own early life, a life which had been private and unobserved. In this section he enters the public world, and that world gradually expands in circumference. The Franklin who does things in this section is the same Franklin who writes it all down. There is no further occasion to note his *errata*, since the period of youthful indiscretion is behind him. (One would find in the *Autobiography* no basis for concluding that blunders, misperceptions, and acts of callousness occur in adulthood as well as before.) The larger mistakes of public men and nations are now his subject.

Franklin does not describe himself as evolving in his perceptions after his twenties. He discovers the value of training women in bookkeeping and business management or the auditory and emotional power of oratory, but he is not altered in his basic identity by these discoveries, as he had been by the discoveries of his youth. Now it is the world around him that is changed by his personality. The militia, the Pennsylvania Hospital, even the building left over from the Great Awakening are all made to fulfill Franklin's notion of a congenial human community: the militia offers citizen protection (and, once established, it parades through town with its swords drawn in his honor); the hospital "for the Reception and Care of poor sick Persons, whether Inhabitants of the Province or Strangers" (A, 199) can only be financed through his sanction and management; the New Building is transformed through his negotiations from a religious assembly place to a school lecture hall. He is careful to ascribe to others those innovations that had been incorrectly attributed to him; the Philadelphia of his *Autobiography* is peopled with citizens of just the sort of public spirit he valued and exemplified.

The absence of evolving perceptions in this section gives the narrative a somewhat more loose-knit and variegated character. From the political dilemmas of the Quakers he shifts to the Franklin stove and then to the founding of the Philadelphia Academy (A, 188–94). Yet he could not describe his life simply as an interminable accumulation of experiences leading to no end. He was not writing *The Education of Benjamin Franklin.* Certain themes of earlier parts have passed; the pewter spoon and china bowl incident had already dramatized his emergence from poverty to affluence. In this section he is most concerned with the creation of reputation.

Much of the playfulness of the first section is gone from the description of these scenes of prospering and planning. His earlier detachment had made that humor possible, but here, though he is thirty to fifty years removed from the events, he is still involved in all the activities he describes. Franklin's humor is at times quite grim. Noting the crowds that attended Whitefield's sermons, he remarks, "it was matter of Speculation to me who was one of the Number, to observe the extraordinary Influence of his Oratory on his Hearers, and how much they admir'd and respected him, notwithstanding his common Abuse of them, by assuring them they were naturally *half Beasts and half Devils*" (A, 175). Following a night of drunken revelry at a treaty conference in Carlisle, the Indian spokesman explains that the Great Spirit must have intended rum for the Indians to get drunk with. Franklin observes that rum seems to be intended "to extirpate these Savages to make room for Cultivators of the Earth" (A, 199). Samuel Keimer or James Ralph might have been sources of amusement, but the Franklin of this section moves in larger groups, where the human tendency towards folly and self-delusion is accentuated by numbers.

Certain large themes that had appeared earlier persist into this sec-

tion. The danger of disputatiousness, which Franklin had first described in Boston and tried to cure through the virtue project, appears
in the Pennsylvania governors he must cope with, particularly Robert
Hunter Morris (A, 212–14). The value of prudent collaboration is
spelled out in the business arrangements he makes as a silent partner
in other printing establishments. The opposed merits of speaking and
writing, a subject for consideration in his dealings with Collins and
Ralph, are brought up in relation to Whitefield. As always his experience is full of practical lessons for others, particularly for the young.
Writing to his European friends in 1788, he reports that he has omitted
materials that would be of no benefit to a young reader (W, 9:665, 676).
He still sees the purpose of the work as "showing him [the young
reader] from my example, and my success in emerging from poverty,
and acquiring some degree of wealth, power, and reputation, the advantages of certain modes of conduct which I observed, and of avoiding the errors which were prejudicial to me (W, 9:675–76).

Despite Franklin's concern about chronology and dates, the distinction between past and present has disappeared in this final section.
Anecdote and history are mixed together; the issues of other generations are still alive in Franklin's retelling, as if all the long years of his
maturity were a kind of indeterminate present. When he describes the
Albany Plan of Union, which he had drawn up in 1755, he still defends
it as a program, although the Revolution had already taken place to
unite the colonies in independence (A, 209–12). His reminiscences
about General Braddock are accompanied by a detailed list of provisions provided for the junior officers in Braddock's army—an example
of his preoccupation with the papers he had recovered in America (A,
221–22). The narrative is curiously proportioned, often underplaying
the most significant achievements of his life. His experiences as a militia commander in frontier Pennsylvania get more attention than his experiments in electricity, perhaps the most important empirical
research of the century. And even more space is given to the political
questions of the 1740s and 1750s. A succession of colonial governors
passes through his pages, each accompanied by a train of musty anecdotes. Though he reports to his European friends that he has made
considerable omissions in the section he is at this point writing, the
reader notices that he found it difficult to abridge or summarize.

The reader does not *see* Franklin in motion and in action as in the
first section. There are places in the narrative where a specific scene is
described, such as Whitefield's sermon for the Georgia orphanage or
the conversations with Governor Morris. But these vignettes do not
give the reader the same view of Franklin as a depicted person, carry-

ing type forms, throwing his friend in the Delaware, or walking down Market Street, that the first section had presented. Conversations make up more of the third section than of the other parts; characteristically the exchange leads to some pithy clarifying statement, usually by Franklin but often by others with whom he concurs. These conversations exemplify mastery: James Logan's crushing retort to William Penn when Penn rebuked him for fighting in self-defense, or Franklin's suggestion to the Presbyterian chaplain that he become a rum steward (A, 187–88, 235). And little in this section suggests that Franklin's mastery is incomplete, except where he comes in contact with the fathomless incompetence and venality of the British imperial administration.

In all aspects of his life Franklin relentlessly searches for a public and representative meaning. Describing his way of learning languages, beginning with useful modern languages and passing eventually to Latin, he argues for his method in place of the classical emphasis common to his time. His publishing ventures are presented as projects undertaken for the common good: the sayings in *Poor Richard's Almanack* discouraged extravagance and encouraged the development of capital in Pennsylvania; the *Pennsylvania Gazette* was "another Means of Communicating Instruction" (A, 164–65). Even the death of his four-year-old son from smallpox is turned into a lesson of the importance of inoculation at an early age.

Out of these projects and instructions emerges a portrait of American society as it is and should be. The Junto, the volunteer fire companies, and the committees that came together to further projects like the college and hospital—all of these are small models of an American society. They are voluntary associations without obvious leadership. To be a member of such a group did not involve sacrificing one's independence of action or belief. All these groups are deliberately pluralist in character, open to all beliefs and economic conditions. They can function effectively not despite the diversity of their membership but because of it; the members can feel that they represent both themselves and the community at large. Self-interest and patriotism become interchangeable. And behind this network of groups we see Franklin himself, silently taking on the drudgery of routine business for the sake of advancing his own initiatives, propagandizing in the name of a committee of friends, allaying traditional hostilities through careful patterns of representation, refusing ever to appear as the motive force he really is.

By contrast, there are failed versions of American society. The Quakers are admirable in profession but ineffectual in practice, stymied by their unwillingness to adjust principle to the demands of experience.

Indians were killing themselves off with drink, freeing the land for the cultivators of the earth. The colonial bureaucracy, the governors and generals sent over from England, proved either incompetent, unimaginative, or hamstrung by their instructions. Against the Quakers Franklin sets the Dunkards, who have no written creed and are therefore able to respond flexibly to the fresh demands of the spirit. Against the arrogance of most colonial officials Franklin notes the abilities of Governor William Shirley, who was "sensible and sagacious... attentive to good Advice from others, capable of forming judicious Plans, quick and active in carrying them into Execution" and who, when others stood on ceremony, found "*a low Seat* the easiest" (*A*, 253–54). The values of the marketplace, where industry, frugality, flexibility, self-discipline, and alertness to the demands of the moment help one thrive, are the values that distinguish one as an American.

Like the London exchange described in Voltaire's *Philosophical Letters*, American society—for which Franklin's Philadelphia is a model—is supposed to consist of diverse but complementary groups. For Franklin as for Voltaire, diversity meant, in particular, diversity of religions, and the *Autobiography* rightly emphasizes that diversity. There are Quakers, Presbyterians, Anglicans, "French prophets," Dunkards, Moravians, and no doubt others. Franklin always donated to their building funds, and he even gave out valuable advice, to Gilbert Tennent, about fundraising and to the zealous Presbyterian chaplain about drawing a good crowd of militiamen for prayers.

It was as a self-declared friend to all religions that Franklin formulated a kind of all-purpose creed, "containing as I thought the Essentials of every known Religion, and being free of every thing that might shock the Professors of any Religion" (*A*, 162). The creed is part of the imagined Society of the Free and Easy; it purports to be a kind of lowest common denominator for all religions, excluding only what is doctrinally parochial:

That there is one God who made all things.
That he governs the World by his Providence.
That he ought to be worshipped by Adoration, Prayer and
    Thanksgiving.
But that the most acceptable Service of God is doing Good to
    Man.
That the Soul is immortal.
And that God will certainly reward Virtue and punish Vice ei-
    ther here or hereafter.

(*A*, 162)

Franklin does not advance a new belief in competition with the existing ones: the all-purpose creed instead converts all beliefs into varia-
tions on a theme. Whatever we believe is merely one particular version
of this basic creed. Religion becomes thereby an unnecessary term for
the definition of the self.[2]

The religious behavior of his countrymen interested Franklin as a social phenomenon. While checking the frontier defenses against the
French and Indians in 1756, Franklin visited a Moravian settlement
and remarks in the *Autobiography* about their marriage practices, services of worship, and mode of communal living (A, 236–37). When
George Whitefield and the Great Awakening arrive in Philadelphia, he
remarks on how "it seem'd as if all the World were growing Religious;
so that one could not walk thro' the Town in an Evening without Hearing Psalms sung in different Families of every Street" (A, 175–76).
Whitefield's power fascinates Franklin without moving him to emula-
tion; he is too much the walking onlooker and noter of semblances.
Doctrine itself is always a source of delusion for Franklin. In the second section he had noted with disapproval the kind of preaching done
by one minister in Philadelphia, whose aim was "rather to make us
Presbyterians than good Citizens" (A, 147). Citizenship was always superior to religious forms of identity, which struck him as not so much
wrong as inhibiting. After noting the refusal of the Dunkards to set
forth their creed, trusting to the future to enlighten them further, he remarks, "This modesty in a Sect is perhaps a singular Instance in the
History of Mankind, every other Sect supposing itself in Possession of
all Truth, and that those who differ are so far in the Wrong: Like a Man
travelling in foggy Weather: Those at some Distance before him on the
Road he sees wrapt up in the Fog, as well as those behind him, and also
the People in the Fields on each side; but near him all appears clear.
Tho' in truth he is as much in the Fog as any of them" (A, 191). The possibility of anyone being out of the fog in religious or philosophical
questions did not occur to Franklin.

Franklin's sense of detachment from religious experience does not
stem from his preference for science as a superior mode of cognition.
When he describes his own experiments in electricity, he has to sandwich the account awkwardly between the administrations of Governor
Morris and Governor Denny. His small innovation in the design of
street lamps and his invention of the Franklin stove are in keeping with
his intention of showing himself as one more ingenious than brilliant.
And the small inventions are of more tangible practical use than the
great conceptual breakthrough on electricity. "Human Felicity," he
notes, to those who would find his street cleaning proposal trifling, "is

produc'd not so much by great Pieces of good Fortune that seldom happen, as by little Advantages that occur every Day" (*A*, 207).

Most of the third section is devoted to Franklin's political life in Philadelphia in the 1740s and 1750s. His involvement in that world is total and unironic, unlike his attitude toward religion or science. Writing after the Revolution, he takes special care to foreshadow the tensions that led to the conflict. Each of the governors who arrive in Pennsylvania is more high-handed and manipulative than the last. And when the French and Indian War breaks out, Franklin is drawn into contact with General Edward Braddock—who is famed among schoolchildren as the commander in the battle called simply "Braddock's Defeat." In a conversation before the campaign against Fort Duquesne, Franklin suggests to the general that his line of march is vulnerable to ambush by Indians. "He smil'd at my Ignorance, and reply'd, 'These Savages may indeed be a formidable Enemy to your raw American Militia; but upon the King's regular and disciplin'd Troops, Sir, it is impossible that they should make any Impression" (*A*, 224). The smile of condescension at the American tradesman would prove a crucial symptom of the conflict twenty years later. "I was conscious of an Impropriety in my Disputing with a military Man in Matters of his Profession," Franklin recalls drily, "and said no more" (*A*, 224).

He then goes on to describe in great detail the upshot of the general's plan of attack. Braddock died in the battle; his successor, Colonel Dunbar, then retreated pell mell back to the settled areas of Pennsylvania, leaving most of his provisions behind and the frontier undefended. "This whole Transaction," Franklin notes, "gave us Americans the first Suspicion that our exalted Ideas of the Prowess of British Regulars had not been well founded" (*A*, 226).

The *Autobiography* records at length the military preparations for the campaign against Fort Duquesne. Trivial rivalries in Pennsylvania colonial politics also take up much of the third section. Franklin gets bogged down. His undimmed powers of recollection combine together with his continued sense of involvement in issues of the 1750s to produce a narrative that seems to move more and more slowly. And instead of hastening his account toward completion, he apparently went back after reaching his fiftieth year in October 1788 and amplified what he had just written. According to J. A. Leo Lemay and P. M. Zall, the most recent editors of the *Autobiography* manuscript, Franklin probably inserted eleven pages, on the Pennsylvania Hospital, paving the city, and sweeping the streets, some time between December 1788 and May 1789.[3]

Franklin was a dying man as he wrote the last pages of the *Autobiog-*

raphy. His handwriting in the manuscript is weak and pain-ridden; in his letters he refers to the pain that kept him from writing for extended periods.[4] Yet he does not hurry his story to a close; it was hard for him to relinquish the sense that he could master his life through writing. By September 1789 he admitted that he could not complete the story (*W*, 10:35). Two months later he sent a copy of the manuscript as thus far completed to Benjamin Vaughan and Le Veillard, asking for their comments. Even after this he continued to write, getting the narrative as far as 1758, the year of his return to England, this time as colonial agent representing the Pennsylvania Assembly in their dispute against the Proprietaries. Those disputes were acrimonious, and Franklin has not lost his sense of the basic and irreconcilable disagreements he experienced in England. Nothing is concluded in the last pages of this abortive fourth part. Franklin died in April 1790.

He probably revised the manuscript copy that was sent to his European friends. That copy, recovered a few years later by his grandson and literary executor William Temple Franklin, has since been lost, and some scholarly controversy has gone on about the extent of Franklin's changes. For our purposes a few observations will suffice. First, the edition of the *Autobiography* that William Temple Franklin finally published in 1817 does not differ structurally from the manuscript in Franklin's own hand that has survived, though many changes in wording appear, some of them no doubt introduced by Temple Franklin. Franklin was therefore sufficiently pleased with his earlier work to make no basic changes in it. Also, as the consensus of scholarly opinion has established, it is fruitless to seek beyond the manuscript we do have in search of Franklin's final intentions.[5] Finally, it is significant that Franklin took some trouble to rework and revise his manuscript. He was a swift and confident writer, not a painstaking one during most of his life; the effort spent on revising the wording of the *Autobiography* is further evidence of the importance of the project to him.

During the 1780s Franklin was asked several times to provide information toward biographical sketches. Each time he firmly refused and insisted that the *Autobiography* in progress should serve as the sufficient record of his life (*W*, 9:533, 550). When he sent copies of the manuscript to his friends in Europe, he insisted that they were not to be copied or published without permission. Neither rival accounts nor imperfect editions were to supplant the work he had spent so much time on.

Only the Notes remain, to suggest what Franklin might have written beyond the point where his narrative breaks off. He wrote only a few pages about his prolonged stay in England, and he seems to have delayed for some months entering into the story of that period of his life. Perhaps he found those years harder to associate with the initial movements from poverty and obscurity with which he had commenced. During the remaining thirty-two years of his life after the narrative ends he lived in America for only eight. Thus the uncompleted *Autobiography* is a more particularly American work than Franklin's life as a whole was. Eighteen years had elapsed since the project had begun, yet despite some differences of emphasis and the rambling political anecdotage of the last pages, the basic assumptions Franklin maintained about his life remained consistent to the end. Becoming Benjamin Franklin had been easy, and recalling was as natural as becoming.

7 Franklin's Identity in the Autobiography

The *Autobiography* has ensured that Franklin is remembered as he wished to be. Concluding his discussion of the Art of Virtue in the second section, he offers a carefully composed portrait of himself that depicts the kind of identity he intended to bequeath to the world. He offers a testimonial here to the bold and arduous project, crediting it with "the constant Felicity of his Life down to his 79th Year in which this is written" (A, 157). The passage stands out somewhat from its context; it was inserted later, added in the wide left-hand column Franklin reserved for inserted materials.[1] The formality of this portrait, drawn for his posterity, is heightened by the unusual use of the third person.

> To *Temperance* he ascribes his long-continu'd Health, and what is still left to him of a good Constitution. To *Industry* and *Frugality* the early Easiness of his Circumstances, and Acquisition of his Fortune, with all that Knowledge which enabled him to be an useful Citizen, and obtain'd for him some Degree of Reputation among the Learned. To *Sincerity* and *Justice* the Confidence of his Country, and the honourable Employs it conferr'd upon him. And to the joint Influence of the whole Mass of the Virtues, even in the imperfect State he was able to acquire them, all that Evenness of Temper, and that Chearfulness in Conversation which makes his Company still sought

for, and agreable even to his younger Acquaintance. I hope
therefore that some of my Descendants may follow the Example and reap the Benefit. (A, 157)

That he has achieved "constant Felicity" in his life is a matter not to
be demonstrated but to be explained. Nor has his been an idiosyncratic or accidental success; contingency has nothing to do with the
conduct of life in Franklin's recollection. He says he has succeeded because of a clear and imitable program, not through his own unique
character or circumstances. The virtues are arrayed about him like at-
tendant figures in a tableau. His life history can in fact be told in summary as an enumeration of virtues and their effects. The mention of
Temperance evokes the frequent references to food in the *Autobiography*: his early vegetarianism, his unusual diet in London, even the food
eaten from his first china bowl. *Industry* and *Frugality* are the themes
of his early obscure years; no one fails, it seems, except by lacking
these. *Sincerity* and *Justice* will be the distinguishing traits of his public years. Together the virtues have given him evenness of temper and
cheerfulness in conversation; they have made him independent of others, but he prides himself on his sociability. The paragraph concludes
with a direct invitation to his posterity to imitate his example; by this
time his posterity is a metaphor for his entire future audience.

Constant Felicity—this is none other than a formula for happiness itself. The virtues he enumerates are not just his own personal mix; they
are the standard for the good life, as lived by anyone at any time. He is
an old man, and from the vantage point of age he can pronounce on
human existence with some air of mastery. It is not easy for Franklin's
reader to respond that this mode of life, though good for Franklin, is
only one of a number of satisfying lives. Franklin insists that the mode
of identity he embodies—one that entails conscious and continual
control over every aspect of life—is the only life worth living through to
the end.

As a result of the *Autobiography* Franklin's life has been understood
to be not a unique occurrence but a model for imitation—or in some
cases derogation. In the nineteenth century it was put to use in school
readers as an example for boys; the record of Franklin's rise to wealth
and public service seems even to have increased in popularity in the
hundred years after his death. In the words of one reader, Jared
Sparks, a Connecticut farm boy who rose to become president of Harvard (and an editor of Franklin's papers), the *Autobiography* "taught
me that circumstances have not a sovereign control over the mind."[2] In
the twentieth century it has become a standard text in our preoccupa-

tion with American self-definition; at this writing there are ten separate paperback editions, not including its appearance, excerpted or in its entirety, in literature anthologies. Its influence on American life is really incalculable.

Even those who have disliked Franklin take him at his word about the character of his life. The real challenge raised against him has been about whether this life is ideal, not about whether it was lived in the first place as Franklin says it was. D. H. Lawrence, his most cogent and hostile critic, accuses Franklin of being the mechanical creation of his own conscious will. "Why the soul of man is a vast forest, and all Benjamin intended was a neat back garden. And we've all got to fit into his kitchen garden scheme of things. Hail Columbia!"[3] The bold and arduous project in particular inspires Lawrence's scorn and rage.

> I am a moral animal. But I am not a moral machine. I don't work with a little set of handles or levers. The Temperance-silence-order-resolution-frugality-industry-sincerity-justice-moderation-cleanliness-tranquillity-chastity-humility keyboard is not going to get me going. I'm really not just an automatic piano with a moral Benjamin getting tunes out of me.[4]

Lawrence sees no difference between Franklin the person and Franklin the representative of a mode of identity. Those who have shared his objections, like those who have seen him as a model, have responded to a cultural image somehow clothed in human form. Both sides have taken the finished product of recollection as the perfect reflection of Franklin's experience.

Even Franklin's biographers, who have other ways of knowing him besides the *Autobiography*, tend to see him as the supreme embodiment of the Enlightenment ideal. Franklin becomes the calm spectator, whose life is the product of conscious decisions and who trucks and barters with others like him in a society voluntarily formed. Carl Van Doren offers a characteristic formulation. "Mind and will, talent and art, strength and ease, wit and grace met in him," he writes in the last page of his biography, "as if nature had been lavish and happy when he was shaped. Nothing seems to have been left out, except a passionate desire, as in most men of genius, to be all ruler, all soldier, all saint, all scholar, all some one gift or merit or success. Franklin's powers were from first to last in a flexible equilibrium. Even his genius could not specialize him. He moved through the world in a humorous mastery of it. . . .And sometimes, with his marvellous range, in spite of his personal tang, he seems to have been more than any single man: a harmonious human multitude."[5] Reaching for a felicitous concluding phrase, Van Doren abandons any recognizable human condition. Even in our own time it is evidently still important to believe that the Enlightenment produced such a mythical being, whether angelic or demonic.

Franklin did not so much submit to the spirit of his own times as exploit it. "This is the Age of Experiments," he writes near the end of the *Autobiography*, and no one was a more gifted and ingenious experimenter, whether in physics, government, or the conduct of life (A, 257). His disposition to experiment and improvise is put forward as a means of increasing rather than lessening the control he maintained over his own behavior. Franklin refused to see his life as a jumble of chance occurrences out of which certain public achievements had sprung. Throughout his life he insisted that his experiences had a discoverable and premeditated pattern. The governing metaphor of the *Autobiography*, the life as a book, dates from a joking epitath he wrote when he was twenty-two. The all-purpose creed and the project for achieving moral perfection date from about the same time. "Life, like a dramatic Piece, should not only be conducted with Regularity, but methinks it should finish handsomely," he wrote to George Whitefield in 1756. "Being now in the last Act, I begin to cast about for something fit to end with. Or if mine be more properly compar'd to an Epigram, as some of its few Lines are but barely tolerable, I am very desirous of concluding with a bright Point" (P, 6:469). (One wonders what the great Methodist thought of the comparison between life and stage plays or witty sayings.) When he wrote to Whitefield, he was only fifty, hardly old enough to imagine himself in the last act. He maintained the attitude that his life was largely behind him, comprehended and in good order, for over thirty years.

Franklin's basic assertion, that his life had been one of "constant Felicity," is too large a claim to go without further examination. Thus far the *Autobiography* has been treated in its own terms, according to Franklin the same trust that a reader grants to an author and a character in a novel. A different kind of look at his life is required in order to assess what kind of identity he attained at different stages, how easy it was to become Benjamin Franklin, and whether such a life was, or remains still, something fit to be imitated.

Part Two
The Life

8 Identity in the Life

Franklin's greatest achievement was the creation of himself. He was at work on that creation all his life, not only in living that life but also in projecting models by which he and his imitators might live it. In his first published prose writings, the *Dogood* letters, he was trying to imagine a believable character appropriate to Boston in the 1720s. In *The Way to Wealth* he tried to convert economic prudence into a basis for a mode of consciousness. When it came time for him to write his *Autobiography*, he could see that Americans were searching for new models of personal and group identity amid the disruption of behavioral paradigms following the Revolution. He was still working on the model of the complete American at his death.

The *Autobiography* started to exercise its spell on readers even before it was published. It was available in manuscript to the French eulogists who would memorialize him in the period of mourning following his death; those eulogies fostered the image of Franklin as the benign and detached spectator of life, a man whose achievements were so natural as to seem normative.[1] Along with that cultural image has come that of the many-sided Franklin, a being who is finally explainable only in terms of his inexhaustible diversity of talents, interests, and capacities.[2] There is also the constantly chuckling and cheery Franklin, the perfect model of sanity. In part such images of Franklin suggest something about the cultural needs which could encourage them. The durability of such impressions has come from a desire to believe that the limits of individual personality can be transcended. In part, it should be clear by now, these versions of Franklin have persisted because Franklin carefully prepared them.

But there was nothing inevitable, or even particularly likely, about his success in the role of Benjamin Franklin the American. Though the *Autobiography* slyly insinuates that anyone could have done the same, at any historical moment and under any circumstances, a closer look at his life will reveal an achievement more troubled and more impressive than he took credit for. Franklin had a history of crises and adaptations, of losses, frustrations, and acceptances, of anger and happiness and fulfillment just like any other human being. He had, in short, a personality, one partly revealed and partly concealed by the express statements about himself in the *Autobiography*. That personality underwent a long development; there was more to it than a list of maxims and a will to regularize his life.

Franklin's identity survives for us through his writings, the *Autobiography*, and a large body of miscellaneous publications in which he revealed and defined himself. Written evidence, however, is by no means wholly satisfactory; writing is notoriously less spontaneous and unguarded than speech. But Franklin used words all his life to conceal and to reveal himself. Though he did not cry out from the depths of his being, he was always busy presenting himself in some way or other, and the presentations together will tell us what we need most to know about the man himself.

Among these materials the first in importance is the *Autobiography*. For a significant part of Franklin's life it is the only surviving witness; how else would we know why he suddenly left for England in 1724 and returned two years later or how he happened to move in with his wife? But to get at the personality behind this impressive contrivance, we need to ask different questions about the *Autobiography* from those asked thus far. Thus we shall need to know not how he achieves success but why success takes for him the forms it did, not how he worked toward moral perfection but why he should have thought such a thing possible and aimed for it.

Beyond the *Autobiography* there are abundant materials from which to construct a portrait of Franklin's developing identity. As the initial epistolary format of the *Autobiography* would suggest, he was at ease in his letters and aware of the self he was presenting to the world. He was a published writer in his early teens, and he was revealing himself in print all his life. Franklin did not acquire the intellectual discipline in law or theology that formed the writing habits of most other Americans who wrote during the colonial period. Though he wrote like them about the divine will or the rights of colonists, he was inclined to give even standard arguments a turn of his own. The volume of Franklin's writings is considerable; at this writing the Yale edition of his *Papers* has reached twenty-five volumes, with twelve busy years of his life yet to go. Finally, there are the responses of others to him, many available in the Yale *Papers*.

Still, defining Franklin's identity is not a simple task. He wrote about himself in great detail in the *Autobiography* and elsewhere, he confessed his own failings repeatedly, and yet those failings seem paltry, once confessed. What do we care if he blundered into intrigues with low women in Philadelphia, or ate and drank too much for his gout, or slept late in the mornings as an old man, or left his papers in disarray? We are accustomed to think that a man's innermost self will appear in his private and intimate moments, away from the roles he must adopt before the world. So with Franklin we face a paradox. To understand Franklin's self we cannot separate him from the larger public America where he played out the last forty years of his life. We cannot expect to find the real Franklin somehow in private life, freed from public roles in order to assume his own personality. It is the private Franklin who is most inscrutable, most invulnerable to examination, always the good companion, always under control. The energies of his inner life were released in the public world, converting the history of his time into a field for self-revelation. This is a grandiose formulation; indeed, no one has such plastic powers over events. Yet Franklin's impact on American history as colonial agent, ambassador, and finally autobiographer is indisputable. We shall not understand that impact unless we see that his involvement in public questions is as much personal as political. If we accept the premise that the strongest feelings point to the deepest parts of the self, we must look for them in Franklin's public rather than his private life. The private Franklin was an indulgent father; the public Franklin broke with his son William over the Revolution and left behind in his will a final bitter rebuke. The private Franklin was a loyal son to Josiah Franklin; the public Franklin turned against his king. The ambassador to France in private dallied with the noble ladies of Paris; the public Franklin presented his exemplary life for the imitation of Americans.

Unless we seek out Franklin in this public world, we are likely to be baffled by his extraordinary self-control. Accustomed to look for life in a person's most intimate surroundings, we find everything in order here, while neglecting to look more carefully at the way in which his public existence expressed his inmost impulses. Franklin's struggles for identity took place in the press and in his unavoidably public letters of the 1760s and 1770s. At the same time America was undergoing a struggle for identity, aroused to self-examination by challenges to its isolation and autonomy. To understand this reciprocal search for identity will lead us back further in the century. Franklin's definition of national character evolved to correspond with the changes in his own image of himself; the America that surrounded the active projector of the 1750s was not the same country that he returned to from France in 1785. Also, Franklin was never simply an observer of national character. From the first he was conscious in varying ways of being its creator.

Franklin's problem of developing and asserting a certain kind of identity can also be seen as a problem in finding or creating an audience. Just as personal identity can only be formed in relation to groups that the self accepts or rejects, the writer must engage a body of readers who can be called his audience. Franklin's literary efforts to assemble an American audience reveal how far he was from the identity needs of his contemporaries and how fragile any such audience would be.

To explore Franklin's sense of himself in its development, we should look for patterns and themes rather than for the accumulation of chronological detail. This is not a biography, but rather a kind of essay, with the essay's freedom to be suggestive rather than definitive. Much of Franklin's life must be left out in this brief sketch, not because of the insignificance of the omitted elements—for all experiences contribute to make or manifest a person's identity—but because selection is necessary in order to see patterns clearly. The details of Franklin's varied life must not distract us from a few basic questions. Why did he aim at so much greater a role in his country and the world than his contemporaries did, and what kept him going, into a time of life when most other men turn to leisure? It is not as if he had no capacity to enjoy life. His casual writings while in France suggest a mellow retirement, when in fact he was steadily at work on complex negotiations. Why was the *Autobiography*—as well as all the other efforts at projecting his identity—so important for him? How is it that he could feel that the life of a conscious outsider should serve as an exemplary life for Americans? Naturally such questions can have no finally satisfying answers, but they are the questions we most wish to ask.

9 Growing Up Different

Franklin was different from the other Americans around him in Boston and Philadelphia. His earliest published writings reveal ambitions and values that were out of keeping with his cultural surroundings, and his recollections in the *Autobiography* confirm that he wanted something not available in America, or even imaginable. The prominence he achieved he seems to have wanted from a very early age, and he grew up in a place where no one else really aspired to that kind of prominence. Fame was thrust upon the other Founding Fathers more or less unexpectedly during the Revolution, but Franklin had been getting ready for it fifty years earlier.[1]

What made him different? The rhetoric of the *Autobiography* is contrived to suppress this question. Its reader is invited to think that Franklin was a representative figure of his times, gifted only with a greater capacity for hard work than most. Since his time he has had a host of imitators, and the culture has authenticated the possibility of his sort of success. But he himself had only a personal vision to go by, and we ask from where such a vision could have come.

To search for the roots of personality, whether public or private, we naturally turn to the events of childhood, to relations with parents and family. More is known about Franklin's early history than about any other American of his social class and time—anecdotes and characterizations about his father and his early childhood. But no key to his distinctiveness emerges soon—the researcher will not find out what "rosebud" means from any of this. His parents, in the *Autobiography* and in the family letters that survive, appear as solid God-fearing working people with no extraordinary qualities. Since they are so perfectly characteristic of their place and time, their very ordinariness associates Franklin the more closely with the culture of Boston. That culture, not any special upbringing or parental relationship, brought him forth.

Josiah Franklin, his father, was an immigrant. He had left Northhamptonshire in 1683 to practice his dissenting beliefs in Puritan Boston, where he was admitted to membership at Old South church. (Judge Samuel Sewall, whose diary tells us much of what we know about the flavor of that Boston, records attending a prayer meeting at the Franklin home.)[2] The year 1683 was rather late for such gestures of faith. The tide of Puritan belief was at its ebb in the late years of Charles II's reign; even in New England the ministers were lamenting the loss of the original impulse of belief. But the Franklin family had a history of determined Protestant convictions.[3] In the *Autobiography* Franklin recounts how his ancestors had read the outlawed English Bible in the days of Queen Mary. The ties that bound Josiah to Boston were of his own choosing. His son would feel the same readiness to pick up and leave for more hospitable surroundings.

Once arrived, Josiah Franklin had had to adapt to the New World economy. There was no call for silk-dyeing, the trade he had been trained in back in England, so he made himself into a tallow chandler and soap maker, disagreeable work in his son's opinion, but gainful. "He had an excellent Constitution of the Body, was of middle Stature, but well set and very strong," the *Autobiography* recalls (*A*, 54). If his reading consisted primarily of the tracts of Puritan doctrine that Boston produced in such abundance, he also had talents in drawing, and he could play the violin to accompany his own singing of hymn tunes of an evening. He was handy with his hands, and his son picked up from him both a fair degree of physical dexterity and strength (Benjamin's fellow workers in London would be amazed at his ability to carry heavy forms of type) and also an interest in mechanical devices.

"But his great Excellence lay in a sound Understanding, and solid Judgment in prudential Matters, both in private and publick Affairs" (*A*, 54–55). Franklin wanted to remember his father as someone involved in public life, even though his father's station in life clearly prevented him from any significant role. "I remember well his being frequently visited by leading People, who consulted him for his Opinion in Affairs of the Town or of the Church he belong'd to and show'd a good deal of Respect for his Judgment and Advice" (*A*, 55). By the time he wrote this, Franklin had long been immersed in the world of public affairs; yet underlying this assertion about his father is an unusual assumption about political life. It is suggested that despite his father's lack of formal education, despite his lack of wealth, despite his not being a minister, the excellence of his character alone was sufficient to give his political judgments weight. In England in Josiah Franklin's day a tradesman would only be making a fool of himself by being concerned with public questions; the upholsterer in Addison's *Tatler* 155 is satirized for reading the newspapers and neglecting his work. But in New England a revolution had taken place in the theoretical relationship of public and private life. Puritanism subjected the believer's life to public scrutiny, calling upon him for public confessions of his own spiritual state and public allegiance to the godly community. Even a tallow chandler was thereby called to a public existence. The proverb about diligence in his calling that Franklin learned from his father promised that the hard-working man would stand before kings. Private virtue assured a public role. The Puritan ideal was, of course, not realized in Massachusetts, a colony whose political life was more and more run by an oligarchy of wealthy merchants, lawyers, and royal place-holders. But Franklin chose here to remember the cultural ideal, in preference to the social reality.

At the family table his father would invite a sensible friend or neighbor and direct the conversation to ingenious and useful subjects. "By this means he turn'd our Attention to what was good, just, and prudent in the Conduct of Life; and little or no Notice was ever taken of what related to the Victuals on the Table, whether it was well or ill drest, in or out of season, of good or bad flavour, preferable or inferior to this or that other thing of the kind; so that I was bro't up in such a perfect Inattention to those Matters as to be quite Indifferent what kind of Food was set before me" (*A*, 55). Franklin recalls his father as one who exerted his authority through subtlety and indirection. It was the sensible friend who seemed to turn the young Franklins' attention toward the good, the just, and the prudent. When Benjamin was caught stealing stones from a construction site, his father did not physically punish him but rather convinced him "that nothing was useful which was not honest" (*A*, 54). His father originally intended Benjamin to be educated as a minister, the one important learned profession of the colony. When Josiah changed his mind, he gave his reasons—that he could not readily afford to pay for such an education and that clergymen were most often poorly paid—to friends while Benjamin was on hand to hear.

Many hearers were on hand in the Franklin family. Benjamin was the youngest boy among seventeen children. His father had married twice and was forty-eight by the time Benjamin was born. In a letter to his sister Jane written in 1760 and then again in his *Autobiography*, Franklin recalled one instance when thirteen Franklin children sat together at the father's table.[4] But that event was a special occasion, inspired by the return of his brother Josiah, who had run away to sea and returned after nine years. Benjamin's oldest half-sisters and half-brothers were old enough to be parents to him and had their own households even in his early childhood. It was difficult to keep track of so large a family. Three years before Benjamin was born, an older brother, Ebenezer, was discovered drowned in a tub of suds, the event recorded in Samuel Sewall's diary.[5] In the circumstances of Benjamin's childhood, it became vital to get more than one's own share of attention.

The traditional sociological distinction between extended and nuclear families does not adequately describe the dynamics of such a family. The Franklin family was an economic unit. An older brother John had already been trained as a tallow chandler, and Benjamin in turn was put to work as the last boy to help his father. Yet the family also produced its own centrifugal forces. There was the attraction of the sea: three sisters married sea captains; a brother-in-law and a nephew of Benjamin's were lost at sea, as was brother Josiah.[6] Benjamin himself longed to go to sea and proved to be adept at boating and swimming. Throughout his childhood he must have seen brothers and sisters continually leaving to live on their own, though sometimes nearby.

About his mother Franklin says little, except that she had good health and nursed all her children. Some letters survive that he sent her from Philadelphia, addressed to "Honoured Mother." It is clear from them that Franklin did not wish to disagree with her openly. He discounted his religious differences with his parents, and he may have concealed from her the illegitimacy of his son William.[7] Often the task of writing to her was turned over to Franklin's scarcely literate wife Deborah. Abiah Franklin was thirty-eight when he was born and lived to be eighty-five (his father lived to be eighty-nine)—"a discreet and virtuous Woman" Franklin had her labeled on her tombstone, words which reveal little that is distinctive. Her father was Peter Folger, a prominent settler of Nantucket who once published a poem rebuking New England for persecuting Baptists and Quakers. Franklin remembered the last lines.

because to be a Libeller,...
    I hate it with my Heart.
From Sherburne Town where now I dwell,
  My Name I do put here,
Without Offence, your real Friend,
    It is Peter Folgier.

(A, 52)

Grandfather Folger had put his name down emphatically, in contrast to his grandson, who contrived through a long writing career a bewildering multitude of pseudonyms and clearly delighted in concealing his identity.

One other parent figure appeared in the Franklin house when Benjamin was nine. His father's older brother, for whom he had been named, arrived from England, already a man of sixty-five. Benjamin Franklin the elder emerges from his nephew's memoirs and his own commonplace book as a recognizable personality—devout, energetic, affectionate, and a little cracked. Like his younger brother, he had left the Church of England late in the reign of Charles II; their common beliefs were a symptom of how close the brothers were. "He was very pious," his namesake recalls, "a great Attender of Sermons of the best Preachers, which he took down in his Shorthand and had with him many Volumes of them" (A, 49). He also collected political pamphlets while in England. Unlike Josiah, the elder Benjamin tried ridiculously to interest himself in politics. He was specially concerned about his namesake and sent him letters from England with advice couched in an earnest doggerel.

Be to thy parents an Obedient son;
Each Day let Duty constantly be Done;
Never give Way to sloth or lust or pride
If free you'd be from Thousand Ills beside...

(A, 49n)

This from an acrostic. Josiah was cool toward poetry, and when his son wrote some ballads on public occurrences, he ridiculed them and warned that poets (like ministers) most often lived in poverty. Both father and uncle were at first in favor of a career in the church for Benjamin; Uncle Benjamin promised his nephew his supply of shorthand sermons—"I suppose as a Stock to set up with" (A, 53). Franklin's tone toward Uncle Benjamin is wry and detached. As a child of seven he had sent his own verses over to Uncle Benjamin and received enthusiastic rhymed praise in response. But once arrived in Boston, the uncle seemed a silly old man. Uncle Benjamin's commonplace book survives, a collection of odd stuff. Where his father was diligent in his calling, Uncle Benjamin was a meddler and a dabbler. Uncle Benjamin was earnest and straightforward, without much sense of the absurd; Josiah was indirect and capable of making his point through ridicule. The uncle wrote poetry; the father encouraged his son's prose. The son recalled tensions between his father and his uncle. "[T]ho' I was a Child I still remember how affectionate their Correspondence was while they were separated," he wrote to his sister Jane, "and the Disputes and Misunderstandings they had when they came to live some time together in the same House."[8]

Franklin's father was clearly the one figure against which Franklin might define himself. His father's saying about diligence in one's calling became a personal emblem that offered the promise of ultimate reward to drudgery. According to his recollection his father was highly conscious of money—the cost of education or apprenticeship, the cost of setting up children in trade, and the dangers of imprudent investment. Even when recalling his father's decision not to invest in his proposed printing press, Franklin seems to have felt no resentment; his father thought him too young, and he was. Josiah Franklin had a gift for restraint. When other parents punished, he dissuaded. He was an exile from his homeland, where he had broken with his relations for religious reasons. Benjamin was to do the same, though it is significant that he never appeals to his father's precedent. The youngest son, he was evidently a favored child, the only one ever designated by his father for any special learning. When Benjamin got into disputes with his older brother James, his father tended to take Benjamin's side, despite James's age and legal standing as master. Only a few letters from Josiah survive. In one of them, dated May 26, 1739, the father describes to his son the Franklin genealogy and possible claims to some armorial crest. "Some think we are of a French extract, which was formerly called Franks, some of a free line, a line free from that vassalage which was common to subjects in days of old: some from a bird of long red legs" (P, 2:229). Father Franklin's rhetorical climax with the bird of long red legs (the frank, an English heron) suggests how seriously he takes the question of ancestry. And one can detect here a glint of his son's sense of humor—sly, almost undetectable at times, directed satirically at the self's own pretensions. There are coats of arms associated with Franklins, he reports, based on his brother Benjamin's research. "However our circumstances have been such as that it hath hardly been worth while to concern ourselves much about these things, any farther than to tickle the fancy a little (P, 2:230).

Franklin refers more than once to the image of the parental table of this God-fearing patriarch and his abundant family. Later in life, however, he developed a pattern of dining apart from others. His vegetarianism was reason for his eating alone as an apprentice. In London his temperance separated him from other journeymen printers at Watts's printing house. There he convinced others to join him in his own dietary customs. As for his father's religious principles, he left them without any accompanying sense of rebellion against his father. Because of his reading schedule he stopped attending public worship, "which my Father used to exact of me when I was under his Care: And which indeed I still thought a Duty; tho' I could not, as it seemed to me, afford the Time to practise it" (A, 63). He did not become a patriarchal figure himself. He had only three children, one who came from outside the marriage and another who died in early childhood. Franklin's father is described as an example to be imitated, but the son himself does not imitate the example.

In a family so large, the parental authority must have been partly diffused among the older siblings. Franklin recalled long after in a bagatelle written to Mme. Brillon in Paris how when he was only seven he had impulsively bought a whistle with all the coins in his pocket. When he returned home whistling, his older brothers and sisters laughed at him for throwing away his money, so that he cried with vexation. But he treated ridicule as a form of discipline and did not resent it; his childhood experience becomes the basis for a little homily on bad investments, whether economic, political, or psychological.[9] As the youngest son Franklin apparently experienced looser discipline than the older children had. His father was wary of forcing him into a trade he would dislike, recalling the older son who had run off to sea rather than dip candles.

Moreover, Josiah was a youngest son himself, born when his own father was fifty-nine and his mother forty. The parent-child interaction is quite different when the parents are younger. If the parents' psychosocial development has been normal, it is somewhat like being raised by grandparents: the older parent has resolved many of the life crises that still vex the younger parent. Franklin was clearly conscious of what it meant to be the youngest son. He looked into a register of births at his father's birthplace in England. "From that Register I perceiv'd that I was the youngest Son of the youngest Son for 5 Generations back" (A, 46). His mother was also a youngest child, born when her father was fifty and her mother probably in her forties (P, 1:lvi). Insofar as the youngest child of elderly parents has a special experience, Franklin's parents were peculiarly equipped to appreciate that experience. In fairy tales the youngest son has a distinctive role; he has a kind of naive wisdom, often contrasted with his oafish older brothers who are incapable of solving the story's special problem. Denied the normal attributes of full adulthood at the beginning of the story, when he remains protected and without skills, he proves yet to have an uncanny sense for what to do. "There is a certain earnest naiveté about him," writes Lawrence. "Like a child. And like a little old man. He has again become as a little child, always as wise as his grandfather, or wiser."[10]

What Franklin recalls about his father suggests a man settled and assured in his identity, requiring nothing from his children to complete himself. Age, and the ego maturity that is supposed to come with age, became an incessant motif in Franklin's writing. Father Abraham in *The Way to Wealth*, Cato in *Busy-Body 3*, *Advice to a Young Tradesman*—Franklin continually depicted situations in which aged wisdom appeared. In his own childhood the standard of behavior was that of age, yet he himself was young. Hence he tried in various ways to mimic aged wisdom, from his first periodical letters, under the *persona* of the seasoned matron Silence Dogood, to his last writings, by which time he had grown into the role. Aged wisdom was a kind of act he put on. He played at being old and wise for so long that when he finally became old he could be perfectly comfortable in the part.

From the fact that his father changed his mind about his son's career and yet allowed him some choice of trades one can deduce that a complex mixture of control and self-direction shaped Franklin's early life. He frustrated his father's intention to make him a tallow chandler, and he had to be persuaded to become his brother's apprentice in the print shop. The independence of judgment he was permitted is exemplified in the stone wharf incident; when caught he tried to argue that he was right to steal stones. Franklin's youthful rebelliousness did not take the form of reaction against parents or higher authorities. He tended from the first to identify with authority and to see himself capable of manipulating it, a tendency which was central to his political life. He quarreled instead with figures he saw as no better than himself. Numerous quarrels of this sort punctuated his early life before he finally settled down with his own printing press.

Franklin recalls himself as an avid reader from early childhood (he could not remember not being able to read), yet he was also a leader of other boys. These two activities traditionally tend to conflict; bookishness can separate a child from the thoughtless vigor of play. Franklin, though, was able to cultivate both a private and a public self simultaneously. Puritan child-raising, as Emory Elliott has pointed out, often led children to introject the mannerisms of piety and moral certainty that they found in their parents and ministers, qualities that would serve to separate them from their fellows and that could not easily be sustained into adolescence.[11] A number of the significant figures of American Puritanism had early histories in which they were publicly taken to be examples of piety or enforcers of school rules—Edward Taylor, Michael Wigglesworth, Jonathan Edwards, Cotton Mather, and others. This alienation from his peers Franklin seems to have escaped. He seems, in fact, to have been uneasy in the presence of social disapproval, such as during his brief tenure as publisher of his brother's newspaper or when he refused to pay his dues to the other compositors at Watts's printing house in London. Young Puritans established their identity by separating themselves from the behavior patterns of their sinful playmates. The independent identity which Franklin found for himself began to emerge later, in adolescence, when he was a secret reader and writer in his brother's print shop.

As a boy Franklin underwent three different kinds of education. Because his father had intended him for the ministry, he was enrolled at the Boston Latin School. He did well in his one year there, rising to the top of his class and then skipping to the next higher grade. Then his father changed his mind and transferred him to a writing and arithmetic school. He was less successful there, doing well in writing but failing in arithmetic. After a year his father took him out of school, and he was apprenticed, first as a tallow chandler (for two years) and then as a printer. From grammar school through apprenticeship he had experienced in quick succession the kinds of education available to an American colonist.

Franklin always smarted from the lack of a traditional formal education, particularly because the status that goes with that education had been dangled before him and then taken away. In his first set of periodical letters (the *Dogood* papers, written while Franklin was himself nearly of college age and working as a printer's apprentice) he wrote a satire of Harvard in the form of an allegorical dream vision.

> I reflected in my Mind on the extream Folly of those Parents, who, blind to their Childrens Dulness, and insensible of the Solidity of the Skulls, because they think their Purses can afford it, will needs send them to the Temple of Learning, where, for want of a suitable Genius, they learn little more than how to carry themselves handsomely, and enter a Room genteely, (which might as well be acquir'd at a Dancing-School,) and

from whence they return, after Abundance of Trouble and
Charge, as great Blockheads as ever, only more proud and self-
conceited. (P, 1:17)

Franklin's epigraph, wrenched out of context from Cicero's de Finibus,
reveals a continuing theme in his educational writings. An sum etiam
nunc vel Graecé loqui vel Latine docendus: am I even now to be taught
to speak either Latin or Greek? When he taught languages to himself,
he learned Latin last, he says, since the modern languages are more immediately serviceable (A, 169). At the end of his life as he reviewed the
fate of his English School in the Philadelphia Academy, he drew an extended comparison between Latin and the useless chapeau bras carried by gentlemen of fashion. Around the same time he told Dr.
Benjamin Rush that Latin and Greek were "the quackery of literature."[12] These references are unexpectedly harsh, perhaps some of the
defensiveness of the autodidact. The Harvard graduates of 1722 could
hardly be said to have learned "to carry themselves handsomely, and
enter a Room genteely" except in the eyes of a sixteen-year-old apprentice who saw that avenue to status and authority closed to him. A hint
of Franklin's buried feeling of inferiority can be heard in his Autobiography as he is describing the establishment of the Library Company.
"This Library afforded me the means of Improvement by constant
Study, for which I set apart an Hour or two each Day; and thus repair'd
in some Degree the Loss of the Learned Education my Father once intended for me" (A, 143). Franklin compensated for his deprivation by
conceiving of it as a virtue; but to do so required a suppression of his
own sense of disappointment.

The bare details of Franklin's family background and early childhood do not explain much. We do discover the roots of certain tendencies in later life. From his father he learned the value of diligence,
prose, mature judgment, and perhaps humor. Yet Franklin was clearly
not a man striving to satisfy his father's ambitions or even to earn his
father's good will. A good part of his father's importance seems to have
been that he left his youngest son alone. When in 1738 Benjamin wrote
a carefully ambiguous letter to his parents in response to his mother's
complaints about his religious unorthodoxy, his father wrote back to
say that they were well satisfied with his answer (P, 2:206). From the
frustration of his desire for a learned education and learned status
Franklin obviously learned a readiness to compensate. But the disposition to compensate does not explain why Franklin was so driven, why
he directed his energies so widely throughout his long life. He was
able, after all, to surpass by far any expectations his culture might have

had for him. No Boston child of the first quarter of the eighteenth century grew up with the ambition to become what Franklin became. His boyhood seems normal. His greatest longing then was to go to sea—not a place where one is likely to find fame. It is in his adolescence that we find the beginnings of his ambition to become someone special before the world. To see how that crisis of identity formation took place, we must look at his city, Boston, and the sort of personal identity that was available for a young apprentice to adopt.

The Boston in which the young Benjamin Franklin played and worked was a seaport town of ten to twelve thousand inhabitants. Unlike the dispersed and fragmented Boston of the later nineteenth and twentieth centuries, Franklin's Boston was a tightly knit settlement of narrow streets on a peninsula. The town had been born in a flush of millennialist zeal, when Bostonians were convinced they were the advance guard of the Protestant Reformation, the very center of human history. Much had happened since that heady moment. An older generation could still recall the series of conflicts in the later seventeenth century: the Half-Way Covenant, King Philip's War, the loss of the original charter, the brief authoritarian rule of Governor Edmund Andros, the imposition of a charter providing for a royal governor, the witchcraft outbreak at Salem, the local controversies surrounding the establishment of the Third Church and the Brattle Street Church. The effect of all of these was to blunt the original colonizing impulse. By 1720 the convulsions were over; Boston was still the center of New England Puritanism, but it was a Puritanism considerably weakened in its energies. The leading exponent and exemplar of the Boston Puritanism of the day was Benjamin Colman, minister at the Brattle Street Church (Uncle Benjamin's church). Unlike his predecessors, who had taken pride in a hard and uncompromising message spoken in the plain and profitable manner, Colman's preaching was sentimental and sublime. "His exact and exquisite Judgment as well as his lively Fancy and Imagination, were employed in every Discourse," writes his biographer, "The choicest Matter presented in Elegant Language and flowing Eloquence."[13] Colman did not aspire to the political influence which ministers had when Massachusetts proudly called itself a theocracy; where an older generation of ministers had sought to lead like prophets, he sought to direct his congregation's taste toward higher experiences, like a literary critic. Socially and politically, the leading figures in Boston were merchants, who together constituted an amorphous and shifting group with no particular sense of cultural mission.[14] Now that the first Puritan impulse was arrested, the town looked nervously over its shoulder at England and Europe, the standard of culture. Boston was the port of entry for new ideas from England, and there were a variety of importers. Colman had brought with him from a lengthy European visit a whiff of Addison and of Augustan poetry. Alongside him Cotton Mather had been an indefatigable proponent of new scientific and cultural ideas, which he was eager to reconcile with the old faith. Even a tradesman like James Franklin, Benjamin's brother and master, had come back from his apprenticeship in England with a taste for the sort of satire and diatribe that flavored the grubby world of English letters. Boston was, in short, a provincial town that had mislaid its original pretensions to cultural centrality. It was a city raised at first to preach the Word but now converted into a seller and a shipper—like young Benjamin, a maker of tallow candles and soap, emblems of cleanliness and dim enlightenment.

Growing up in this Boston, then, meant becoming an American provincial. But Franklin would not accept the identities presented to him by his times. From his first struggles with his brother one can see the ambition to be more than his circumstances demanded of him. It was not enough for him just to rise in the world economically, to become a successful merchant or tradesman. He wanted to create a public identity for himself of a kind quite unforeseen, to address an audience not yet gathered, to play a role not yet created. A recurring image appears in his *Autobiography*: young Benjamin visited or invited in by older, more influential men. Governor Keith of Pennsylvania, Governor Burnet of New York, the Mr. Lyons who introduced him to Mandeville, Sir Hans Sloane of the Royal Society, the assemblymen of New Jersey—standing before kings began early for Franklin, who later on even kept a running count of how many real kings he had stood before (five in all). Yet he also wished to be independent, operating on his own and under his own terms. He broke with his brother and then later with Keimer, his employer, in search of that independence. His identity needs—acknowledgment and independence—were in tension with each other, perhaps even contradictory, but he pursued both actively. Perhaps his need for both traces to his status as a favored child. Often the favored child who leaves home has trouble reconciling himself with the realization that he is just another person in the eyes of the world. Franklin never really accepted that reduced status, so his adolescence was much embroiled until he arrived at a sort of temporary working truce between his ambitions and the world.

Franklin's basic problem then, through his adolescence and beyond, was the achievement of the right sense of identity. We know that identity is a matter of reciprocal connection between self and society; a young person accepts the role of minister, tallow chandler, or printer and in that acceptance develops a sense of himself as a whole person, distinguishable from others. In eighteenth-century America in particular, that process of identity adoption was less predefined than in the more stable and complex societies of Europe. To arrive at one's work, social rank, companions, and family, all the features which externally define a person's identity, required a range of decisions not elsewhere possible. For those who wished to alter their identities or create new ones, America offered the occasion. Southern planters like William Byrd of Westover and Quaker merchants like Samuel Powel wanted to be English gentlemen. The crowds who flocked to the preachers of the Great Awakening wanted to be members of God's elect, an intangible but greatly valued identity. There were even a shocking number of colonists who apparently decided they wanted to be Indians and deserted the settlements entirely. Identities in the colonies were indeterminate and flexible, and a person might be called to do several things. Edward Taylor was a minister, physician, and farmer (and only in private a poet); Samuel Sewall was a merchant, judge, lay preacher, and author. A person could rise in the world, like Sir William Phips, who rose from common sailor to governor of Massachusetts; or fall, like Franklin's erstwhile employer Samuel Keimer, who ended his life working as a poor journeyman in Barbados. Society did not encompass the self as it did in Europe, and it could not offer so complex a set of identities. Franklin's own father was obliged to change trades upon arriving in Boston. Adaptability and flexibility were vital, and in the exercise of that adaptability could come a sense of personal independence.[15]

The partial breakdown in the structure of existing identities imported from Europe produced two potential results. One possibility was anomie and crises of identity. Around the edges of the biographies of famous colonials one can see examples of the wreckage of personality. Cotton Mather's son Increase cracked under the strain of too much ancestry; he drank, philandered, ran into debt, and was at last lost at sea. Jonathan Edwards's uncle Joseph Hawley desired spiritual rebirth along with the other citizens of Northampton in 1735, but he could not find it and cut his throat. Franklin's *Autobiography* includes numerous instances, some among close friends, of the dangers of personal disintegration. But, in the unsettled conditions of colonial America, the ego might take charge of identity-formation in ways quite unknown before. In the stiff admonitions to himself in Washington's copybook, in the passages of fumbling and driven ambition in John Adams's diary, and in Franklin's resolutions and lists of virtues, we seem to see a generation creating itself. The generation of Revolutionary leaders, to whom one must add Franklin, though he was much older, was free of the self-destructive duties of sonship that had hamstrung the second and third generations of Puritans. They had made themselves into their own fathers.[16]

Naturally where personal identity is so much a conscious creation, national identity must similarly appear to be within the self's control. Traditional groups, Freud argued, are defined by their acknowledgment of a father-leader. Only the sanction of this father-leader's love for his children could be sufficient to overcome the hostilities of group members toward each other. But this notion of paternal power had lost much of its force in England during the eighteenth century, and Americans in particular had constituted themselves as a collection of fatherless groups. The New England ideal of theocracy meant that the sustaining father was not human, and the God of New England, unlike the Anglican God, could not be reliably employed to sanction social arrangements. The king, father symbol in England, was far away, and the father-surrogates who governed the colonies were frequently contemptible. The tie of group fatherhood was thus largely unavailable for colonial Americans.[17]

Lacking a viable father-leader to sanction a pattern of social order and unite the members of the society, the American colonists were forced into a tensely guarded equality with each other. Those social class distinctions that survived the passage to America did help to alleviate mutual tensions. Slavery surely encouraged solidarity among whites, especially since blacks comprised around a quarter of the colonial population. Fear of the French and Indians also encouraged solidarity. But within the fatherless group of brothers it was vital that nothing disrupt the uneasy equilibrium. This insistence on equality manifested itself in the persisting references to safeguarding the people's liberties, often against nebulous and insubstantial threats. The young tradesmen of the Junto asked each other at every meeting, "Have you lately observed any encroachment on the just liberties of the people?" (P, 1:258). The leaders of colonial America distrusted the people, but they distrusted each other no less. Men in public life were praised not as leaders but as preservers of the people's rights. At the death of Andrew Hamilton, the defender of John Peter Zenger and a Speaker of the Pennsylvania Assembly, Franklin printed his eulogy in the *Pennsylvania Gazette*. "He lived not without Enemies: For, as he was himself open and honest, he took pains to unmask the Hypocrite, and boldly censured the Knave, without regard to Station and Profession. Such, therefore, may exult at his Death" (P, 2:327). This is strange praise. Hamilton is not described as a good man living in wicked times, yet the enemies he has made are somehow to his credit. The eulogy posits a world where mutual hostility is the norm. Colonial society was a society without heroes. Even Cotton Mather's descriptions of Sir William Phips's alleged daring deeds are less dramatic than his descriptions of simple yeomen fighting the Indians on their own.[18] These tensions among brothers persist into the period of nationhood. The history of the American Revolution is filled with evidence of this mutual jealousy which impeded the common effort: the quarrels among Adams, Deane, Lee, Izard, and Franklin in the American commission in Paris, the pecking order among American generals, Benedict Arnold's aggrieved desertion to the British. Yet the very extent of these hostilities is a sign of some group cohesion, since they acknowledge a common relationship.

Along with this intense and uneasy local identity, the colonists passively acknowledged themselves to be Englishmen. Being English was not so much a national identity in America as a political allegiance. The English symbols of unity were particularly weak in the eighteenth century. The dynasty of Hanover was an embarrassing necessity to Whigs and without legitimacy to many Tories. Except for a brief moment under the elder Pitt, English political leaders were uninspiring. The history of the seventeenth century had discredited both monarchy and republicanism, in the forms of Cromwell and the Stuarts. Americans exploited the advantages of this anomalous and unbinding identity. They could claim that the assertion of their own liberty and independence was in fact an affirmation of their identity as Englishmen. Shortly after starting the *Pennsylvania Gazette* Franklin printed an account of Massachusetts controversies between the governor and the legislature over the governor's salary.

> Their happy Mother Country will perhaps observe with Pleasure, that tho' her gallant Cocks and matchless Dogs abate their native Fire and Intrepidity when transported to a Foreign Clime (as the common Notion is) yet her SONS in the remotest Part of the Earth, and even to the third and fourth Descent, still retain that ardent Spirit of Liberty, and that undaunted Courage in the Defence of it, which has in every Age so gloriously distinguished BRITONS and ENGLISHMEN from all the Rest of Mankind.[19]

A note of defensiveness about the American environment is detectable, and the exaggerated declaration of kinship while defying the royal authority betrays a strain that will be felt more strongly forty years later. But Franklin is still seeking independence as an aspect of British identity.

The adolescent Franklin thus had two group identities available to him: an intense and unstable local identity in Massachusetts or Pennsylvania and an English identity which was a product of abstraction rather than of emotional attachment. He also had the option of leaving the colonies behind entirely and becoming an Englishman once he had arrived in London in 1724. But he resisted all those identities, in the forms offered to him. In Boston particularly he was in the end completely isolated; there was no place for him, no one who would employ him or publish him.

In what Franklin tells about his early years we see a young man whose conception of himself bore little resemblance to the world's conception of him. In frustration he thrust his imagined character at others to be acknowledged and admired, and it was repeatedly rejected.

The *Autobiography* describes Franklin's continual and unsatisfied attempts during his early years to maintain various close relationships. His brother, his friends John Collins and James Ralph, Samuel Keimer, Deborah Read, his would-be benefactor Governor Keith—all these relationships foundered, for a variety of reasons. The route was not easy from this young Franklin's identity struggles to the state of humorous self-possession in which the *Autobiography* was written.

The twelve-year-old Franklin was somewhat reluctant to apprentice himself to his brother; he still longed for the sea. But his father kept pressuring him, and eventually he signed the indentures that committed his time to his brother until he turned twenty-one. Once on the job he learned the trade quickly, to the point where he felt his brother could teach him no more. Problems soon began between the two of them. James was nine years older, an awkward age difference for two brothers who were supposed to be master and apprentice. When Benjamin was only a small child, his brother had been sent to England to be apprenticed as a printer. When he returned, he brought his own press, paid for by his father; he set up shop on his own when he was only twenty. From his own writings as well as from his brother's recollection, James Franklin appears to have been impetuous and irascible. A middle child (Benjamin was his next surviving younger brother), he does not seem to have gotten on well with authority figures. He could not convince his father to support him in his disputes with brother Benjamin; his father openly regretted having paid so much to set him up in printing. With the ministers of Boston and the General Court he got in trouble as the publisher of the *New-England Courant*.

The *Courant* was Boston's third newspaper (not including the short-lived *Public Occurrences* of 1690). Like the other scrawny newspapers that were beginning to appear in the colonies, it carried little news; instead it was a forum for a small group of contributors, the Couranteers, who entertained the town with light-hearted affectations of the distant cosmopolitan standard in London. The paper first appeared at the beginning of a smallpox epidemic in 1721 when Cotton Mather and Zabdiel Boylston were promoting inoculation as a means of keeping the disease under control. James Franklin quickly began to publish the views of the opposers of inoculation, who represented the majority of the community, and thus brought on himself the wrath of the Mathers. In all ways James seemed determined to provoke the authorities. "I *cannot but pity poor* Franklin," remarked old Increase Mather, "*who tho but a young Man, it may be speedily he must appear before the Judgement seat of GOD.*"[20] James responded with spirit. "[T]he Law of Nature, not only *allows*, but obliges every Man to defend himself against his Enemies, how great and good soever they may appear."[21] The symbols of learning and power in Boston did not intimidate him. When Cotton Mather's son Samuel published a letter attacking the *Courant* and signed it "John Harvard," James Franklin pounced on him.

> Notwithstanding which, a young scribbling Collegian, who has just Learning enough to make a Fool of himself, has taken it in his Head to *put a stop to this Wickedness* (as he calls it) by a letter in the last week's *Gazette*. Poor Boy! When your Letter comes to be *seen in other Countries,* (under the Umbrage of Authority,) *what* indeed *will they think* of New England! They will certainly conclude, There is *bloody Fishing* of nonsense *at* Cambridge *and sad Work at the* Colledge.[22]

It was in the midst of these hostilities that Benjamin began his writing career.

While working in his brother's print shop, Franklin taught himself how to write. He had been writing poetry even in childhood; his brother published two doggerel ballads he wrote about local events. But when he entered into a writing competition with his friend John Collins, Collins had the better prose, in the opinion of Franklin's father, who discovered the exchange. What Franklin needed was a model, which he discovered in Addison's *Spectator*. The Couranteers were particularly influenced by the *Spectator*, which they tended to cite as if its authority was everywhere acknowledged. Eight volumes of the *Spectator* were part of the *Courant* library, apparently brought back from London by James with his press. Benjamin purchased a volume of his own (he remembered it as the third), and formulated for himself a program of self-education by which he might imitate Addison's prose. In choosing Addison, Franklin could not have done better. "Whoever wishes to attain an English style, familiar but not coarse, and elegant but not ostentatious, must give his days and nights to the volumes of Addison," counseled Dr. Johnson in *The Lives of the Poets*. Over fifty years earlier, Franklin had done just that.[23]

Franklin's early writings in Boston are not merely of literary interest. Not even the *Autobiography* tells so much about what he was and what he wanted to be, as a sixteen-year-old apprentice. The ballads he wrote were lost, but his first periodical essays survive, in part because his complete set of the *Courant* has survived, with the initials of contributors apparently written in his hand in the margins. Franklin began writing for the public in his adolescence, in the midst of that period during which young people must struggle to discover who they are. Franklin's earliest self-assertions were thus quite public. In his later writing the necessities of advocacy or the perception that his readers must not be offended softened the display of self, but young Franklin had nothing he wished to advocate more than the proposition that he was in some way special. Behind the mask of his fictive authoress he could display his own command of English prose, his resentment at Harvard students who were receiving an education he was denied, his contempt for what passed for poetry in New England. These short essays, with their surface of simpering reasonability and their covert assertions of mastery, reveal the problems of identity that Franklin would return to all his life.

At the same time he was learning to write, Franklin was reading a fresh assortment of books, some of them borrowed from the *Courant* office and the Couranteers. In large part, Franklin's recollection of these adolescent years in Boston is a history of books read. The satisfaction he notes in coming upon these books is like Jonathan Edwards's, who was at the same time discovering Newton, Locke, and others in the recent Dummer book bequest to Yale; both young Edwards and young Franklin felt a restlessness about the stale present which could not be lifted by any of the minds around them. There is a secretive quality in Franklin's descriptions of his reading, as there would be about his writing as well. Some of his books he borrowed by knowing booksellers' apprentices; those had to be returned quickly and in good condition before they were missed. He could read and work on his writings only at night or before work or on Sundays, "when I contrived to be in the Printing House alone, evading as much as I could the common Attendance on publick Worship, which my Father used to exact of me when I was under his Care" (A, 63). At this point he still accepted public worship as a duty, but he neglected that duty and secluded himself away to read in the empty print shop. Later, when he describes his diligence in appearing to be industrious, he compares reading to a secret sexual liaison. "[A] Book, indeed, sometimes debauch'd me from my Work; but that was seldom, snug, and gave no Scandal" (A, 126). The Franklin who is so genially open in his *Autobiography* reveals in that account a pattern of concealments and withdrawals from society. He is not ashamed of those concealments; rather he seems to feel a pleasure in the snugness of hiding with a book from the eyes of others. His first prose writing for publication was also submitted anonymously to his brother's newspaper, written in a disguised hand and slipped under the door of the shop at night. The next day James and the Couranteers discovered it. "They read it, commented on it in my Hearing, and I had the exquisite Pleasure, of finding it met with their Approbation, and that in their different Guesses at the Author none were named but Men of some Character among us for Learning and Ingenuity" (A, 68). Concealment for Franklin was connected with being looked for; there was exquisite pleasure in that enhanced status.

Franklin managed to get still more time to himself for reading through a disagreement with his brother about their eating arrangements. One of the books he had read had convinced him to become a vegetarian, so he refused to eat the boarding house food that his brother and the other apprentices ate. (His father had tried to inculcate a disregard for food, but instead Franklin was continually aware of what and how he ate.)[24] James complained of his unreasonable eating requirements, so Benjamin proposed a solution by which James would pay him directly the expense of his meals. "Rather than fight for his rights, Franklin withdrew from hostilities," notes Richard Bushman, who has examined this episode cogently in the light of psychoanalytic theory. "Though sharp words may well have passed across the dinner table, in recounting the episode he presented himself as placid and utterly noncombative, preferring to withdraw rather than inconvenience anyone."[25] Franklin emphatically disliked open hostilities. "Above all things I dislike family quarrels," he wrote to his sister in 1757, "and when they happen among my relations, nothing gives me more pain."[26]

Forced to a confrontation by his angry colleague Arthur Lee in 1778, he wrote, "I do not like to answer angry Letters. I hate Disputes. I am old, cannot have long to live, have much to do and no time for Altercation" (W, 7:132). As a youngest boy he would be less likely to win family quarrels, without the aid of parents. This attitude toward mutual hostility separated Franklin psychologically from other colonial Americans who were bound up in the web of family rivalries and mutual hostilities which characterized colonial society as a whole. Instead, Franklin tried, as Bushman points out, to strike mutually advantageous bargains, such as the one with his brother, which allowed him more time to himself and more money for books.[27]

In one of his books he came upon a description of the Socratic method, which led him to Xenophon's *Memorabilia* where the method was more fully depicted. "I was charm'd with it, adopted it, dropt my abrupt Contradiction, and positive Argumentation, and put on the humble Enquirer and Doubter" (A, 64). As Franklin's metaphor indicates, the humble inquirer and doubter is a role that Franklin tried playing, one that gave him considerable argumentative advantages among his more forthright, blustering companions. Unlike his later self, the adolescent Franklin was an enthusiastic arguer, not merely out of interest in ideas but just as importantly as a display of ego in contest with other egos. Ideas, like identities, he liked to put on to see how they would look—the Socratic method, vegetarianism, religious skepticism, Addisonian good sense. During these adolescent years he worked, or considered working, as a journeyman printer, author of periodical letters and philosophical treatises, editor, swimming instructor, and merchant's clerk. The process of growing up required that he discard a variety of experimental work identities, leaving only printer and writer.

Franklin's public writing career was launched in the midst of continuing friction between his brother and the authorities of the colony. The sixteen-year-old apprentice was thus involved in conflict in two directions. His brother was unhappy with his insubordinate attitude and unwilling to acknowledge his precocious talents. Outside the print shop the Mathers were counterattacking; Samuel Mather, the son of Cotton, seized on a mixed metaphor in one of Franklin's *Dogood* papers and held it up for ridicule.[28] Franklin's earliest writing habits were formed in response to this two-front war. He dealt with the complexities of the situation by an ingenious use of masks. He kept his real identity as author hidden long enough to secure his standing with his jealous brother, whose campaign of raillery against the authorities his writings somewhat supported. The *persona* for his periodical letters was a New

England matron named "Silence Dogood." The name referred unmistakably to Cotton Mather, who had written *Essays to do Good* and who could never be silent in pulpit or press. Yet Silence Dogood does not serve to make Mather ridiculous. The tenth essay is a straightforward proposal (adapted from Defoe's *Essay upon Projects*) for friendly societies to insure widows, exactly the kind of project Mather would have endorsed (P, 1:32). Similarly, *Dogood 6* is a little sermon against pride of appearance. Franklin bore no malice toward Cotton Mather; late in his life he wrote to Samuel Mather about visiting Cotton at his house and receiving some seasonable advice.

The other Couranteers displayed a cheerful defiance of the community and flailed away at its standards. Matthew Gardner in particular, the most versatile of them, was one of the significant early influences on Franklin's writing.[29] But Franklin could not long feel comfortable in their company. He learned from them, he was flattered by their approval, but he could find no continuing satisfaction in being a member of a coterie. At those times when he was trying to be purely satirical as opposed to humorous, as in the dream vision of Harvard, the satire tends to be bland and vague. Later on in Philadelphia he addresses his adversary Samuel Keimer as Cretico, "thou sowre Philosopher," but then hurries to insist that *"if any bad Characters happen to be drawn in the Course of these Papers, they mean no particular Person"* and that *"Cretico lives in a neighboring Province"* (P, 1:121). In the best of his early writing satire, humor, and direct statement are all mixed together in constantly shifting proportions, so that the reader is always off balance. Silence Dogood is not wholly an object of satire, but neither is she wholly the medium through which the world is to be perceived. She is naive enough to be discombobulated by Boston's night life but shrewd enough to laugh out loud at her husband's fumbling attempts at courtship. Franklin had acquired his writing style by imitating Addison, but his own writing never has the static, lapidary quality of Addison's. Tone and distance are always in motion, keeping Franklin from being imprisoned in an attitude.

What Franklin could find in Addison was a control over personal emotion which is almost unnerving in its completeness. "Since I have raised to myself so great an Audience," Addison writes in *Spectator 10*, "I shall spare no Pains to make their Instruction agreeable, and their Diversion useful. For which Reasons I shall endeavour to enliven Morality with Wit, and to temper Wit with Morality, that my Readers may, if possible, both Ways find their Account in the Speculation of the Day."[30] One can see why the young Franklin might be drawn to the elegant and gelatinous smoothness of this passionless prose, so different, for example, from the frantic raucousness of Cotton Mather. Addison, with Steele his collaborator, perfected the periodical essay, a genre of considerable importance in the century. Periodical essays appeared regularly in newspapers, rubbing up against the records of public occurrences, but their distinctive trait was that they had no urgent occasion. Insofar as the essays of Addison attempt to sway the reader, it is toward a cultural attitude, not a political judgment. That attitude is insinuated by presupposing its universal acceptance. Opposing views are courteously ignored, as one would ignore a breach of taste. "He is so cool, so infuriatingly sensible," writes C. S. Lewis, comparing Addison to the great Tory satirists, "and yet he effects more than they. A satiric portrait by Pope or Swift is like a thunderclap; the Addisonian method is more like the slow operations of ordinary nature, loosening stones, blunting outlines, modifying a whole landscape with 'silent overgrowings' so that the change can never quite be reversed again."[31] There is no brilliance of manner in an essay of Addison's, but there is a sense of control, over its material and its audience, that the beleaguered and ambitious apprentice in Boston hungered for.

But in important ways Addison's model of a writer addressing society did not fit the American colonies. Addison was the calm spokesman for an ascendant Whig merchant oligarchy, comfortably writing from a London that was the conscious center of growing political and cultural power. Franklin's early imitations of Addison appeared in raw American villages on the edge of a wilderness. In some ways Franklin was conscious of his differences from Addison and tried to adapt his writing to his circumstances. His *persona* is different from Addison's. The Spectator himself is a silent and detached observer; Silence Dogood is talkative and a frank meddler, like Franklin's later *persona*, the Busy-Body. The Spectator is born of an old landed family; Mistress Dogood is the widow of a rural Puritan minister. But what she sees around her often looks and sounds like Addison's London. When she strolls the streets of Boston at night, the young men she sees and hears are not recognizable natives of New England.

> As it grew later, I observed, that many pensive Youths with down Looks and a slow Pace, would be ever now and then crying out on the Cruelty of their Mistresses; others with a more rapid Pace and chearful Air, would be swinging their Canes and clapping their Cheeks, and whispering at certain Intervals, *I'm certain I shall have her! This is more than I expected! How charmingly she talks!* &c. (P, 1:42)

Franklin has substituted literary perceptions for authentic ones. His affectation of the Addisonian style in these years meant the adoption of a posture of cultural conservatism. He pretended that Silence Dogood was addressing people of leisure and breeding; her real audience was the citizens of Boston.[32]

From his earliest writings Franklin professes a concern for the betterment of his countrymen. The *personae* through whom he speaks as a young printer and almanac-maker—Mistress Dogood, the Busy-Body, Poor Richard, and others—are all intimately part of society, unlike Franklin himself, and are created to act in his place. "It is undoubtedly the Duty of all Persons to serve the Country they live in, according to their Abilities," Mistress Dogood writes (*P*, 1:13). By the end of his life, when he was writing the *Autobiography* in 1788, Franklin interpreted such professions as part of his long educational campaign. "I considered my Newspaper also as another Means of Communicating Instruction, and in that View frequently reprinted in it Extracts from the Spectator and other moral Writers, and sometimes publish'd little Pieces of my own which had been first compos'd for Reading in our Junto" (*A*, 165). But the good intentions announced in the 1720s and 1730s have the ring of a derived piety. Like his master Addison, Franklin seems to be addressing a persisting and indefinite present, and the audience he addresses lacks distinctive characteristics. The *Busy-Body's* Philadelphia is a blurred version of Addison's London, where young men carry satires around in their pockets and a kind of simple amiability characterizes most social relations.

It is difficult to detect in these early years a consistent idea of American distinctiveness which Franklin seems conscious of. He is not addressing an audience of Americans, nor is he much aware of being an American. As a young man in Philadelphia and London he showed little sense of allegiance to place. What had begun as a business trip to London ended in a stay of a year and a half; even on the verge of leaving for Philadelphia he considered staying behind instead to teach swimming to the nobility. Franklin's earliest attempts at public recognition were gestures undirected at any particular community. In the 1720s Franklin was not fully conscious of society, so his *personae* appear to have no local habitation.

While Mistress Dogood was making her biweekly appearance in the *Courant*, James Franklin was pushing his feud with the authorities still further. At one point he was jailed; finally he was forbidden to publish the paper. As a device to get around the prohibition Benjamin was made the nominal publisher and his apprenticeship indentures supposedly voided, though a new set was privately made up. "A very flimsy Scheme it was," he remarks in the *Autobiography*; the new indentures had dubious legal standing. While James was in jail, Benjamin had Mistress Dogood quote long passages from a British defense of freedom of the press and from *Cato's Letters* by Trenchard and Gordon. By appealing to these already classic statements of Whig political philosophy, he tried to escape from the level of raillery and personal hostility that was sufficient for his brother and the other Couranteers. He had charge of the paper during the month while his brother was in jail, and he claims that he "made bold to give our Rulers some Rubs in it" (A, 69). But he was obviously uncomfortable to be cut off from the community. Perhaps, as Leo Lemay argues, *Dogood 9* contains an attack on Judge Samuel Sewall, who had committed James Franklin to jail. Whether true or not, the attack is concealed behind a reference to the despised former governor Joseph Dudley, a much safer target.[33] Even in attack Benjamin preferred subtlety, trapping his opponents in an unexpected similitude that diminishes them. His own aggressions were not displayed overtly in his writings; rather his writings release aggression in play.[34]

In the first issue of the *Courant* published under Benjamin's name, the new publisher adopted a detached tone not seen before in the paper's lively history. The new *Courant*, he assured its readers, would avoid "Party Pamphlets, malicious Scribbles, and Billingsgate Ribaldry"; it would devote itself to the "Diversion and Merriment of the Reader. Pieces of Pleasancy and Mirth have a secret Charm in them to allay the Heats and Tumors of our Spirits, and to make a Man forget his restless Resentments. They have a strange Power to tune the harsh Disorders of the Soul, and reduce us to a serene and placid State of Mind" (P, 1:49). The new *Courant* will serve the public good by disarming aggression and calming the normally tense relations between men. The new publisher speaks impersonally and collectively, unlike James Franklin, who spoke in his own irascible person. The writers for the *Courant*, the announcement said, are a society bound together by allegiance to a symbolic leader, old Janus the Couranteer, who is henceforth master of their revels and the recipient of letters to the paper. Old Janus, a figure made up of contrasting masks, was an apt symbol for the seventeen-year-old publisher.

Though his own writings from this time seem conciliatory and amiable in tone, Franklin recalls himself as embroiled in controversy. When brother James was arraigned before the Council of the General Court (the colonial legislature), Benjamin was also brought in and examined, but then released, probably on the grounds that as an apprentice he could not legally testify against his master. He felt he was getting a reputation in Boston "as a young Genius that had a Turn for Libelling and Satyr" (A, 69). New England society valued precociousness. Cotton Mather and Jonathan Edwards both manifested their talents young, graduated from college before they were seventeen, and rose on the basis of their precociousness to influential pulpits in their early twenties. But there was a condition exacted for such rewards: an unwavering allegiance to, and even celebration of, the group values which the precocious one had so early mastered. Franklin was conscious of that requirement, and he knew he was violating it. His religious opinions were also alienating him from the community; "my indiscrete Disputations about Religion began to make me pointed at with Horror by good People, as an Infidel or Atheist" (A, 71). It is important to recognize that Franklin was more emotionally involved in the mutual hostilities of Boston and later of Philadelphia than he ever wanted to acknowledge.

Though Benjamin was nominally the publisher of the newspaper, his brother James had the actual control. From February 1723 onward, the *Courant* appeared under the name of Benjamin Franklin, leaving Benjamin vulnerable for the gestures against the government which James wished to make. Benjamin always sought concealment and control; here he found exposure combined with powerlessness. He reflected at this time "that I had already made myself a little obnoxious to the governing Party; and from the arbitrary Proceedings of the Assembly in my Brother's Case it was likely I might if I stay'd soon bring myself into Scrapes" (A, 71). His legal status as apprentice or journeyman in his brother's shop was completely ambiguous. Confronting his brother on one side and a disapproving community on the other, he finally found his situation intolerable. "At length a fresh Difference arising between my Brother and me, I took upon me to assert my Freedom" (A, 70).

But once out of his brother's employ, he could find no work with other printers in Boston; they had been warned by James not to hire the renegade. So despite his father's disapproval (here the father sided with the brother-master), and in advance of attempts to have him stopped, he left by boat for New York and eventually Philadelphia.

The breaking of his indentures Franklin himself felt to be wrong. Though he may have had a legal right to do so, he knew that he was running out on an agreement with his brother to which he had voluntarily consented. Indentures were an important legal contract; those who broke them could be brought back to work by law. In July 1722 Josiah Franklin advertised in the *Courant* for his runaway indentured Irish servant William Tinsley, "about 20 Years of Age and heavy in his going..."[35] Forty shillings would go to anyone who apprehended the man. Josiah did not suffer passively the loss of an apprentice and would hardly have approved of his youngest son absconding. But it was not his father Franklin was running out on; it was his brother, the brother who had taught him his trade and whom he had defended in print himself.

Franklin was conscious of doing wrong, though he later rationalized his departure on the grounds of his brother's "harsh and tyrannical Treatment" (A, 69). Though he confesses this as his first *erratum* and thus somewhat defuses his own guilt, he was clearly bothered by his actions for a long time after. Ten years later he visited his brother in Newport where James had moved his press. James was in declining health, and Benjamin undertook to take on James Junior as his own apprentice and then even set his nephew up as a printer at his own expense. "Thus it was that I made my Brother ample Amends for the Service I had depriv'd him of by leaving him so early" (A, 170).

Franklin was acting here as he would always act when the pressures on him from others became too great. He withdrew. Withdrawal from hostilities became one of the basic patterns of his life.[36] He withdrew from Boston and conflict with James; he withdrew from conflicts with his adolescent friends and from Samuel Keimer; eventually he withdrew from the British Empire, to which he had once felt a powerful attachment. It was easier for him to work with people from whom he was protected by a certain distance. Closer relationships turned out badly. Franklin was not close to any of the other Founding Fathers with whom he was associated.[37] They were younger men; even Washington was younger than his own son William. Separated from him in experience and in the extent of reputations, they were nonetheless his collaborators in the Revolution. There were other patterns of withdrawal in his life. Reading meant for him a sort of withdrawal, alone in the empty print shop at noon or on Sunday mornings. Concealment was another form of withdrawal, whether concealment of authorship or the concealment of a group's existence, such as his Junto would practice. Early in his life, though, he did form some strong personal attachments, to his friends Collins and Ralph and to a kindly Quaker merchant, Thomas Denham. His relationship to his brother was obviously close enough to leave him a troubled mixture of feelings when it broke up. When all these relationships collapsed, through estrangement or death, Franklin turned away from all friendships in which any vulnerable part of himself was given to another person. He formed useful, cordial friendships with others whom he could use and who could use him. He married prudently, to a woman unlikely to accompany his restless mind or to seduce him from the world of free speculation with an overwhelming tenderness. He preserved, at a certain nearly undetectable psychic cost, his freedom from constraining ties with other people.

10 Early Years of Independence

The next distinct stage of Franklin's life was spent in Philadelphia and then in London. He was seventeen years old when he arrived in Philadelphia, twenty when he returned there from London in 1726. Unlike most other young men of his age, of whatever social class, he had considerable independence. That independence had come to him abruptly and dramatically, through his journey from Boston to Philadelphia described so vividly in his *Autobiography*. Now he was to confront the problems of independence. There were problems in getting along with friends, benefactors, and work associates. He had also declared his independence from religion, and that departure presented him with a further sense of being uncontrolled. His need for public acknowledgment, whetted in Boston, was unfulfillable in London, despite his best efforts. Finally he had to control his own freedom himself, to renounce or postpone the greatest of his vague ambitions, and to make a new start. To do this, he sailed home to America, resolved to change his life.

Here, as in the last chapter, the *Autobiography* must be examined not for its rhetoric but for its information on the young Franklin's inner state. The affection Franklin felt in 1771 for his earlier self leads us to trust his account, but it is a story with an assured future; only in passing remarks does Franklin hint at the anxieties that went with independence. "I lived very agreeably, forgetting Boston as much as I could..." (A, 79). "We had together consumed all my Pistoles, and now just rubb'd on from hand to mouth" (A, 96). "He left me with a small Legacy in a nuncupative Will, as a Token of his Kindness for me, and he left me once more to the wide World" (A, 107). In Boston his work had connected him to his family; now his employers and fellow workers were bound to him only by economic ties. There had once been a little spare money to buy books with; now he could be rich enough to show off his gold coins on a visit to the old print shop or deep in debt and without means to get out. Away from his family he had to count on friends to confirm his sense of himself, and there he met serious disappointments.

Franklin's passage on ship from Boston to escape his brother was arranged by his friend John Collins. This was the same friend who had competed with him in writing before he began his self-taught course in Addisonian prose. Not long afterwards, Collins joined him in Philadelphia, after having spent a short time in New York. As a youth Collins had had "the Advantage of more time for reading, and Studying and a wonderful Genius for Mathematical Learning in which he far outstript me" (A, 84). In Boston he had seemed highly promising; Franklin had known him since the two were children and as an apprentice spent "most of my Hours of Leisure for Conversation...with him" (A, 84). But away from Boston Collins fell apart. From his conversations about religion with Franklin he became an unbeliever; more important, he began to drink heavily. Franklin was obliged to pay his debts because his drinking made him unemployable. Eventually the two quarreled while on an outing on the Delaware. Collins refused to take his turn at rowing; in an ensuing tussle Franklin threw him overboard and would not let him back in the boat until Collins was exhausted. By the time of this incident Collins owed Franklin a considerable sum of money and had disgusted him with his drunken disintegration. Not long after, Collins left for Barbados and was never heard from again, leaving Franklin with only sour memories of bad debts and of a cruel trick played in angry exasperation on a river afternoon.

What Franklin wanted in this period was some sort of mentor, someone fit to guide him in independence, to introduce him to workable goals and the means of achieving them. One candidate for the position of mentor appeared quite suddenly. Through Franklin's brother-in-law, a sea captain, the governor of Pennsylvania discovered who the young journeyman was and what his past experience in Boston had been. Governor Keith then called on Franklin and soon offered to fund Franklin's own printing press—just what his father had done for his elder brother—if he would go over to England and select the equipment. But when Franklin arrived in London, he discovered that Keith had provided no money at all; it had all been a fantasy of the governor's, a talented and impoverished aristocrat who lived by his wits and his appearance of good nature. Even fifty years later in the *Autobiography* Franklin could not suppress the sense of hurt and bewilderment he had felt at this capricious reversal.

Accompanying him from Philadelphia to London was James Ralph, the next close friend in Franklin's life. Like Collins, Ralph was a young clerk, a lover of reading and a free spirit. Franklin and Ralph lodged together in London once Franklin realized he was stranded there. Ralph, the older of the two, had been to London before and showed Franklin around. He sought work in the theatre, then as a writer, and eventually as a country schoolmaster; Franklin at the same time found work in a printing house. LIke Collins, Ralph borrowed considerable money from Franklin. In the country, where he went to teach, he took on Franklin's name, the ultimate loan, on the grounds that he did not wish to mar his future literary fame with the association of having taught school. Franklin thought Ralph's ambitions to poetry a dangerous delusion and took pains to convince him to forget them. While Ralph was in the country, Franklin was getting to know Ralph's woman in London, a little milliner. She had lost her reputation and work on Ralph's account, and turned to Franklin to help her out. "I grew fond of her Company, and being at this time under no Religious Restraints, and presuming on my Importance to her, I attempted Familiarities (another Erratum) which she repuls'd with a proper Resentment and acquainted him [Ralph] with my Behavior" (*A*, 99). This clumsy and thoughtless move brought an end to the friendship with Ralph, who announced that he considered all past debts canceled. By this time Ralph owed Franklin twenty-seven pounds, a sum large enough for Franklin to remember it precisely over forty years later. "I lov'd him notwithstanding, for he had many amiable Qualities" (*A*, 106). Franklin's talents and ambitions at this stage in his life had little plausible audience beyond what Ralph could provide. Franklin loved Ralph; the loss of his friendship was in a sense irreplaceable.

There are striking parallels in his friendships with Collins and Ralph. There is a pattern of abandoning or demeaning women, a mutual renunciation of conventional responsibilities. Ralph deserted his wife and Franklin his fiancée in order for them to go to England; according to the story Collins invented to get Franklin his passage to Philadelphia, Franklin was escaping marriage to a girl he had impregnated. Franklin and Collins conducted an extended debate on the education of women, the sort of debate that inevitably reduces its subject to rhetorical formulations. Franklin was drawn to both Ralph and Collins for their wit and engaged in writing contests with each. For the young Franklin friendship involved rivalry; these two friendships seem to have soured in part because of his own aggressiveness. He allowed himself to be used by them to the point where he lost a lot of money, some of it not his own. There is a certain crude manipulative cruelty on both sides in his relations with the two of them that nevertheless coexisted with a deep attachment for them. Forty years later he still remembers them well. All three had deserted conventional moral- ity and the status designated for them as clerk and apprentice. Like the Rousseau who describes his own youth in his *Confessions*, they had cut loose from the models of selfhood that could have offered sustaining emotional rewards and chosen instead to be exiles and outsiders. Franklin's friendships, like Rousseau's, were intense and frustrating, broken apart by the strain of competing egos. Unlike Rousseau, though, Franklin came eventually to be comfortable with his own emotional isolation, substituting good humor and cordiality for passionate friendship.

At work in Philadelphia and London Franklin had other problems, though he was better able to adjust to those. The printer for whom he worked in Philadelphia was Samuel Keimer, a man whose personality emerges vividly from Franklin's narration. From the first, Franklin was unimpressed with him. In the *Autobiography* he recounts how Keimer was outsmarted by the rival publisher, Bradford, who brought young Franklin by to find work for him and then, not identifying himself, lured the obtuse Keimer into revealing his business plans. Franklin stood by and watched silently. Religious fanatic, glutton, incompetent, petty manipulator, slob—Keimer was not equipped to inspire any respect for his authority in his new employee, who was already his superior in all aspects of printing. "At this time he did not profess any particular Religion, but something of all on occasion; was very ignorant of the World, and had, as I afterwards found, a good deal of the Knave in his Composition" (A, 79). Not long after starting work for Keimer, Franklin was quietly angling to set up on his own.

At Watts's printing house in London, Franklin stood out from the other employees for his physical strength and for his practice of drinking water rather than beer for lunch. "The water American," they called him. He ran into trouble with his workmates when he moved from the pressroom to the composing room and there refused to pay the dues that the journeyman required of new workers. Franklin objected that he had already paid with the pressmen, and his master agreed. But here the protection of authority to which Franklin was so prone to turn for help could not protect him against the group solidarity of the compositors, who ostracized him and messed up his work. He gave in and paid. The episode was a characteristic conflict in Franklin's life, setting at variance his tendency to seek the protection of superiors against his urge to be accepted by his peers. Once accepted by the compositors, he was able to have his way with them and even convinced many of them to leave off beer. Among them he was known as "a pretty good Riggite, that is a jocular verbal Satyrist" (A, 101); humor was a means of maintaining dominance.

London was a larger field for attention of the sort that Franklin liked to get, but there, instead of being a promising young man who could chat with governors (two already, he notes), he was just a laborer in a print shop. In America the means of getting attention had been literary, and the young Franklin had a pride in his reasoning and philosophical powers as overweening as Ralph's in his poetry. Having read William Wollaston's *Religion of Nature Delineated* as an edition of it was coming off the press where he worked, he decided to turn his own mind to the problems of free will and determinism. Wollaston's waffling discussion passed as profound among enlightened circles in the eighteenth century who preferred not to examine their metaphysical assumptions too carefully. Franklin's response to it, *A Dissertation on Liberty and Necessity, Pleasure and Pain*, which he dedicated to Ralph, is little more than a slick manipulation of commonplaces, uninformed by any real urge to resolve a philosophical problem; it lacks Wollaston's earnestness and ends by positing a universe in which good and evil are meaningless names. "To say it was His Will Things should be otherwise than they are, is to say Somewhat hath contradicted His Will, and broken His Measures, which is impossible because inconsistent with his Power; therefore we must allow that all Things exist now in a Manner agreeable to His Will, and in consequence of that are all equally Good, and therefore equally esteemed by Him" (P, 1:63). Jonathan Edwards would later address this same topic with different, more interesting conclusions in *The Freedom of the Will*. The pamphlet did have partially the desired effect, however, for it came to the attention of his employer, who, although impressed, disapproved of its amoral conclusions.

Another metaphysician, a Dr. Lyons, read the pamphlet and introduced Franklin to clubs and coffee houses, where he met one prominent author of the time, Bernard Mandeville. With an acquaintance at another club he tried to arrange an introduction to Sir Isaac Newton, then eighty-three, but the meeting never took place. In the *Autobiography* Franklin recalls that Sir Hans Sloane, one of the most distinguished scientists in England and secretary for the Royal Society, wrote to him asking to see an asbestos purse Franklin had brought with him from America. In fact, Franklin himself wrote to Sloane about the purse. The memory lapse is revealing. Franklin altered the encounter to make it fit with other experiences of unsolicited attention from the great. In the beginning phrases of his letter, Franklin describes himself as "Having lately been in the Northern Parts of America," as if he were a world traveler rather than a young American provincial; his postscript adds, "I expect to be out of Town in 2 or 3 Days, and therefore beg an immediate Answer," (P, 1:54).

In London Franklin had to seek out attention, and his need for an admiring audience comes out touchingly in an episode in the *Autobiography*. On a warm day off from work Franklin and a group of acquaintances went to Chelsea on an excursion. Franklin had taught one of his companions how to swim; from his days in Boston he had been a good swimmer, and in his bookish way he had even studied the subject in a book by a certain Thevenot. "In our Return, at the Request of the Company . . . I stript and leapt into the River, and swam from near Chelsea to Blackfryars, performing on the Way many Feats of Activity both upon and under the Water, that surpriz'd and pleas'd those to whom they were Novelties. I had from a Child been ever delighted with this Exercise, had studied and practis'd all Thevenot's Motions and Positions, added some of my own, aiming at the graceful and easy, as well as the Useful. All these I took this Occasion of exhibiting to the Company, and was much flatter'd by their Admiration" (A, 103-4). On Franklin swam, past Westminster and the Inns of Court, no doubt attracting some notice, since he was swimming through a well-populated area, performing various stunts to impress friends and passers-by. He had studied Thevenot as he had Addison, aiming to master and if possible exceed his source—"aiming at the graceful and easy, as well as the Useful." The would-be moral philosopher was only nineteen, already free of any sense of priorities by which water sports might be a study unworthy of one concerned with liberty and necessity, pleasure and pain.

Franklin thought enough of his swimming to consider teaching it. But he was going nowhere in London; soon he would have had to admit to himself that in English society he was nobody. Only in the light of his future successes does his career in London seem a presage. By themselves his pretensions to public recognition, his feats of activity in and out of the water, were as hopeless and fantastical as his friend Ralph's attempts at epic poetry. So he joined up with a Quaker merchant, Thomas Denham, who had crossed the Atlantic with him and was now ready to return to Philadelphia. Denham was Franklin's real mentor, a man of character and good advice. Franklin left the printing house to work for him as a clerk, the only time he ever actually left the trade of printing before he finally retired from it. Without the sort of guidance which Denham provided, it is uncertain whether Franklin could ever have gone beyond the futile gestures at personal advancement in London. Franklin had not done much with his independence, and he had sense enough to realize he needed help. In one version of the story of his first arrival in Philadelphia (a version that appeared in the *London Gazette* in 1778), Franklin described how he had been befriended the first day there by a wealthy citizen of Philadelphia who found him in distress and *"unknowing where to go, or what to do."*[1] This version comes to us second hand and somewhat contradicts the firsthand account in the *Autobiography*. But its ultimate source is evidently Franklin, and it reflects his consciousness of the importance of finding a mentor.

The return to America represented a sort of moratorium from the kind of search for public acknowledgment that Franklin had been engaging in. Erik Erikson talks about the moratorium, a period many young people require, as "a span of time after they have ceased being children, but before their deeds and works count toward a future identity."[2] The adolescent must sort out the counter claims of freedom and discipline, adventure and tradition; when he cannot do so, he often retreats into a withdrawn state during which his energies are regimented and his ambitions relinquished.[3] Raised with no satisfying identity models around him but in the company of books of the early Enlightenment (Locke, Addison, Defoe, Shaftesbury, Clarke), which held out the promise of personal autonomy and successful individual action, Franklin could not at nineteen reconcile his acquired values with his situation. How was he to put that identity model into effect? The identity model he had formed for himself was independent, irreligious, and personally assertive, qualities which, as exercised, were getting him nowhere or even into trouble. Franklin was of course not in serious psychological distress, so far as we can tell. He was still working and engaged with his surroundings. But in relation to his ideal of a self, he felt unfulfilled and unsatisfied.

The symptoms of the stage or moratorium he was entering can be found in the writing he did on board ship back to Philadelphia, consisting of a journal which he kept and a plan of action he set down. These records of his early life he preserved and even carried with him to London so that he could refer to them while writing the first part of the *Autobiography*. In the nearly three-month long voyage he had plenty of time to note the natural phenomena: the changing wind and water, the tropic birds with their long ribbonlike tails, the tiny crabs that attach themselves to branches of gulf weed. About those things he was already in the habit of conducting observations and extemporaneous experiments. About his experiences with the other passengers he was concerned to find useful lessons; even after a game of checkers he notes the kind of frame of mind which produces success—boldness and an indifference to the money bet (P, 1:75). He is especially conscious, in several entries, of the need to adjust to society and to the expectations which society makes.

> Man is a sociable being, and it is for aught I know one of the worst of punishments to be excluded from society. I have read of fine things on the subject of solitude, and I know 'tis a common boast in the mouths of those that affect to be thought wise, *that they are never less alone than when alone*. I acknowledge solitude an agreeable refreshment to a busy mind; but were these thinking people obliged to be always alone, I am apt to think they would quickly find their very being insupportable to them (P, 1:85).

In part the vividness and reiteration of this theme in Franklin's journal make clear that he desperately wanted to rejoin society, a feeling reinforced by the experience of being long at sea. En route, his ship spoke another ship bound in the same direction. "There is really something strangely cheering to the spirits in the meeting of a ship at sea, containing a society of creatures of the same species and in the same circumstances with ourselves, after we had been long separated and excommunicated as it were from the rest of mankind. My heart fluttered in my breast with joy when I saw so many human countenances, and I could scarce refrain from that kind of laughter which proceeds from some degree of inward pleasure" (P, 1:91). He recalls a story of someone confined alone in the Bastille and forced to playing little tricks to preserve his sanity. "One of the philosophers, I think it was Plato, used to say, that he had rather be the veriest stupid block in nature, than the possessor of all knowledge without some intelligent being to communicate it to" (P, 1:86). In other passages, dealing with a military martinet and with a religious hypocrite, he reflects on the values of mild discipline and sincerity. The necessity of society is connected in his mind with the strategies of successful leadership. He is not evoking in these passages the mutual emotional sustenance which is to be found in other people. Other people are necessary, not to fulfill him but to hear and see him. A man is not sufficient audience for himself.

Along with the journal he also drew up a "Plan of Conduct," by which he hoped to be guided in his new life.

> Those who write of the art of poetry teach us that if we would write what may be worth the reading, we ought always, before we begin, to form a regular plan and design of our piece: otherwise, we shall be in danger of incongruity. I am apt to think it is the same as to life. I have never fixed a regular design in life; by which means it has been a confused variety of different scenes. I am now entering upon a new one: let me, therefore, make some resolutions, and form some scheme of action, that, henceforth, I may live in all respects like a rational creature. (P, 1:99–100)

One can see here the beginnings of that detachment from an earlier self, the disposition to treat his own life as an object, which would later appear in his *Autobiography*. He describes a past life that has had no direction or design, and he wants to impose a design on what is to follow. Life is compared to a literary composition, and Franklin shows little inclination to acknowledge the inevitable differences between life and art. (The equation of his life to a work of art was to become a continuing motif in his thought.) A considerable regimentation of self would be required to bring his life into line with his demands on it. Looking back on this "Plan of Conduct" in his *Autobiography*, Franklin gives his earlier self its first real commendation awarded for something more than natural talent. The "Plan" is "the more remarkable, as being form'd when I was so young, and yet being pretty faithfully adhered to quite thro' to old Age" (A, 106).

In the "Plan" he resolved to be frugal and industrious, and he saw that those restraints would be necessary for a long time. Though he had broken with Ralph some time before leaving for America (eliminating that drain on his funds) and though he recalls himself as different from his debt-stricken beer-drinking workmates at Watts's, he was so poor at the end of his stay in London that Denham had to pay his passage back and advance him money on his salary.[4] So he resolved not to "divert my mind from my business by any foolish project of growing suddenly rich" (P, 1:100). So far as other people were concerned, he was resolved to be truthful, to "aim at sincerity in every word and action—the most amiable excellence in a rational being" (P, 1:100). He was also going to speak ill of no one and to excuse the faults of others. His former disposition, as a "pretty good Riggite" or as a "young Genius that had a Turn for Libelling and Satyr," would have to be rigorously suppressed. His underlying concern would be to avoid the danger of offending others. Sincerity, "the most amiable excellence in a rational being," is, as we know, distinguishable from authenticity; Franklin was not trying to bring his inner feelings into line with his projected outward behavior. Instead he was preparing an identity that could function effectively in Philadelphia.

Once arrived, he went to work as a clerk for Denham, an arrangement that was satisfying. "We lodg'd and boarded together, he counsell'd me as a Father, having a sincere Regard for me: I respected and lov'd him" (A, 107). But the arrangement lasted only a few months. Early in 1727 both became seriously ill at the same time; Denham died and Franklin nearly did. Franklin had pleurisy; "I suffered a good deal, gave up the Point in my own mind, and was rather disappointed when I found my Self recovering; regretting in some degree that I must now some time or other have all that disagreeable Work to do over again" (A, 107). He would have no ailment so serious until he was quite old. Franklin was apparently not frightened by death in this first flirtation. Dying meant for him not a confrontation with the ultimate but a rather disagreeable job; the tone he takes is one of somewhat amused peevishness. He had not struggled to live on; he had given up. People whom he knew died, but when he refers to death in this passage and elsewhere, he does not treat it as a personified abstraction. Not long after this, he composed his own epitaph, comparing himself to a discarded book, so he could joke about his own death. With his friend Osborne he made a serious agreement that the first to die would visit the other to brief him on conditions after death. Osborne died first, "[b]ut he never fulfilled his Promise" (A, 92). In the *Dissertation on Liberty and Necessity* he had vigorously denied the existence of any afterlife of the traditional kind, because the mind would lack contact with sensory experiences which stimulate it to activity (P, 1:69–70). I do not know whether Franklin, who had just turned twenty-one, actually wanted to die, but I think his disappointment at living once again was genuine. If dying was a disagreeable work, so was the severe self-discipline which he had directed himself to do in his "Plan of Conduct"; death would have saved him from that. And his mentor whom he loved, the man who had replaced the father he had left behind, was dying. The interlude of being loved and guided, of living in a kind of protected space, was over.

One other adjustment would have to be made as Franklin set out on his own. He wanted a conception of the universe that would answer his needs. Some time earlier he had discarded formal religion, and even before that he had felt so little regard for it that he read books on Sunday morning rather than attending church. His *Dissertation* had been a manifesto of unbelief that rejected both the revealed religion of his father and the natural religion of Wollaston and the early Deists. According to the *Dissertation* the universe was an elaborately conceived piece of machinery in which the possibility of individual human agency could only be a delusion. In that respect he was imagining a universe as devoid of contingency as the universe of pure Calvinism. But Franklin was uneasy with this account. He could see no place where his reasoning was lacking, but it seemed wrong to see it this way. Others had cast off belief as he had and been corrupted by unbelief, he considered, thinking of Collins, Ralph, and Keith. "I began to suspect that this Doctrine tho' it might be true, was not very useful. My London Pamphlet...appear'd now not so clever a Performance as I once thought it; and I doubted whether some Error had not insinuated itself unperceiv'd into my Argument, so as to infect all that follow'd, as is common in metaphysical Reasonings" (*A*, 114). He himself could find nothing wrong with his reasoning; the very reasoning process itself seemed indicted by the bad effects of discovering no basis for values. He tried again, this time arguing that because all societies in all ages prayed, the universe must be organized by God to make such appeals meaningful. This manuscript he put away and eventually lost. "The great uncertainty I found in metaphysical reasonings disgusted me, and I quitted that kind of reading and study for others more satisfactory" (*W*, 7:412).

Instead, he worked out a theology and a liturgy of his own, laid out in 1728 as his *Articles of Belief and Acts of Religion*. He begins the Articles with a little treatise on divine beings. The creator of all things, he posits, could have no reason to concern himself with "such an inconsiderable Nothing as Man" (*P*, 1:102). His perception of helplessness led him to surmise that there must be lesser beings or gods in the divine hierarchy, each with his own sphere of control. "It is that particular wise and good God, who is the Author and Owner of our System, that I propose for the Object of my Praise and Adoration" (*P*, 1:103). Franklin had by this time experienced the indifference of the very great; he had gotten on by attaching himself to prominent figures who were well above him in rank but disposed to help him out. The divine being Franklin joined up with was not to be worshipped in a humble and contrite spirit, like the God of the Puritans. "Being mindful that before I address the DEITY, my Soul ought to be calm and Serene, free from Passion and Perturbation, or otherwise elevated with Rational Joy and

Pleasure, I ought to use a Countenance that expresses a filial Respect, mixt with a kind of Smiling, that signifies inward Joy, and Satisfaction, and Admiration" (P, 1:104). And Franklin's prayer was not that his will be submerged in the divine will, but rather, "Increase in me that Wisdom which discovers my truest Interests" (A, 153).

If Franklin had left the Puritans and their religion behind, he had not left the need for some sort of religious experiences. Their worship was public and communal, his private and concealed. The idea implicit in his *Dissertation* that the ultimate Creator utterly transcends human experience was carried over into his acts of worship, as was the notion in his unpublished thesis, that prayer is the evidence of a genuine freedom of action. In his social experience Franklin was especially concerned to ingratiate himself with authority figures and to appear to them as good-natured, respectful, and willing to work. As below, so above. He concluded that there must be a god who could be similarly approached. Prayer was important to him because it implied a universe where a person could alter by actions or appeals the basic nature of things.

There is something quite bizarre in this improvised theology and liturgy—the assumption that by himself in Philadelphia Franklin could discover the basic hierarchy of beings in the universe, an order quite different in fact from anything thought of before. His self-confidence had not been damaged by the London experience; it had merely gone underground. Later in life he withdrew from such speculations behind the provisions of the all-purpose creed. Conventional morality, he was persuaded, made good sense whether ordained or not. Now, returned to Philadelphia, his energies more focused, his sights lowered, and his illusions suspended, he would make his way disguised as what people saw him to be, a hard-working printer with little money. Whether it had been God, his own local god, or chance that had preserved him, Franklin did not know. But he had a clear sense of being fortunate to survive these early years of independence.

11 Success in Philadelphia

In 1726 Franklin returned to Philadelphia to stay. The next twenty years of his life were years of self-discipline and self-denial, just as his plan of conduct had enjoined. Having suppressed his needs for self-display and for intimate friendships, he found for himself a network of working partnerships and tactics of covert social and political manipulation. He married, an arrangement by which he gained a reliable source of cheap labor and sexual gratification. And he found for himself the right distance from others at which he could work.

After Denham's death he went back to work for Keimer, who was bumbling along as ineffectually as before. Soon after, an opportunity arose to start his own print shop in collaboration with a partner he had met at Keimer's. That shop gradually caught on; he was able to buy out his partner, print a newspaper and then an almanac, and to start a series of printing ventures in other cities. These years from 1726 to 1748, when he retired from actively running his printing business, were busy and promising; if we are to follow the development of his sense of identity, they are interesting for the kind of tactics used in forming and defining relationships with others. The Franklin in need of self-display led a buried existence through these years, surfacing only occasionally (as in the Hemphill controversy), and kept fed by slow increments of public acknowledgment.

Between 1726 and 1748, Franklin was finding a role for himself in Philadelphia. The city afforded him a number of possibilities that would never have been available in Boston, and was amazingly well suited for his intended self-development. To be sure, his relationship to it was at first almost accidental; he had left Boston heading first for New York. In two ways he was distant from Philadelphia: he had been born elsewhere, and his stay in London left a lasting impression of what a great, culturally central city was really like. But despite long stays in London and Paris, he kept the identity he had earlier chosen. The association of Franklin with Philadelphia has in fact been one of those inevitable and symbolic linkages whereby a great man and a city seem mutually to define each other, in the same way that Dante is linked with Florence, Socrates with Athens, or Dickens with London. Franklin always came back to Philadelphia; it was the city that he loved.

Philadelphia held a special place in the imagination of the eighteenth century. When Voltaire mentioned it in his *Philosophical Letters*, he wrote that in Philadelphia William Penn had created an image of the golden age, a city of tolerance, commerce, and peace. The reality, as Franklin knew, was rather different; in 1764 he commented wryly about Voltaire's impression: "While we sit for our Picture to that able Painter, tis no small Advantage to us, that he views us at a favorable Distance" (*P*, 9:367). But the cultural image of Philadelphia, first given expression in Voltaire's influential work, persisted through the century. It was perpetuated in Raynal's *Histoire des deux Indes* and entered into the French mythology about America which Franklin so adroitly exploited during the Revolution. Even in America Philadelphia seemed, certainly at the time of the Revolution, a center of culture and prosperity. John Adams records the open-eyed wonderment of the New England delegates to the Continental Congress when they saw the worldly and sophisticated Philadelphians.[1]

Founded by William Penn in 1682, Philadelphia was born out of a religious impulse, but an impulse different from that of Boston. It was to be a refuge, not a city on a hill. The Reformation to the first settlers of Boston had seemed a battle still to be won; by the time Philadelphia got started, the Reformation was over. Boston had been both a vulnerable outpost in the midst of a wilderness and a port facing the Atlantic. Philadelphia grew up when English colonization was already a successful experiment. Though it was a port, it lay well inland, surrounded by good farmland on all sides, and by peaceable Indians with whom the Quakers observed scrupulously considerate relations.

Philadelphia was a planned city, with a street pattern laid out from its founding. In its organization there were no special foci of attention, such as in L'Enfant's Washington or Bernini's Baroque modifications of Rome; the pattern was a simple grid, with streets running parallel and perpendicular to the Delaware River. The existence of such a grid implied expansion along the extended lines of the inhabited streets, a contrast with Boston, hemmed in during the eighteenth century on its peninsula, or New York, crowded into one end of a narrow island.

William Penn had invited diversity from the start by his policy of toleration. Diversity, of course, meant diversity of religions; even by the time Franklin arrived there were significant numbers of Anglicans, Presbyterians, and Baptists along with the Quakers. The Quakers controlled the provincial assembly, but that control was a holding action, a political control exercised by people basically uninterested in political ties. Toleration and diversity did not lead necessarily to harmonious group relations. Governing the colony were William Penn's descendants, three mediocre brothers who had deserted the Quaker persuasion and looked upon Pennsylvania as a large personal estate. William Penn's toleration had opened the colony up to all Protestant sects, who vied with each other for precedence. No sense of special calling united Pennsylvania the way New England was united, and its economy was too mixed to foster the agrarian solidarity of the southern colonies. What held Pennsylvania together was trade and certain voluntary associations for mutual benefit, for example the fire companies of Philadelphia.[2] The Enlightenment model of a society comprised of independent and self-interested individuals was realized in Pennsylvania as nowhere else.

Insofar as any group could, the Quakers set the tone for the community in the first half of the eighteenth century. By this time less a mode of belief than an ethic, Quakerism stressed sincerity, simplicity of living and appearance, diligence in business, group cohesiveness, and the avoidance of hostility. All these were elements of that new identity which Franklin was seeking for himself. In the *Autobiography* Franklin praises the somewhat meddlesome candor of the Quakers. A Quaker woman aboard ship had warned him against two young women who prove to be whores and thieves. When he drew up his list of virtues, it was a Quaker who pointed out to him that he particularly needed to add Humility to the list, "having kindly inform'd me that I was generally thought proud; that my Pride show'd itself frequently in Conversation; that I was not content with being in the right when discussing any Point, but was overbearing and rather insolent; of which he convinc'd me by mentioning several Instances" (A, 158–59). Thomas Denham had been a Quaker, as were several of the Junto members; later, two prominent Quakers, James Logan of Philadelphia and Peter Collinson of London, would be associated with his rise to prominence as an experimenter and man of letters.

But in one crucial respect Franklin could not follow the example of the Quakers. Their first loyalty was to a personal inspiration whose claims could not be compromised with the needs of any human community. His great need, on the contrary, was for a community to which he could offer a rational and convinced allegiance. The Quakers were united in a professed belief which made political action virtually unthinkable. Their kingdom was not of this world, and their emphasis on personal salvation entailed a virtual denial of national identity. Group action among the Quakers was not considered civic or national. The Quaker yearly meeting, an assembly of Quakers in good standing, controlled the group's relations with the society at large. In consultation with the Quaker community in London, the Philadelphia yearly meeting decided on Quaker positions on issues before the Pennsylvania Assembly, and Quaker legislators tended to vote as a bloc.[3] The yearly meeting even arbitrated civil disputes among the Quakers, thus keeping them out of the courts. This gathering was not a group legislature to which the Quakers attributed governing powers. Founded on the irreducible and inviolable sanctity of personal insights, Quaker belief could concede no determining force to any human group. Living with the Quakers reinforced Franklin's internal resistance to authority, a resistance which would later be in tension with his sense of British and then of American identity. But he had imbibed in Boston the Puritan sense of national mission, and when his career of civic activities fully began in the mid 1740s, he continually invoked the rhetoric of common solidarity.

A number of the social complexities of Boston did not appear in Philadelphia because of the Quakers. There was, as yet in the 1730s, no firmly entrenched aristocracy such as Boston already had, and the monied group was socially divided into Quakers and non-Quakers. There were, of course, circles in which Franklin could not travel and which would never really receive him, but a history of social mobility blurred the lines of class. Of special significance to Franklin was the absence of a Harvard College enforcing an unbridgeable gap between educated people and tradesmen. The Quakers were for their own reasons as put off by classical education as Franklin was. Even the government of Pennsylvania was simpler. The Pennsylvania Assembly was a unicameral legislature; the governor's council, which in other colonies functioned as a second house, had there no legislative functions. Philadelphia was a city packed in closely in a few blocks next to the Delaware; rich and poor lived in close proximity to each other.[4] It was a city of small entrepreneurs, some poor, some wealthy, united by nothing so much as the disposition to trade with each other.

It did not take Franklin long to line up the financial backing to establish his own printing business. By 1728, two years after returning to Philadelphia, including his earlier stay, he had published nothing; Philadelphia had far less publishing activity than Boston, and the only newspaper, the *American Weekly Mercury*, was a modest affair run by Andrew Bradford, one of Franklin's competitors. Soon after getting his own press he began planning a newspaper of his own. Before he could do so, however, Keimer heard of his plans and hurried into print with his own contender, grandiosely titled the *Universal Instructor in all Arts and Sciences: and Pennsylvania Gazette*. To undercut the newspaper, Franklin went to Bradford and bolstered its lackluster pages with a new series of periodical essays, this time under the *persona* of the *Busy-Body*. These essays give us the best evidence available on the state of Franklin's developing sense of himself and of his audience as he was getting established in Philadelphia.

The *Busy-Body* series, like the *Silence Dogood* essays, was an adaptation of Addison that promised to provide mild diversion to a community deprived of literary entertainment. In both series Franklin's persona says less than what he himself thinks of a subject, and the disparity is obvious enough that the alert reader will look more closely at the assertions. When Silence Dogood had denounced pride of apparel, and in particular the dangers to church and state of wearing hoop petticoats, her earnest adaptations of Boston pulpit rhetoric could only make the real guardians of propriety look faintly ridiculous. She was, after all, not really a minister's widow, as her readers well knew; no self-respecting woman would have let her prose appear in the racy pages of the *Courant*.[5] Similarly, the Busy-Body remarks in his first number that he is writing "not out of the least Vanity, I assure you, or Desire of showing my Parts, but purely for the Good of my Country" (*P*, 1:114–15). There were surely readers in Philadelphia who might have been alerted to the *persona's* exhibitionist tendencies by this reference to showing his parts.

But there are subtle differences between those two sets of periodical essays that suggest the new life Franklin was trying to lead. He was writing from different motives, and he sought a different rapport with his readers. *Silence Dogood* had been written as a display of his precocious talents; the *Busy-Body* was conceived as a device to distract attention from a potential rival. The very names operate differently. "Busy-Body" is self-mocking; "Silence Dogood" directs mockery outward, at women and the clergy. One can detect in *Silence Dogood* a vein of buried lower class consciousness: the poor do not go to Harvard, she notes; her audience, she writes in the first number, will want to know whether the author is "*poor* or *rich*, *old* or *young*, a *Schollar* or a *Leather Apron Man*, &c" (P, 1:9). The Busy-Body insists instead on offering images of a society in which economic differences are not important, where a poor man of integrity is honored by the rich and powerful. If this is Franklin's wish-fulfillment, it is also well-calculated to prepare a place for him in this society.

The Busy-Body announced in his first number that he was concerned not merely with entertainment but with shaping the morals of the community.

> And tho' Reformation is properly the concern of every Man; that is, *Everyone ought to mend One*; yet 'tis too true in this Case, that *what is every Body's Business is no Body's Business*, and the business is done accordingly. I, therefore, upon mature Deliberation, think fit to take *no Body's Business* wholly into my own Hands; and, out of Zeal for the Publick Good, design to erect my Self into a Kind of *Censor Morum*; proposing with your Allowance, to make Use of the *Weekly Mercury* as a Vehicle in which my Remonstrances shall be convey'd to the World. (P, 1:115)

The tone here is light, too light, in fact, to be altogether satirical. In the occasional pieces Franklin would later do for the *Pennsylvania Gazette*, he would often satirize gossips, but the Busy-Body is not ridiculous. His reasoning represents not a gratuitous absurdity but a community value taken casually for granted. The humor also implied a subtly asserted independence; what is collective duty for the Quakers and Puritans becomes a free option for the Busy-Body.

In the *Busy-Body* Franklin several times sets up two opposing characters, one the ideal and the other its opposite. Ridentius is a scoffer, intimidating others with his ridicule; Eugenius is his good-natured opposite, who "takes more Delight in applying the Wit of his Friends, than in being admir'd himself: And if any one of the Company is so unfortunate as to be touch'd a little too nearly, he will make Use of some ingenious Artifice to turn the Edge of Ridicule another Way, choosing rather to make even himself a publick Jest, than be at the Pain of seeing his Friend in Confusion" (P, 1:118). Eugenius represents the right uses for humor which Franklin was trying to employ, after seeing the dangers to himself of wrong uses. Also in the *Busy-Body* there appears for the first time a character of continuing importance to Franklin—the simple rustic philosopher, who is universally respected despite his simplicity and humbleness of origins. Cato is this character's name in this first incarnation. He is dressed "in the plainest Country Garb," wearing homespun and thick shoes.

> Why was this Man receiv'd with such concurring Respect from every Person in the Room, even from those who had never known him or seen him before? It was not an exquisite Form of Person, or Grandeur of Dress that struck us with Admiration. I believe long Habits of Virtue have a sensible Effect on the Countenance... The Consciousness of his own innate Worth and unshaken Integrity renders him calm and undaunted in the Presence of the most Great and Powerful, and upon the most extraordinary Occasions. His strict Justice and known Impartiality make him the Arbitrator and Decider of all Differences that arise for many Miles around him, without putting his Neighbors to the Charge, Perplexity and Uncertainty of Law-Suits. (P, 1:119–20)

These are the very terms that Franklin uses to describe his own father in the *Autobiography*—a simple man of acknowledged integrity, consulted about disputes, and respected by the great. Cato, however, is not a character but an abstraction; insofar as Franklin is treating his father here, he has converted him into a complex of admirable qualities, lacking even the quality of fatherhood. This Cato is alone, not the busy patriarch his father was. The context in which he appears is a praise of virtue, which is associated with the controlling of passions. His opposite is Cretico, a thinly disguised portrait of the egregious Keimer, whom Franklin accused of trying to intimidate his employees and of devoting himself to musty authors rather than to the knowledge of mankind.

Franklin then tries to deny that Keimer is the real subject of this portrait by disclaiming that he has anyone in particular in mind. His own aggressions, however, had not yet been brought into perfect control. As the series of letters proceeded, he found it necessary to deny even more strenuously that his portraits were intended maliciously.[6] Keimer in turn accused him of being two different people: one a "Free-thinker of the Peripatetick Sect" who affected an air of superiority and detachment from other people, the other "an Understrapper to a Press," not a philosopher but a mere working nobody (P, 1:134). Keimer's angry characterization of young Franklin is rather acute: it was not easy to be a detached speculator on philosophical questions while laboring at the printing press, yet Franklin sought to have things both ways. And Keimer's comment emphasizes how hard it must have been for Franklin to pass himself off as the innocuous Busy-Body to people who could remember his satirical and irreligious impulses.

Keimer was, however, only a temporary hindrance to the development of Franklin's reputation in Philadelphia. Others were noticing his intelligence, amiability, and industriousness. Franklin seems to have hoarded the memory of compliments received from Isaac Decow, Dr. Baird, and others; forty years later he could recite them verbatim in his *Autobiography*. (He also remembered the discouraging predictions of one Samuel Mickle, a "Croaker"; Franklin recalls with considerable satisfaction how Mickle's pessimism cost him money by preventing him from buying a house before the prices rose.) Franklin kept a running count of the influential friends he was accumulating. "These Friends were afterwards of great Use to me, as I occasionally was to some of them. They all continued their Regard for me as long as they lived" (A, 113). Now that he was back in Philadelphia, he had a more realistic sense of how the political lines of force in the colony operated. He established ties with members of the ruling oligarchy rather than with the governor, who could never hold more than a temporary and vulnerable position of power.

Keimer eventually gave up on his newspaper and sold it to Franklin, who quickly made it a going concern. Three years later, in 1732, he started an even more successful venture, *Poor Richard's Almanack*. He had in part been forced into it by the loss to his rival of the printing contracts of all the other almanacs.[7] Franklin's principal competition at this time was the almanac of Titan Leeds; as a device to call attention to his own production, Franklin had Poor Richard predict astrologically Leeds's death. By this time such a prediction was rather an old trick; Swift had done the same thing in 1708 under the name of Isaac Bickerstaff. Franklin was not averse to borrowing an old idea, however, knowing that his readers would neither know nor perhaps care whether it was original

As space fillers Franklin included maxims and pithy sayings which he adapted from a variety of other sources. In the third section of the *Autobiography* he claims that these maxims inculcated industry and frugality, but it has been long recognized that a much wider variety of sayings appeared.[8] The first almanac, for example, included maxims about the wisdom of being married, of not overstaying visits, of not dealing with villains, and even of not writing on walls (P, 1:293, 298, 303, 302). Later he would assemble those maxims dealing with industry and frugality into the famous Preface to *Poor Richard Improved* of 1758, but throughout the period of his authorship a wide range of imitation folk wisdom appeared in the almanac. In the *Autobiography* Franklin describes himself as an educator of his poorer countrymen, "conveying Instruction among the common People, who bought scarce any other Books" (*A*, 164); but it would be more accurate to say, at least of the almanacs, that he carefully adjusted himself to his sense of the common people's tastes.

Many of these early ventures, including the *Busy-Body*, the *Pennsylvania Gazette*, and the pamphlet on paper currency, were assisted by a body of Franklin's acquaintances who had formed themselves together under the name the Junto. The word *junto* in contemporary usage suggested a group of political plotters, a secret cabal, and though the name was no doubt humorously adopted, the group was in a sense plotting secretly for its own political advancement. The Junto consisted primarily of up-and-coming young tradesmen; each Friday evening they would gather to discuss both a series of continuing items of business, the Standing Queries, and also individual queries brought by each member on morals, politics, or natural philosophy. "Our Debates were to be under the Direction of a President, and to be conducted in the sincere Spirit of Enquiry after Truth, without Fondness for Dispute, or Desire for Victory; and to prevent Warmth all Expressions of Positiveness in Opinion, or of direct Contradiction, were after some time made contraband and prohibited under small pecuniary Penalties" (*A*, 117).

The Junto served Franklin as a substitute for intimate friendships; the aggressions he had formerly shown in dealing with particular others could there be diffused and redirected within the group. His success at using the Junto is indicative of his readiness to use people as tools, not that the other members were exploited but rather that his relations with them were a means rather than an end. He had always worked well in groups, readily rising to the position of leader, as he had while building the wharf as a child, among the Couranteers, and in the press room at Watts's printing house. Thus he had set out to collect around him a group that would provide the intellectual stimulation he had found with Collins and Ralph. Just as important, the Junto would provide the same reinforcement his friends formerly offered for his freedom from a fixed identity. They too were on the rise. The secrecy of the Junto offered the illusion of intimacy; its set format restrained displays of aggressiveness and attempts at domination. Franklin could not love the Junto as he had loved Collins and Ralph, but he also could not be betrayed by it.

The Junto Standing Queries reveal a striking emphasis on public scrutiny of individual behavior.

3. Hath any citizen in your knowledge failed in his business lately, and what have you heard of the cause?

4. Have you lately heard of any citizen's thriving well, and by what means?...

6. Do you know of any fellow citizen, who has lately done a worthy action, deserving praise and imitation? or who has committed an error proper for us to be warned against and avoid?...

12. Hath any deserving stranger arrived in town since last meeting, that you heard of? and what have you heard or observed of his character or merits? and whether think you, it lies in the power of the Junto to oblige him, or encourage him as he deserves?

13. Do you know of any deserving young beginner lately set up, whom it lies in the power of the Junto any way to encourage?...

16. Hath any body attacked your reputation lately? and what can the Junto do towards securing it?

(P, 1:257–58)

Well might Franklin and Breintnall (another Junto member) style themselves the Busy-Body. The Standing Queries organize systematically the group awareness of what everyone is doing that is characteristic of small towns. (Philadelphia in 1727 had fewer than 12,000 inhabitants.)[9] But this apparent meddlesomeness was accompanied by the more philosophical queries brought to the meetings by each member:

Can a Man arrive at Perfection in this Life as some Believe; or is it impossible as others believe?...What general Conduct of Life is most suitable for Men in such Circumstances as most of the Members of the Junto are; Or, of the many Schemes of Living which are in our Power to pursue, which will be most probably conducive to our Happiness. (P, 1:261, 263)

For the young tradesmen it was apparently natural to shift from the organized gossip of the Standing Queries to the abstract question of the evening. Somehow individual behavior and philosophical ideas were viewed in the same perspective. The Standing Queries apparently served to liberate Junto members from the group values of the surrounding community, bringing those values into consciousness through dialectic almost as a sort of group therapy. Together the members were able to assume the role of dispassionate, social observers, a necessary role for young men who wish to alter their status positions in society. The Junto served to provide potent mutual support for those aspirations.

The Junto Standing Queries also pointed Franklin inevitably into politics. For all members, the meetings were a weekly reminder and reinforcement of their identities as public-spirited citizens, as well as a base of support for group action. Part of the group's constitution provided that members do business with each other and refer business to each other. Out of the Junto came also the foundation for the network of public action committees which Franklin would later organize. Paradoxically, Franklin's very identity as an outsider in Philadelphia required that he pursue a public life. He had freed himself and was kept continually free of that unconscious absorption into a community which both emotionally supports and politically weakens a person who might otherwise have been drawn to political action and public reputation. Franklin required from the world of publicly visible actions that sustaining reflection of himself that he could get nowhere else. He needed finally to create for himself a country.

Before he could deal with those public questions, certain private needs had to be taken care of. He needed to be freed from the desperate exigencies of single life, but he was not in a strong bargaining position for choosing a mate. By this time he had developed a pattern of shabby and mutually demeaning encounters with women. Manipulative and self-centered relationships with women or attitudes toward women accompanied his friendships with Collins and Ralph; there had been, for example, Ralph's woman, Mrs. T., the little milliner whom Franklin had tried to seduce after she was financially indebted to him. The obverse side of such attitudes appears in a letter to his little sister Jane written shortly after he returned to Philadelphia. "Sister, farewell," writes the twenty-one-year-old Franklin, "and remember that modesty, as it makes the most homely virgin amiable and charming, so the want of it infallibly renders the most perfect beauty disagreeable and odious" (P, 1:100).

There had been one young woman whom he had planned once to marry. Before leaving for England in 1724 he had been boarding in the house of John Read, a carpenter who owned a fair-sized house on Market Street. Living there, Franklin got to know Read's daughter Deborah, then fifteen years old. He had remembered her from his first day in Philadelphia, when she had laughed at him for walking along with great puffy rolls under each arm. Deborah Read was the young woman he saw most often, and before long they were engaged. "I had a great Respect and Affection for her, and had some Reason to believe she had the same for me," in the rather opaque words of the *Autobiography* (*A*, 89). But any wedding was postponed until his return from the trip to England, and when he arrived there and decided to stay for a while he unceremoniously dumped her. Another *erratum*, he admits.

When he returned he found that she had contracted a disastrous and abortive marriage with a bigamous potter who had since absconded, leaving considerable debts. He in turn, once he had gotten the printing business started, courted a young woman whose parents abruptly forbade his suit when they discovered he wanted the usual dowry settlement. The affair had been engineered by the wife of one of the Junto members, and the parents had seemed accomplices, but they suddenly declared that he would be a poor financial risk. Probably some indications about the potential engagement had reached his family in Boston. "I am not about to be married as you have heard," he wrote to his older sister Sarah, slipping the cryptic announcement in among family inquiries and reports of travel plans (*P*, 1:171).

At the same time Franklin had been sexually active. "[T]hat hard-to-be-governed Passion of Youth, had hurried me frequently into Intrigues with low Women that fell in my Way, which were attended with some Expence and great Inconvenience, besides a continual Risque to my Health by a Distemper which of all Things I dreaded, tho' by great good Luck I escaped it" (*A*, 128). As in other cases of aggressive behavior, Franklin insists on his own passivity; these women had fallen in his way. And it was they who had exploited him; "from the Expence," he writes in a crossed-out phrase in the *Autobiography*, these intrigues "were rather more prejudicial to me than to them" (*A*, 115n). One of these women presented him with a son, William Franklin, and the expense he describes was in part the cost of the disreputable mother's upkeep for the rest of her life.[10]

When Franklin scouted around for a wife after his collapsed romance, he found no parents with desirable daughters willing to fork over the expected dowry money, "the Business of a Printer being generally thought a poor one" (*A*, 128). But there was Deborah Read, whom he still felt guilty about. He began seeing her again, and only a few months after the other affair had broken off, she moved in as his common-law wife (her earlier marriage making it impossible for them to be legally married). Both were making the best of things.

Deborah Franklin was a plain-looking, unlettered woman, but very loyal to her husband. She did have some property to bring to the marriage, a house on Market Street that was deeded to Franklin a few years after they moved in together. (Franklin's mother-in-law was given the right in the deed to occupy part of the property for ninety-nine years, for rent of one peppercorn per year.) Why did Franklin not choose a wife more like himself in her intelligence and interests? Probably no such woman could have been found in Philadelphia among the social classes who would marry a daughter to a young debt-ridden printer. Deborah's illiteracy was to be expected; the Philadelphia Quakers did not have the same concern about education, whether for men or for women, as there had been in Puritan Boston. Later in life Franklin would be repeatedly fascinated by experiences of educated and intelligent women, but at twenty-four the very idea of one must have been foreign to him.

Franklin always talked about marriage as something to be submitted to with good-humored resignation. He did not think it important to find some particular and special woman; later on in life he could think of no real argument against the Moravian custom of marriage by lot. He was not embarrassed by his son's illegitimacy and in fact later arranged to have William appointed royal governor of New Jersey. When William in turn had his own illegitimate son, William Temple Franklin, the grandfather looked after the boy in England while his father was in America. Marriage for Franklin was a device for satisfying a natural instinct, not a cultural rite. It was not supposed to limit or direct the male self, but rather to complete and strengthen that self to act in the world. "It is the most natural State of Man, and therefore the State in which you are most likely to find solid Happiness," he writes in a famous letter of advice, the so-called "Old Mistress's Apologue." "It is the Man and Woman united that make the compleat human Being. Separate, she wants his Force of Body and Strength of Reason; he, her Softness, Sensibility and acute Discernment. Together they are more likely to succeed in the World. A single Man has not nearly the Value he would have in that State of Union. He is an incomplete Animal. He resembles the odd Half of a Pair of Scissars. If you get a prudent healthy Wife, your Industry in your Profession, with her good OEconomy, will be a Fortune sufficient" (P, 3:30). Yet these arguments for marriage are prudential rather than moral, and there are certainly alternatives to the violent natural inclinations his correspondent describes. The male self must be served. With professed unwillingness Franklin suggests another possibility; he lists eight reasons for choosing an older woman as a mistress. Franklin treats the sexual appetite as something irrelevant to a person's basic definition of himself.

Shortly after his marriage, Franklin became a mason and entered actively into the activities of the Philadelphia lodge. Only three years later he was elected Grand Master. There were several reasons for his involvement with masonry, an involvement that lasted the rest of his life though he does not allude to it in his *Autobiography*. As a mason he was in contact with prominent Philadelphians on a footing of fellow membership. In the masonic rituals he found a further alternative to religion, and his engagement in them must have helped his credibility as an earnest young man. The secrecy of the rituals was akin to that of the Junto and of many of his own writings. It was a few months after joining St. John's Lodge that he drafted his proposal, reproduced in the *Autobiography*, for a United Party of Virtue, another secret society whose members underwent a program of collective self-discipline.

The masons, marriage, and the Junto were all means to public acceptance and respectability, forms of voluntary discipline for Franklin. In the nearly twenty years between the *Busy-Body* and his retirement from business, Franklin was involved in almost no extensive writing venture. He had suppressed his talent for controversy and his urge to bring himself into prominence. But there was one exception, a short interlude during which he wrote voluminously and vehemently. In 1734 a new Presbyterian minister named Samuel Hemphill arrived in town. He quickly gained a reputation as an excellent preacher, and Franklin joined the crowd of his hearers. His sermons "had little of the dogmatic kind, but inculcated strongly the Practice of Virtue, or what in the religious Stile are called Good Works."[11] But traditional Presbyterians were less impressed, believing that salvation was to be through grace and not works, and they met in synod to suspend him from the ministry.

Franklin, who had reconciled himself with the church as community but not as doctrine, threw himself into the controversy without regard to any sense of his status as an outsider. "I became his zealous Partisan, and contributed all I could to raise a Party in his favour," he writes in the *Autobiography*: "and we combated for him for a while with some Hopes of Success" (*A*, 167). He objected to the denial of Hemphill's free expression and defended the teaching of morality rather than dogma. Hemphill clearly differed from the Westminster Confession, so Franklin used the traditional radical Protestant argument, that the Reformation must be further reformed. At first, in his initial contribution to the controversy, a "Dialogue between Two Presbyterians," Franklin adopted a benign and good-tempered tone. "There are Men of unquestionable Good Sense as well as Piety" among the synod who would be sitting to decide Hemphill's case, and Franklin claimed to trust their judgment (*P*, 2:31). By the end of the controversy, however, his writing displayed a polemical vigor and a taste for harsh unequivocal assertion which he had resisted earlier. The doctrine of man's fall is "a Notion invented, a Bugbear set up by Priests (whether *Popish* or *Presbyterian* I know not) to fright and scare an unthinking Populace out of their Senses, and inspire them with Terror, to answer the little selfish Ends of the Inventors and Propagators" (P, 2:114). Also, despite his later claim that he had always found the doctrine of Calvinism unintelligible, he proved a sharp controversialist in these pamphlets.

Significantly, Franklin did not perceive the controversy as an internal question to be decided by Presbyterians. He even denied that the church had the right to exclude members who believed differently. "Now, the Case between a whole Society and one Man, is exactly the same as between Man and Man; the Number of Persons on one side, and their Fewness on the other, does not make any Alteration in it" (P, 2:78). Franklin was determined to be related to society on his own terms. The community should be open for redefinition by its members. Looking back on the Hemphill episode in his *Autobiography*, Franklin ironically notes the transitoriness of religious controversies.

> There was much Scribbling pro and con upon the Occasion; and finding that tho' an elegant Preacher he was but a poor Writer, I lent him my Pen and wrote for him two or three Pamphlets, and one Piece in the Gazette of April 1735. Those Pamphlets, as is generally the Case with controversial Writings, tho' eagerly read at the time, were soon out of Vogue, and I question whether a single copy of them now exists. (A, 167)

As he does elsewhere in the *Autobiography*, Franklin underplays his own past emotional involvement, but the pamphlets themselves survive to attest to the urgency of the question for him. His place in society, his right to define his own terms of relationship to the community, was here brought into question. It was a problem that would surface again in the years before the Revolution.

As Franklin became more sure of his place in the community, he began to undertake a series of public projects which would alter the character of life in Philadelphia and eventually serve as his model of what American society should be. His first venture, in 1729, was a proposal to increase the supply of paper currency; not only would struggling entrepreneurs gain by a fluid and inflating currency, but printers would be needed for the paper notes. In 1731 he and the Junto members formed the Library Company. Soon after came the Union Fire Company, a volunteer fire company that also served as a social club for its members. He served as clerk of the Provincial Assembly, as postmaster, as justice of the peace, and later as member of the Philadelphia Council and of the Assembly. He invented the Franklin stove in 1742 and four years later began his experiments in electricity. He published proposals which led to the founding of the American Philosophical Society, the Pennsylvania colonial militia, and the Academy at Philadelphia (later the University of Pennsylvania). He assisted in establishing the Pennsylvania Hospital and the first fire insurance company in America. These are the highlights. Through most of this period he was also managing his printing house, the *Pennsylvania Gazette, Poor Richard's Almanack*, a short-lived magazine *The General Magazine*, and a network of collaborative printing ventures. Franklin was not involved in these projects alone; several were the initiatives of other men, to whom he lent his ingenuity and his pen. He came to be regarded as the greatest expediter of projects in Philadelphia; Gilbert Tennent, the prominent Presbyterian leader of the Great Awakening, turned to him for advice on how to raise money for his new church. From being an active projector himself he developed the credibility that made his support a necessary authentication for the proposals of others.

Following early frustrations in getting support for the Library Company, Franklin devised a set of tactics for getting things done in the city. There would first be an anonymous pamphlet or article in the *Pennsylvania Gazette* which would describe a problem and suggest a solution. Then, shortly after, a committee would be formed, comprised of members from the Junto and from different groups in the community. It would be necessary to secure the favor, or at least the neutrality, of the important powers in the colony—the Proprietaries, the Quakers, the non-Quaker gentry. In other words, whatever the project, it was essential to take it out of politics, ·or from the intergroup bickering that passed for politics in Pennsylvania. Like the Busy-Body, Franklin wanted to be "no Party man, but a general Meddler" (P, 1:121). The basis for financing the project would be public subscriptions or a lottery. The names of the subscribers and the amounts subscribed would be included in the committee's records, so members of the monied and influential class would know who had given liberally and who had been tight-fisted. Credit for the success of the project would go to no one; the credit of being benefactors was widely diffused, and the envy of the prominent few toward the initiator would be largely eliminated.

Particularly in electoral politics it was important to minimize the appearance of aggressiveness. In 1747 another candidate for Franklin's longtime post as clerk of the Pennsylvania Assembly suggested that he resign.

> My Answer to him was, that I had read or heard of some Public Man, who made it a Rule never to ask for an Office, and

> never to refuse one when offer'd to him. I approve, says I, of
> this Rule, and will practise it with a small Addition; I shall
> never *ask*, never *refuse*, nor ever *resign* an Office. If they will
> have my Office of Clerk to dispose of to another, they shall take
> it from me. I will not by giving it up lose my right of some time
> or other making Reprisals on my Adversaries. (*A*, 185)

On being challenged Franklin displayed a kind of defensive passivity.
However public-spirited he might have been, however denying of hostility, he still realized the possible need of making reprisals on his enemies. But he denied having ambitions himself. In 1751 he was elected
to the Assembly. "My Election to this Trust was repeated every Year for
Ten Years, without my ever asking any Elector for his Vote, or signify-
ing either directly or indirectly any Desire of being chosen" (*A*, 197). In
actuality Franklin assured that votes for him were energetically solic-
ited by others (*A*, 197n).

Even during this active period of community involvement Franklin
held himself off from full identification with his city, preferring to see
himself as a sojourner in Philadelphia. In a will drawn up in 1750 he
gives thanks to God "That he gave me to live so long in a Land of Liberty, with a People that I love, and rais'd me, tho' a Stranger, so many
Friends among them; bestowing on me moreover a loving and prudent
Wife, and dutiful Children" (*P*, 3:481). Even his wife and family did not
finally bind him to his adoptive place. To be fully a Philadelphian, he
knew, meant to be wholeheartedly a member of one of the squabbling
groups that composed the city. His separate status was thus a declaration of neutrality, since a deeper commitment to the society had to
mean a commitment to only a part of the society and consequently alienation from the rest of it.

By withholding full identification from the Presbyterians, the Anglicans, and later the enthusiasts who followed George Whitefield, Franklin found a special status for himself in relation to all of them. Thomas
Penn fretted over Franklin's status as early as 1748, believing him "a
dangerous Man...of a very uneasy Spirit. However as he is a Sort of
Tribune of the People, he must be treated with regard" (*P*, 3:481). Much
later John Adams pointed out Franklin's versatile relations with different religious groups.

> While he had the singular felicity to enjoy the entire esteem
> and affection of all the philosophers of every denomination, he
> was not less regarded by all the sects and denominations of
> Christians. The Catholics thought him almost a Catholic. The

Church of England claimed him as one of them. The Presbyterians thought him half a Presbyterian, and the Friends believed him a wet Quaker. The dissenting clergymen in England and America were among the most distinguished asserters and propagators of his renown. Indeed, all sects considered him, and I believe justly, a friend to unlimited toleration in matters of religion.[12]

Because he was not fully within any group, a nonparticipant in the continuing rite of group solidarity, he could act for the group in acknowledging the world outside which the internal rites denied. Like Talleyrand in Revolutionary France or Maxim Litvinov in Stalinist Russia, his ideological cosmopolitanism was a tacitly accepted deviance that licensed him as agent to the world.

For the most part Franklin was able to maintain in Philadelphia the role of the privileged outsider. Even the controversies and fervor of the Great Awakening could not shake him; he became a personal friend of George Whitefield, the greatest evangelical preacher of his day. Whitefield's supporters erected for public meetings the so-called New Building, with a board of trustees carefully balanced to avoid giving predominance to any group in Protestant Philadelphia. A vacancy arose which would have obliged the board to name a second member of some sect to the board. "At length one mention'd me, with the Observation that I was merely an honest Man, and of no Sect at all; which prevail'd with them to chuse me" (A, 194). The Autobiography reveals Franklin's unrealized ambitions to be a quasi-religious leader himself, as the founder of the Society of the Free and Easy and the propagator of the all-purpose creed. But these ambitions had to be suppressed if he was to accomplish good works in Philadelphia.

The projects that Franklin undertook to advance became, in a way, a means of self-expression. Onto them he projected his own sense of independence. All the institutions he helped to found were set up so that no one group or individual could dominate, nor could anyone claim these benefactions as his own. His prominence in Philadelphia was largely built on his involvement in civic good works, yet his style had nothing to do with noblesse oblige. Private benevolence of Squire Allworthy's kind was the accepted English model in the eighteenth century; it confirmed the social hierarchy through the personal tie between giver and receiver. Franklin's benevolence, on the other hand, was public and representative rather than personal.[13] He found a model for his own style of good works in the parable of the Good Samaritan. Soliciting funds for the Pennsylvania Hospital in his newspaper, he drew out an elaborate and very personal application of the parable.

> For this one Thing, (in that beautiful Parable of the Traveller wounded by Thieves) the Samaritan (who was esteemed no better than a *Heretick*, or an *Infidel* by the *Orthodox* of those Times) is preferred to the Priest and the Levite; because he did not, like them, pass by, regardless of the Distress of his Brother Mortal; but when he came to the Place where the half-dead Traveller lay, *he had Compassion on him, and went to him and bound up his Wounds, pouring in Oil and Wine, and set him on his own Beast, and brought him to an Inn, and took Care of him.* (P, 4:148–49)

The Samaritan was religiously unorthodox; Franklin generally sought to downplay his own unbelief through a display of good works. Charity for him was based not on the duties inherent in a fixed order of society but on the vicissitudes which happen to all. "We are in this World mutual Hosts to each other; the Circumstances and Fortunes of Men and Families are continually changing; in the Course of a few Years we have seen the Rich become Poor, and the Poor Rich; the Children of the Wealthy languishing in Want and Misery, and those of their Servants lifted into Estates, and abounding in the good Things of this Life" (P, 4:149). Just as we are all mutual hosts, so we are all guests and sojourners in a fluid society. Self-protection in a world of incalculable changes is the basis for charity.

If Franklin's projects altered Philadelphia, his recollecting imagination remade it even more considerably in the *Autobiography*. For one thing, his associates in the Junto and on other committees, because they are not really characterized and seem to act always in unison, appear to be only extensions of his will. For another, the respectful solicitude which he always paid to the colony's older and more influential men—Andrew Hamilton, James Logan, Richard Peters, and others—a solicitude that is evident in his surviving letters to them, does not fully appear in his *Autobiography* as a precondition to his successes. The reader of the *Autobiography* is unaware that the Franklins were not really part of high society in the province, even after Franklin had retired from his trade. And the *Autobiography* transformed Philadelphia into an ideal of religious toleration. The New Building was constructed, he states, for members of any belief in the world, "so that even if the Mufti of Constantinople were to send a Missionary to preach Mahometanism to us, he would find a Pulpit at his Service" (A, 176). The New

Building was erected as a place for George Whitefield to preach the revived Calvinism of the Great Awakening. It would have been a great surprise to his followers on the building's board of trustees to hear that Franklin was extending its use so ecumenically.

Franklin's plans for the Academy at Philadelphia (later to be the University of Pennsylvania) illustrate particularly well how his public improvements mirrored his self-image. What better way to propagate a mode of identity than to establish a school curriculum that imitates one's own education? He had been deprived of a learned education as a boy, after having the prospect held out before him; now he could create a Harvard College of his own. As early as 1743 he had drawn up a proposal, but the time was not ripe. Six years later his *Proposals Relating to the Education of Youth in Pennsylvania* appeared, supposedly published at the request of "some publick-spirited Gentlemen" (*P,* 3:307). A year later the plan for the Academy was completed; the school opened in January 1751.

His *Proposals* appear to be drawn from extended reading in the theory of education. The pamphlet features long passages from various sources in the footnotes, and it is prefaced with a sort of bibliography that describes those sources. In fact, however, the basic ideas and emphases were Franklin's own; the sources offer less a basis than a pretext for his proposals.[14] He specifies at the beginning that the school is supposed to satisfy a public need. The first generation of colonial leaders was old or dead, men whose formal education in Europe had trained them for public service; the next generation has fallen short of their abilities. As for the American youth, "the best Capacities require Cultivation, it being truly with them, as with the best Ground, which unless well tilled and sowed with profitable Seed, produces only ranker Weeds" (*P,* 3:399). The subjects to be taught are selected for their appropriateness in preparing students for public life. The students are to study oratory, along with its modern counterpart, political journalism (*P,* 3:412–13). They are to study the history of colonies, "which should be accompanied with Observations on their Rise, Encrease, Use to Great-Britain, Encouragements, Discouragements, &c. the Means to make them flourish, secure their Liberties, &c" (*P,* 3:415). True merit, he concludes, consists in "an *Inclination* join'd with an *Ability* to serve Mankind, one's Country, Friends and Family" (*P,* 3:419). As always, Franklin could hardly conceive of genuine human worth existing only in a private sphere.

The leading metaphor Franklin uses for education comes from horticulture, a familiar source, but given here a strange twist. "And if Men may, and frequently do, catch such a Taste for cultivating Flowers, for

Planting, Grafting, Inoculating, and the like, as to despise all other Amusements for their Sake, why may not we expect they should acquire a Relish for that *more useful* Culture of young Minds" (*P,* 3:400–401). He is referring not to the teachers but to the prominent Philadelphia citizens who will serve as trustees for the Academy; these people, he imagines, will visit the school frequently and take a direct personal interest in the students. Probably Franklin's youth in Boston would have encouraged such an idea; in the early eighteenth century such visitations were an important yearly ritual for the entire Boston community.[15] The visits of the trustees to the projected Academy would also give students the opportunity to show off their abilities and promise, as the young Franklin had done.

Two areas of study concerned Franklin in particular, and all knowledge was subordinated to or comprehended in those categories. English and history, his primary areas, receive about equal attention as the program is developed in his *Proposals* and later in his *Idea of the English School.* By *English* Franklin meant the study of writing and speaking; he emphasizes, for example, the teaching of letter writing. This is a very distinctive emphasis. Already Franklin had experienced the value of correspondence in his own self-advancement. His letters had by then given him access to political decision making and scientific research. The letter also creates an equality of status between the correspondents; there he did not need to fear being taken for an upstart tradesman. The students were to master English prose style in the same way Franklin had, by competitions and imitation of the *Spectator* and other models.[16] *History,* the other major heading, includes a large body of material that might have fallen under the heading of philosophy. The basis for morality and the necessity of a public religion are to be revealed by history; it will teach the effects of oratory and the advantages of forming civil societies; even science and technology are to be presented as the history of nature and the history of commerce (*P,* 3:412–13, 415–18). This immense consolidation is Franklin's most original contribution to the theory of education proposed for the Academy. It must be an unusual sort of history that can offer all these lessons. In part this embrace of history clearly stemmed from an impulse central to the Enlightenment: the disposition to study matters in terms of their origins as opposed to their basic natures or ultimate ends. This examination of history, though, is not at all dispassionate or open-ended. "Indeed," he writes in the Proposals, "the general Tendency of Reading good History, must be, to fix in the Minds of Youth deep Impressions of the Beauty and Usefulness of Virtue of all Kinds, Publick Spirit, Fortitude, &c" (*P,* 3:412).

The study of history especially encourages adaptability, a principal goal of his educational program. History is always taking fresh shapes from the present which is constantly depositing new material into it. Although he never deserted the belief that history has meanings and patterns, Franklin was also inclined to anticipate vicissitudes and reversals of fortune. Classifying all studies as variants of history would eliminate the possibility of a curriculum based on a fixed order of elements or a designation of classic works, since new history is continually reordering knowledge. The Pennsylvania he would train students for was a place in transition; they would need broad capabilities. "Thus instructed," he writes at the end of the *Idea of the English School*, "Youth will come out of this school fitted for learning any Business, Calling or Profession.[17]

The model for education in the Academy is Franklin's own self-education. His students were to write by imitating the *Spectator*; they would be motivated by a series of small competitions. Even Franklin the printer's finicky concern for clear handwriting and correct spelling is represented in the curriculum. But here Franklin was unable to remodel the city to conform to his own likeness. Once the Academy was established, the prevailing views of education, which stressed the classical languages, gradually overcame Franklin's. His hand-picked rector, William Smith, proved to be a traditionalist, and Franklin watched with helpless indignation as his English School withered in the 1760s. It would not be through formal education that Franklin would form the character of the new generation of Americans.

Though he was much involved, the Academy was only one of his projects. At the same time that he was promoting the school, he was writing *Poor Richard Improved*, conducting experiments on electricity, serving as Provincial Grand Master of Masons in Philadelphia, and carrying on an active and already published correspondence. He committed himself to no one project to the exclusion of others. When he describes these civic improvements in his *Autobiography*, he implies that they were not accomplished just for themselves, in response to immediate and unrelated needs, but as part of a larger conception of the city and the nation. His writings in furtherance of those projects bear out his claim to having had such a grand design. In this he was quite by himself, except insofar as he was able to muster others to help materialize his visions. Such a perspective is nonexistent among his American contemporaries in 1750.

Politically he was an American before it was really possible to be one. In 1751 he attained one of the few offices that dealt with all the colonies, the deputy postmaster-generalship. He was the principal force behind the Albany Congress of 1754 and its neglected proposals for colonial unification. He was among the first colonials to advocate a common and coordinated defense against the French. The constitutions of the Academy make clear his aim of serving a national need. It was important for him to see himself as a citizen of an imperial domain. As inheritors of that dream fulfilled, we ourselves do not readily recognize how easily that dream could have seemed to be only an extravagant delusion, the fevered imaginings of a busy small-town printer. In 1750 there was still a long way to go before Franklin's conception of American identity would be believed by any besides him.

Around 1750 Franklin's life changed in ways that the *Autobiography* scarcely reflects. The period of life he had planned for in his shipboard resolutions on the way back to Philadelphia was over. The self-abnegation and application to business that he had committed himself to were no longer necessary. The success of his printing business, the *Gazette*, the *Almanack*, and a network of lucrative silent partnerships in printing businesses around the colonies had left him well off. In 1748 he signed a partnership agreement with David Hall that left him free of the active management of his printing business; at age forty-two he was, in effect, retired. Around 1746 his portrait was painted by the best of the itinerant American painters of the day, Robert Feke. In his study of the portraits of Franklin, Charles Coleman Sellers describes how Franklin wished to be depicted. "What we see in the portrait is that the subject chose to dress in the style of a successful tradesman, neither wearing his own hair as many contemporaries did, nor assuming the wig style of professional men and gentlemen of leisure." But the pose, Sellers notes, is at odds with the attire. "If the costume is bourgeois, this at least is aristocratic."[18] He stands erect and assured, his head cocked to one side, his right hand open to his side in a gesture that traditionally suggests the power to dispose of matters by a wave of the hand. It is a pose that suggests something beyond bourgeois contentment with commercial success.

Industry and frugality had done it. Franklin was readily disposed to recommend those qualities to others, for he felt that they had helped him. But industry and frugality were dispositions he had not really internalized; they were means, not ends. He worked hard so he could retire early. He intended to spend the moderate fortune he had acquired on himself, not preserve it for his posterity. "I have assured him" he wrote to his mother, referring to his son, "that I intend to spend what little I have, my self; if it pleases God that I live long enough: And as he by no means wants Sense, he can see by my going on, that I am like to be as good as my Word" (P, 3:475). Franklin had rather simple tastes for clothes, accommodations, and possessions; if he seemed frugal, it was out of disinterest in consumption.

Around 1747 he became interested in electricity, and together with a group of friends he performed, during the next four years, the experiments that first established his international reputation. At times he was fully absorbed in the problem, an unusual condition for him, since he tended to divide his attention. In September 1748 he wrote with satisfaction of the leisure he now enjoyed, in a letter to the New York gentleman scientist Cadwallader Colden. He writes that he was discouraging talk of electing him to the Pennsylvania Assembly. "Thus you see I am in a fair Way of having no other Tasks than such as I shall like to give my self, and of enjoying what I look upon as a great Happiness, Leisure to read, study, make Experiments, and converse at large with such ingenious and worthy Men as are pleas'd to honour me with their Friendship or Acquaintance, on such Points as may produce something for the common Benefit of Mankind, uninterrupted by the little Cares and Fatigues of Business" (P, 3:318). That Franklin should have thought of science as a pursuit of a gentleman's leisure shows its real place in his life. He stayed with the problems of electricity that he and his friends had first identified, and he resolved them in a brilliant series of conjectures and experiments. When those problems were solved, he turned to other, more sustaining concerns. He did not see any great imminent public benefit to the phenomenon he was describing; it was largely a game for him, characterized by electrified portraits of the king and imagined banquets where a turkey could be killed by an electric shock and everyone would drink from electrified bumpers. At one point he admits in passing that he was "[c]hagrin'd a little that We have hitherto been able to discover Nothing in this Way of Use to Mankind" (P, 3:364), but he then came up with the identification of electricity and lightning, and consequently with the idea of the lightning rod. There he had found a satisfying climax to his researches, a simple, easily implemented solution to one of the continual predicaments of nature.

"I flatter'd myself that by the sufficient tho' moderate Fortune I had acquir'd, I had secur'd Leisure during the rest of my Life, for Philosophical Studies and Amusements," he writes in the *Autobiography*, ". . . but the Publick now considering me as a Man of Leisure, laid hold of me for their Purposes" (A, 196). The truth was rather that his freedom from daily work had enabled him to range more widely in his efforts to transform his public surroundings; like the models of elderly virtue he often wrote of, he presented himself as being called to public service without seeking it. Only five days after his letter to Colden announcing his preference for leisure and experimentation, he was elected to the Philadelphia Common Council. His more basic attitudes he expressed in a letter to Colden two years later, when his interest in electricity had run its course. He warns Colden against too great a love for "Philosophical Amusements." "Had Newton been Pilot but of a single common Ship, the finest of his Discoveries would scarce have excus'd, or atton'd for his abandoning the Helm one Hour in Time of Danger; how much less if she had carried the Fate of the Commonwealth.[19] Public life was immensely more important then mere philosophical or scientific speculation.

It was natural for Franklin to pose the relationship between the philosopher and the nation in this insistent way. He had come to feel that his experience specially suited him for what he saw as the most important public functions. He was always describing the circumstances of Philadelphia or the American colonies as a whole in terms of analogies to his own experience. In 1743, in his "Proposals for Promoting Useful Knowledge among the British plantations in America," he projects his own experience onto the American scene as a whole. "The first Drudgery of Settling new Colonies, which confines the Attention of People to mere Necessities, is now pretty well over; and there are many in every Province in Circumstances that set them at Ease, and afford Leisure to cultivate the finer Arts, and improve the common Stock of Knowledge" (P, 2:380). This was his own history, an evolution from the drudgery of getting established to the leisure which promotes arts and sciences. The inclination to see his experience as a metaphor for the manners and situation of a rising people appeared long before he began writing the *Autobiography*. Franklin placed himself at the center of American history; few men in his generation in America were even aware that history was taking place.[20]

During the years following his return to Philadelphia, Franklin had developed a sense of what Americans were like. Silence Dogood, his first draft of an American, had been only in part an inhabitant of Boston; the rest of her had belonged in Addison's London. But the task of outdistancing his rivals in the printing business sharpened his sense of the American reading public. He invented Richard Saunders the astrologer and gave him an almanac as a means of reaching the widest possible audience, and when he quit active publishing he continued and even expanded the almanac. If his projects in Philadelphia suggested what he wished the country to be, his almanacs were adjusted to what it was.

Poor Richard himself was the purported almanac-maker whose work

Franklin printed each year. Franklin the printer received the profits, Poor Richard admitted, but the good-natured astrologer did not resent the loss. Richard Saunders was a sort of scientist himself, a student of the stars, and a reader and writer, living with a wife who harassed and ridiculed him for his impracticality. Contentment and simplicity characterized him. He had no capacity for irony, and he wished to live by the maxims he printed. Poor Richard knew that he was no great original mind, and he admitted to borrowing many of the maxims and snatches of poetry that filled out his almanac.

Franklin had to invent Poor Richard to reach the American audience he wished to address. It was an audience undefined by religion, beyond a very generalized Protestantism that might even embrace people with no developed opinions at all. His readers would appreciate quips about the dry doctrine preached in New England or about the odd speech mannerisms that could be heard around the colonies (P, 2:226–27). It was a rural and a tradesman audience, and the occasional disdain in the maxims for the pretensions of nobility and the greediness of lawyers implied attitudes that might later have been called populist. "A Plowman on his Legs is higher than a Gentleman on his Knees," says the almanac for 1746 (P, 3:63). The maxims themselves appear to confirm attitudes already held, rather than persuading the reader to a new viewpoint. Poor Richard's simple-wittedness and generalized good intentions authorized him to pass off as common wisdom opinions that were really Franklin's own possibly unorthodox views. "Different Sects like different clocks, may be all near the matter, tho' they don't quite agree," says the almanac for 1749 (P, 3:341). The view, though Franklin's own, appears in a context of anonymous folk wisdom which authorizes it as a general truth.[21] Despite the apparent sufficiency of each expression there was a new supply of epigrams each year, usually saying what had been said already. His audience valued novelty of expression rather than originality of thought.

At first Franklin filled the almanacs with many folksy and rather undidactic epigrams. "Neither a Fortress nor a Maidenhead will hold out long after they begin to parly," writes Poor Richard in 1734 (P, 1:354). Eventually he offered short passages of broadly instructional material, capsule biographies of worthy men like Newton, Locke, and Bacon, for example. Luther and Calvin are included, both praised primarily for their temperateness at eating and their industriousness. Among these accounts Franklin liked to feature stories of the great who had fallen or returned to a private station—Richard Cromwell, the Protector's son, for example, or Stanislas, the former king of Poland. The implicit message in these references seems to be to content oneself with common life and beware of aspirations to greatness, hardly a lesson Franklin himself would have embraced. The epigrams all pose limits to the human desires for self-indulgence, self-display, and superior understanding; they insist that one must live within those limits, which are imposed by nature and the human condition. "No gains without pains," says the almanac for 1745 (P, 3:6). There is no greater, more complex, more beautiful, or more fulfilling life beyond the boundaries of this prudential wisdom. As yet there is no assertion that the mode of existence bounded by these maxims is distinctively American; nothing is permitted to qualify the universality of this wisdom, except that its authority is cheery, bumbling Poor Richard. Franklin had found his American audience, but he had not yet seen how they might be different from those he still considered to be his fellow Englishmen.

Poor Richard's Almanack was a public project in which Franklin's role was only partly hidden. The leisure he found in the 1740s permitted him also to write more freely, and he celebrated his release from earlier constraints with various comic pieces that apparently circulated among friends without danger of being published under his name and bringing embarrassment to him. One of those is his so-called "Old Mistress's Apologue"; another is the "Speech of Polly Baker," published in 1747 and not identified as Franklin's until more than thirty years later. It is a kind of hoax, a supposed courtroom speech from a woman quite unlike the simpering housewives that Franklin occasionally invented as *personae*. She is a kind of woman not really seen before in fiction.[22]

Polly Baker is brought to court in Connecticut upon the birth of her fifth illegitimate child. Instead of accepting the court's verdict, however, she delivers a spirited defense of her conduct.

> Abstracted from the Law, I cannot conceive (may it please your Honours) what the Nature of my Offence is. I have brought Five fine Children into the World, at the Risque of my Life; I have mantain'd them well by my own Industry, without burthening the Township, and would have done it better, if it had not been for the heavy Charges and Fines I have paid. Can it be a Crime (in the Nature of Things I mean) to add to the Number of the King's Subjects, in a new Country that really wants People? I own it, I should think it a Praiseworthy, rather than a punishable Action. (P, 3:124)

Brusquely setting aside the law in this case, she points to her own service to the commonwealth as a breeder, a service which, moreover, has put her to considerable inconvenience. Though she has already produced five illegitimate children, she still insists on seeing herself as the very epitome of self-control, a model of disinterested public service. She has not seduced any married man; in fact she would be quite happy to be married. "I must be stupefied to the last Degree, not to prefer the Honourable State of Wedlock, to the Condition I have lived in. I always was, and still am willing to enter into it; and doubt not my behaving well in it, having all the Industry, Frugality, Fertility, and Skill in Oeconomy, appertaining to a good Wife's Character" (P, 3:124).

In his earliest writings Franklin had played with the idea of sexuality. "Women are the prime Causes of a great many Male Enormities," Silence Dogood had intimated.[23] But despite the opportunities available, there is no more hint of sexuality in Polly Baker's argument than in any other legal brief. "Industry, Frugality, Fertility, and Skill in Oeconomy"—her qualifications do not include sexiness. Polly Baker is in fact a tough independent woman who wants only to be left alone by the state. She is clearly unimpressed by the sanctions that the church has leveled against her.

> I own, I do not think as you do; for, if I thought what you call a Sin, was really such, I could not presumptuously commit it. But, how can it be believed, that Heaven is angry at my having Children, when to the little done by me towards it, God has been pleased to add his Divine Skill and admirable Workmanship in the Formation of their Bodies, and crown'd it, by furnishing them with rational and immortal Souls. (P, 3:125)

She is the earliest known ancestor of Hester Prynne, a woman making do by herself in a new continent, out of the shelter of traditional morality. She needs no man to fulfill her, though having one would be a convenience.

Polly Baker inhabits a society in which the idea of deference has lost its meaning. So far as she is concerned, she has done her duty to increase and multiply, despite considerable artificial barriers (codes of law and religion, courts and penal systems); she has done that which nature and the best interests of the society required, "and therefore ought, in my humble Opinion, instead of a Whipping, to have a Statue erected in my Memory" (P, 3:125). Polly Baker is no zany, unconsciously reducing to absurdity the idea of self-sufficiency. Her sense of herself, it turns out, corresponds to what her society sees in her; her speech succeeds so well that the embarrassed magistrate who has fathered her children marries her the next day. American society in the middle of the eighteenth century had not set aside deference quite so completely, but the American self was working itself loose from society in a way which Franklin captures here. Polly Baker is so real as an American that Abbé Raynal could treat the story as factual in his ency-clopedic *Histoire philosophique et politique des etablissements et du commerce des Européens dans les deux Indes.*

Like Franklin in the Hemphill case, Polly Baker is determined to de-fine her own relationship to society. Franklin was always inclined to talk about how he was performing disinterested public service to the community, as Polly Baker claims to be doing, but he was also aware of himself as a wheeler-dealer, a successful businessman, and a person ultimately concerned with feeding the demands of a large and peculiar vanity. Polly Baker is thus an absurd variant of his own situation.

"The Speech of Polly Baker" is a convenient example of Franklin's sense of humor, a defining trait of his well before this midcareer point at which we have paused. Though the piece was misunderstood in Franklin's own time to be a reflection on the severe domestic laws of Connecticut, "Polly Baker" is not really satirical. The humor of the sit-uation is shared by all parties, Polly Baker and the discomfited magis-trates together. There is no ideal alternative which the reader is invited to consider. Franklin's wit is not like Swift's; he has no demanding ideal of human behavior to which individual failings are compared. His humor is not intended to clarify the social relationships described.

So strong was Franklin's humorous impulse that he worried about keeping it in control. Planning his program of achieving moral perfec-tion, he mentions "wishing to break a Habit I was getting into of Prat-tling, Punning and Joking" (A, 151). Earlier he had noticed that his habits of libeling and satire got him into trouble in Boston. In the pages of his newspaper Keimer warned his adversary and former employee of the dangers of imprudent wit. "It requires a great Genius and much good Nature to manage with Decency and Humanity the Way of Writ-ing which the Busy-Body would seem to imitate" (P, 1:121). (Keimer al-ready had reasons to be wary of his former employee's sense of humor.) Especially among the Quakers, who were as a group notably and even proudly without humor, it was hazardous to appear to treat serious matters lightly. But Franklin was still a man who would laugh heartily at a joke, as he would not deny (P, 2:200).

His humor ranged from the naive and deliberately inoffensive note of *Poor Richard* to the near-ribaldry of his private letters. *Poor Richard* was to be read by anyone literate enough to read an almanac; its humor had to be as obvious as possible. On the other hand, in those letters or bagatelles which he wrote for a discreet and trusted audience he could reach for a more intimate amusement. There he could assume a reader who would pretend to be decorous but who has in fact a larger tolerance for the titillating. His strategy then was to be outrageous while maintaining a straight face. Franklin loved to tease his sister Jane Mecom, a proper Boston lady. In the context of a discussion of hypocrites who disdain good works and prefer right sentiments, he says, "they have inverted the good old verse, and say now

'A man of deeds and not of words
Is like a garden full of ——'

I have forgot the rhyme, but remember 'tis something the very reverse of perfume. So much by way of commentary."[24] His sister, supplying the rhyme, would be in complicity with the joke—a joke told also at the expense of the sort of homely rhymed wisdom that Franklin himself was so good at producing.

Humor provided him partly a mechanism for disarming antagonisms, both his own and those of others. In a letter addressed "Dear Jemmy" to his wife's cousin James Read, he offers jocular reasons for why he is staying out of a family squabble. "Are you an attorney by profession, and do you know no better, how to chuse a proper court in which to bring your action? Would you submit to the decision of a husband, a cause between you and his wife? Don't you know, that all wives are in the right?" (P, 3:40). As early as his days with the New-England Courant he had written of the capacity of humor "to allay the Heats and Tumors of our Spirits, and to make a Man forget his restless Resentments" (P, 1:49). He considered humor to be an inborn socializing impulse, the most effective check against the powerful aggressions which seemed endemic in the societies where he lived. It was thus both a mode for the most distinctive sort of self-expression and a means of perpetuating a sense of community with others. And humor required and furthered a sense of elasticity and adaptability; it was based on surprise and disrupted the settled ways of seeing and doing. "And therefore in many Cases it would not be quite absurd if a Man were to thank God for his Vanity among the other Comforts of Life." The mind that could thus comically upend convention would not be likely to get entrapped in constricting systems of discourse.

Humor of Franklin's kind (and perhaps humor of any kind) derives from an essentially intellectual command of life.[25] He could joke about marriage with his wife's cousin or the recipient of the "Old Mistress's Apologue" or the readers of "The Speech of Polly Baker" because he was not much emotionally involved in his own marriage. He and his wife had only two children, one of whom died quite young of small pox. Whatever the hard-to-be-governed passion of youth had been like before marriage, he had no trouble keeping his hands off Deborah. He mourned for the dead child a long time, and he blamed himself for not having him inoculated. This is about as close to private sorrow or a sense of the reality of human suffering as Franklin ever gets. In part he had carried into his own theology the Puritan belief in a blissful after-life. At the death of his brother John he wrote to console his step-neice, "Our friend and we were invited abroad on a party of pleasure, which is to last for ever. His chair was ready first, and he is gone before us. We could not all conveniently start together; and why should you and I be grieved at this, since we are soon to follow, and know where to find him?" (P, 6:407). The graciousness of the sentiment suggests the degree to which control over such experiences had been internalized. Death had no sting; no terrifying otherness lurked at the edges of daily human life.

Franklin in 1750 was beginning to look beyond Philadelphia, to an incipient country only beginning to form in his mind, and to Europe, where his scientific reputation would soon establish a foothold for him. He had a large sense of possibilities, and he was alert to the climate of opinion at a time when the greatest products of the Enlightenment were being published. Writing to Whitefield, he describes his interest in finding some large enterprise which would represent a culmination of his life. Uncommitted to ideology, except for that ideology of the Enlightenment that promulgated the sovereignty of the independent self, he was being drawn more and more deeply into the politics of the colony and the empire, thinking all the while that in political action he would find the most vivid field for self-expression. He would know great frustration before he could propagate his sense of identity and mode of consciousness in a new nation.

12 Frustration and Failure in England

In the last forty years of his life Franklin was divided between two conflicting images of collective life. One was a vision of empire, a powerful, complex, and expanding cosmopolis ruled by a benevolent and virtuous king. The other was what might be called the provincial vision—a people isolated from the great world, living lives of simplicity, self-sufficiency, and virtue. The one alternative was dynamic, culturally rich, and British; the other was stable, culturally rudimentary, and American. The years of Franklin's life that the *Autobiography* does not cover became a drama in which these two cultural ideals contested for dominance in his mind. The choice between the two was, I believe, the most important problem in those years of Franklin's life.

There were psychological implications to the alternatives as well. Both visions made strong appeals to the identity which Franklin had created for himself. The ambition that had driven him to his material prosperity, his civic improvements, and his scientific experiments attracted him to the excitements of empire. Empire meant a firm sense of group membership; citizenship in it was neither voluntary or adventitious. Empire also implied ties to a king, the symbolic father; all of Franklin's instincts to align himself with authority figures were aroused in the early 1760s by the accession of the young George III. For one who had spent the first half of his life looking for a national audience, the British Empire seemed a vast theatre, with the London press a stage on which he could perform. American colonists had a name they habitually used for Great Britain before the Revolution. They called it "home." It was home for Franklin for most of eighteen years; he found there a graciousness, civility, and freedom from bickering in the conduct of daily life which made it seem greatly unlike Boston or Philadelphia. One's identity there did not need to be protected from others or specially fostered, nor need one feel a special responsibility to keep things going in Philadelphia.

To be an American, on the other hand, implied a freedom from the complex pattern of authority relations which held the empire together. To be an American in the years following 1765 meant to be an insurgent, a rebel—an identity that recalled Franklin's youth in Boston. Affirming his identity as an American required him to see himself as the child of his own works, not of some symbolic father. American identity also implied the acceptance of certain limitations; the straitened life of industry and frugality which Franklin had adopted for the sake of getting himself established in Philadelphia would have to be a national norm and the guarantor of virtue. Membership in the American community was voluntary; it demanded, moreover, a continuous effort in order to hold the group in some sort of cohesion. For Franklin to be an American also involved accepting a special role in relation to his colleagues, the younger revolutionaries. His prestige was crucial to establish the plausibility of the revolutionary movement. Franklin took on, in fact, a symbolic relationship to the new country. He was needed in America; he had been a bothersome irrelevance in England.

To subordinate the complexities of Franklin's last forty years to the terms of this problem entails neglecting a great deal of what he wrote and did. Once committed to public life, he pursued that life actively and on a variety of different fronts. I shall not be dealing with his continuing scientific interest, his economic ideas, or his diplomatic maneuverings—in fact with many of the areas in which Franklin is important to the history of the eighteenth century. It is usually forgotten, though, that there had to be some good reason for Franklin to remain in public life. He did not have much to gain financially, though he was not indifferent to some possible rewards when he was in England. Strong attractions called him to private life; other colonials of his own generation, men like William Allen or Cadwallader Colden, tried to avoid the controversies preceding the Revolution, and Franklin certainly could have done so with dignity. He could have sat out the revolution, that is, if he had not been Benjamin Franklin. But he had the kind of identity that needed public life in which to flourish, a public life of the right kind. He believed it was possible to alter or abolish connections with a society, and a society to which he could give his allegiance would have to reflect his own self-definition. The British Empire and the American republic were the options. Forced by events to pick one, he chose to be a citizen rather than a subject.

Direct confrontation with the possibilities of English identity came to Franklin as a result of his voyage to England in 1757 to serve as the agent of the Pennsylvania Assembly to the Proprietors of the colony and the British government. The preparation and delays before that voyage and the voyage itself constitute a considerable passage in the *Autobiography*; in its suggestions of great anticipations and its foreshadowings of future frustrations, it served to evoke the momentous transition between the past in Philadelphia and his future in England.

By the time Franklin was leaving Philadelphia he had become a popular and controversial figure in Pennsylvania politics. "The People happen to love me," he wrote Peter Collinson, describing somewhat apologetically an incident when about fifty of the men in his militia regiment decided to accompany him a few miles on a journey from Philadelphia, their swords drawn in his honor (P, 7:13–14; A, 238–39). Around this time an anonymous admirer expressed what must have been a widespread sense of enthusiasm for Franklin as a mover and a shaker:

> Who plann'd the Scheme the Associates to unite?
> Who wrote *plain truth* to bring that scheme to light?
> Who bid Yon Academick structure rise?
> 'Behold the Man!' each lisping babe replies.
> Who schemed Yon Hospital for the helpless poor?
> And op'd to charitable use each folding door.
> Our Countrys cause, what senator defends?
> Void of all partial, or all private ends.

The same admirer was also perhaps the first to imagine an often repeated scene, the apotheosis at the "great Tribunal" of Franklin as American representative among the immortal thinkers:

> There Bacon Newton will our F——lin greet.
> And place him in his Electrisic seat.
> 'Ore Europe, Asia, Africk's scienc'd Fame,
> The Royal Medal will exalt thy name;
> Transfer the Palm by thy great genius won
> And proudly own America's great son.
>
> (P, 7:73–74)

Such sentiments indicate that Franklin's reputation was beginning to seem out of scale in Philadelphia.

Franklin had been ready to leave two and a half months before the packet finally took off from New York. He had made up a new will and set his affairs in order regarding his postmaster's job and his silent partnership at Franklin & Hall. But Lord Loudoun, the general in charge of the British forces in the colonies, had asked him to delay his departure a few days to consult and to await certain letters Loudoun was writing to the ministry. Franklin then waited in frustration as Loudoun delayed making decision after decision. In the meantime the French were attacking the northern frontier. "On the whole," he recollects in the *Autobiography*, "I then wonder'd much, how such a Man came to be entrusted with so important a Business as the Conduct of a great Army: but having since seen more of the great World, and the means of obtaining and Motives for giving Places and employments, my Wonder is diminished" (A, 253). Franklin had grown up in a society where incompetence soon brought on its own punishment, as it had for Keimer or Franklin's erstwhile partner Meredith. Loudoun had replaced William Shirley, whom Franklin thought a better man. "For tho' Shirley was not a bred Soldier, he was sensible and sagacious in himself, and attentive to good Advice from others, capable of forming judicious Plans, quick and active in carrying them into Execution" (A, 253). Franklin found Shirley's traits especially admirable, but Loudoun, a trained soldier and a Scottish peer, had the job. The root cause of the Revolution was manifested here, in the incomprehensible preference given to breeding over native ability.

Before leaving, Franklin waited on Loudoun and asked to be reimbursed for personal expenses incurred in outfitting Braddock's campaign of two years earlier. He had current expenses while waiting that he hoped the payment would defray, and he had charged no commission for his services. "O Sir, says he, you must not think of persuading us that you are no Gainer. We understand better those Affairs, and know that every one concern'd in supplying the Army finds means in doing it to fill his own Pockets" (A, 255). Loudoun was not being critical; he knew the way of the world, where government contractors profiteer as a matter of course. But Franklin's public identity, as his anonymous admirer had written, was that of a man "Void of all partial, or all private ends." Such behavior in a tradesman was incomprehensible to Loudoun, and his skepticism suggested how great the challenge of representing America would be.

Finally the boat took off, and after its trim was changed began to sail well. Franklin remarks at length about the way the boat's sailing characteristics could be altered by trial and error and suggests that further, more systematic experimentation might improve ship design. Different people work separately and without coordination on the hull design, the rigging, the lading, and the actual management of the ship at sea. "This is the Age of Experiments" (A, 257), Franklin asserts, but ship design and sailing were the product of unexamined tradition. There was a near disaster as the ship sailed through the fog near the Scilly Islands, impressing Franklin with the wisdom of establishing good lighthouses back in America.

Young William Franklin was also along on the voyage, a self-consciously dashing young man who was eager to sample the delights of London. But the object of the trip was to replace the proprietary government. In London the Penn brothers were waiting for the elder Franklin, confident that his efforts to pressure them would be frustrated. "I think I wrote you before," Thomas Penn had imparted to his agent Richard Peters, "that Mr. Franklin's popularity is nothing here, and that he will be looked very coldly upon by great People, there are very few of any consequence that have heard of his Electrical Experiments, those matters being attended to by a particular Sett of People, many of whom of the greatest consequence I know well, but it is quite another sort of People, who are to determine the Dispute between us" (P, 7:111n). In Franklin's eyes it may have been the Age of Experiments, but the "great People" were not interested in experiments.

The origins of Franklin's problems in England from 1757 to 1775 can be detected along his journey there. He was devoted to the rational alteration of the world, whether in ship design or in government; England was impervious to such an interest. He stood for an ideal of disinterested public service, and it was the most cynical and corrupt period in British political history.

In his years in England Franklin met with much misunderstanding of America, but also with a freshly aroused curiosity about it. In the 1760s Europe was beginning to understand America in quite a new way. America was a theatre of increasing importance in the dynastic wars of the eighteenth century. North America in particular, which had formerly seemed far less noteworthy than South America or the Caribbean area, took on a new prominence.[1] As Franklin himself had noted, the population of British America was growing dramatically. The Enlightenment *philosophes*, with their interest in comparisons among societies and their urge to displace Christianity from the center of human history, wanted to take account of the American continents. Much of the new information about America was confused and even nonsensical. Franklin had met one European source of confused information, Peter Kalm, the Swedish scientist, and some of Kalm's strange stories had been fed to him by the playful Philadelphia printer (P, 4:53–54). And the comte de Buffon, the most eminent naturalist of his day, described America as a late and incomplete creation, peopled with defective plant and animal species and a weak, unsociable breed of humans. On the other hand Voltaire could take as the hero of his philosophical tale *L'Ingenu* a Huron Indian of impeccable courage, virtue, and natural-born critical acumen. Whether monstrous or natural, America appeared to be an anomaly destructive of past conceptions of man, society, and the physical universe.

Into this confusion in 1757 stepped Franklin, Fellow of the Royal Society, America's most distinguished citizen, agent of the Pennsylvania Assembly and soon of other colonies as well. Almost by himself, Franklin formed the image of America to the European world in the fifteen years before the Revolution. "I am very sorry, that you intend soon to leave our Hemisphere," David Hume would write to Franklin in 1762, shortly before Franklin's first term as colonial agent was over. "America has sent us many good things, Gold, Silver, Sugar, Tobacco, Indigo &c.: But you are the first Philosopher, and indeed the first Great Man of Letters for whom we are beholden to her" (P, 10:81–82). Hume's catalogue of raw products suggests the way in which America had been seen as unpopulated by civilized human beings, just a vast estate which Europe owned. Franklin's existence suggested that America might also be capable of civilization.

In various ways Franklin had tried to come up with a comprehensive view of America before leaving it. He had tried to unite it politically in 1754 at the Albany Congress. He had thought about American demography, and his speculations had been published in *Observations Concerning the Increase of Mankind*. And on the packet boat to England he had written what was to become his most famous work next to his *Autobiography*, the Preface to *Poor Richard Improved 1758*, known to posterity as *The Way to Wealth*.

The 1758 Preface marked the end of his participation in *Poor Richard's Almanack*. As an anthology of the maxims he had used as filler for the previous twenty-six years, *The Way to Wealth* represented a kind of final statement to the audience he had thus far accumulated. Once published, it was soon reprinted. In the eighteenth century alone, *The Way to Wealth* went through 144 known editions and was translated into fifteen languages. In 1777, at the beginning of its European vogue, the *Courier de l'Europe* reprinted it at the recommendation of a Scottish reader, who called it the "quintessence of the wisdom accumulated in all ages" (P, 7:328–29, 337).

The Way to Wealth consists of an extended exhortation surrounded by a narrative frame. In the narrative frame the almanac-maker Richard Saunders joins a crowd waiting for an auction to begin. In the crowd is Father Abraham, "a plain clean old Man, with white Locks," who is asked to comment on taxes and the times. He offers a sermon on industry and frugality, taking as his text maxims from past *Poor Richard's Almanacks*. Father Abraham is another in the series of wise old men who are consulted by the community at large—Franklin's own father, Cato in the *Busy-Body*, and eventually Franklin himself. The rustic simplicity of Father Abraham would later be attributed to Franklin himself once he arrived in France. Moreover, Father Abraham's name, to a descendant of the Puritans, implied more that just any wise old man; it pointed to a typological parallel to the history of Israel. Franklin had taken on the role of father to the chosen people.

Self-sufficiency is the reiterated moral of Father Abraham's speech. The interrelations for a complex society are like a drug, robbing one of self-awareness. Enmeshed in subtle ties with others, one can never find one's footing in a separate and unique existence. Despite the homely form of its maxims, *The Way to Wealth* projects an austere and lonely model of human behavior. Franklin deliberately excluded all of the humorous maxims he had written; no intimacy is permitted between his narrator and the reader. There are only two classes of people, creditors and debtors. Debt is the worst possible danger, "But ah, think what you do when you run into Debt: *You give to another Power over your Liberty*" (P, 7:47–48). Collective action is unimaginable. "Trusting too much to others Care is the Ruin of many; for, as the Almanack says, *In the Affairs of This World, Men are saved, not by Faith, but by the Want of it*" (P, 7:344). The maxims are the ethic of an agrarian republic. Industry and frugality, the principal virtues, are not valuable in themselves. They are necessary to secure independence from others in a station of life where the alternative is helpless vulnerability to master, creditor, or tax collector.

Franklin had offered economic instruction in earlier writings as well. "Hints for those that would be Rich" appeared in *Poor Richard* for 1737: "Advice to a Young Tradesman written by an old One" was published as part of a manual to young men entering business, written while Franklin himself was withdrawing from active business (P, 2:165; 3:304–8). In those two discussions debt was treated as a necessary condition to making money; it is important to impress one's creditors with evidence of industriousness. Risk capital obliges men to rely on each other; Franklin, whose career as a printer consisted of a complex and profitable series of partnerships, certainly understood the importance of this interdependence. Max Weber set forth the classic discussion of this kind of interdependence in *The Protestant Ethic and the Spirit of Capitalism*. "The capitalistic economy of the present day is an immense cosmos into which the individual is born, and which presents itself to him, at least as an individual as an unalterable order of things in which he must live. It forces the individual, in so far as he is involved in the system of market relationships, to conform to capitalistic rules of action."[2] Weber cites Franklin's "Hints for those that would be Rich" and "Advice to a Young Tradesman" as perfect prototypes of this unalterable order of things. But *The Way to Wealth*, far more influential than the earlier two treatises, has a significantly different aim. A decent subsistence based on economic self-sufficiency is the ideal there. *The Way to Wealth* is no more conducive to mass accumulation than are the economic arguments for self-sufficiency Thoreau puts forward in *Walden*.

At the end of Father Abraham's speech, the auction opens, and his audience rushes in to spend money as if it has never heard him, but Poor Richard is still intoxicated with the sound of his own wisdom, echoed back to him from so august a source. "The frequent Mention he made of me must have tired any one else, but my Vanity was wonderfully delighted with it, though I was conscious that not a tenth Part of the Wisdom was my own which he ascribed to me, but rather the *Gleanings* I had made of the Sense of all Ages and Nations" (P, 7:350). So convinced is he by that harangue that he alone heeds the precepts of Poor Richard; he decides he can do without the material for a new coat that he has come to buy. Poor Richard's innocent vanity, which he shared with many of the personae of Franklin's periodical essays, is a prelude to the more complex vanity candidly admitted at the beginning of the *Autobiography*.

The two personae of *The Way to Wealth* seem to be at odds with each other—the simple and virtuous philosopher and the ridiculous astrologer. But the two are aspects linked together as a principle of balance. As in the *Autobiography*, Franklin's perspective is elusive; if we try to catch him on either side of the line between seriousness and self-parody, he dances out of reach.[3] The care which he has taken to avoid being held to an opinion is evidence of a certain self-consciousness about his advice-giving. Why else his gratuitously subtle narrative frame? Franklin was acutely aware throughout his life of the opinions held about him. By leaving his own intentions in doubt in *The Way to Wealth*, he anticipated the criticism of his own and future times—that he was only a snuff-colored little American tradesman without any values beyond the narrowly utilitarian. The subtleties of perspective also help to disguise his utter seriousness. He believed in the agrarian virtues of *The Way to Wealth*, and he believed that like any virtues they could be taught by precept, just as his *Autobiography* would later teach by example.

The America projected in *The Way to Wealth* is a limited place, no empire open for massive exploitation. Another version of the same view can be found in the *Increase of Mankind*, written in 1751 and published first in 1755 with several reprintings shortly after (P, 4:226). In that essay Franklin was trying for the first time seriously to coordinate English and American identities. He could see the most important event then occurring in American history—the growth in population among the colonists, both from natural increase and from immigration. That increase and the unlimited availability of land which made it possible were giving the American economy distinctive characteristics. Economic realities in America were basically different from those in Europe. Europe was fully settled; America was not, nor would it be for a long time. "[N]otwithstanding this Increase [in population], so vast is the Territory of North-America, that it will require many Ages to settle it fully; and till it is fully settled, Labour will never be cheap here, where no Man continues long a Labourer for others, but gets a Plantation of his own, no Man continues long a Journeyman to a Trade, but goes among those new Settlers, and sets up for himself, &c." (P, 4:228). The physical realities of America conspired to foster the ideal of agrarian independence for which *The Way to Wealth* proposed an ethic.

A variety of occasions lay behind the writing of the *Increase of Mankind*, so it is organized not as a cumulative argument but in numbered and loosely linked paragraphs. His audience was English—he had sent it first to Peter Collinson and Richard Jackson in London—and he was trying to clarify for that audience how basically different America was from Europe. Besides the observations on population that he wished as an investigator to report, he was also concerned to allay suspicions about American manufacturers; restricting colonial manufacturers would hardly be necessary or wise where the cost of labor was inevitably so high. British and American economic needs were different and hence complementary, he implied. The essay predicts that in a century "the greatest Number of Englishmen will be on this Side of the Water." This prediction of future American greatness occasions a paean to the resulting British Empire. "What an Accession of Power to the British Empire by Sea as well as Land! What Increase of Trade and Navigation!" (P, 4:233). Franklin voices here for the first time what would become a continuing theme of his, that the future power, perhaps even the future center, of the British empire lay in America.

The essay also expresses some anxieties about the growing German population in Pennsylvania. Franklin's readiness to embrace all groups as citizens of his country came at a later stage. No one reading the *Autobiography*, with its tolerant and bemused attitude toward Moravians, Dunkards, and others, would suspect that Franklin had once held non-English groups in suspicion. Writing here in the 1750s, he is an English chauvinist expressing a distinct hostility to the blacks and Germans who comprised significant minorities of the colonial population.

> Why should the Palatine Boors be suffered to swarm into our Settlements, and by herding together establish their Language and Manners to the Exclusion of ours? Why should Pennsylvania, founded by the English, become a Colony of *Aliens*, who will shortly be so numerous as to Germanize us instead of our Anglifying them, and will never adopt our Language or Customs, any more than they can acquire our Complexion. (P, 4:234)

Entering Pennsylvania at a rate of 7,000 a year, the Pennsylvania Dutch constituted at mid-century a third of the colony's population, by far the largest body of non-English-speaking immigrants in America. Until the 1750s, moreover, they kept aloof from the colony's political life. In 1732 Franklin had tried to start a German-language newspaper, the *Philadelphische Zeitung*, but that enterprise got nowhere. In his pamphlet *Plain Truth* (1747) he closed by exhorting the "*brave and steady* GERMANS" to join the militia he was advocating (P, 3:203). To his disappointment they did not join in the defense preparations against the French. When war became imminent again ten years later, Franklin and other leading English colonists became anxious about the loyalists of the Pennsylvania Dutch. They established a short-lived system of charity schools to teach the Germans English. More forcible measures of assimilation were contemplated, including restriction of the franchise to English speakers, restricted immigration to Pennsylvania, and restraints on the use of German.[4] In the *Increase of Mankind* the Germans seem such a problem that Franklin attributes to them, by implication at least, a different skin color from the English.

In 1753 Franklin treated the German problem more fully in a letter to Collinson. His distrust for these foreigners he expresses in the characteristic language of the Enlightenment toward disapproved groups. The implications of the swarming and herding images introduced in the *Increase of Mankind* are developed further; the very industriousness of the Germans is menacing. The Germans show signs of being unfit for any civil society, Franklin suggests to Collinson. They quarrel among themselves continually and pay no attention to their ministers. Disputatiousness over religion was a special mark for the Enlightenment of a debased state of mind. The language barrier creates confusion and disorder among English institutions. The Germans are ripe for subversion by the French. Their unwillingness to learn English is a symptom of an unsociable nature.

It should be added that Franklin's disparaging remarks about the Germans were not intended for publication and did not appear in the editions over which he had direct control (P, 4:226). He seems even in the original draft to have had second thoughts. After praising the whiteness of the English over the swarthiness or blackness of other peoples (Africans, Spaniards, Italians, French, Russians, Swedes, and most Germans), he adds as a final sentence, "But perhaps I am partial to the Complexion of my Country, for such Kind of Partiality is natural to Mankind" (P, 4:234). The reference to the Germans would later get him into trouble; his political opponents would discover the earlier edition of the *Increase of Mankind* and make it an issue with which to defeat him while he was back in Philadelphia running for the Assembly in 1764. He would learn the necessary lesson that to affirm Englishness as a superior identity was bad politics for an American.

The problem with the Pennsylvania Dutch underlines an already existing disparity between the group identities Franklin wished to possess simultaneously. To be English meant a feeling of ethnic solidarity with the mother country, and the very term "mother country" implied a parent-child relationship. At the end of his 1753 letter to Collinson, Franklin includes a fervent exhortation for benign parental treatment, "O let not Britain seek to oppress us, but like an affectionate parent endeavour to secure freedom to her children; they may be able one day to assist her in defending her own—Whereas a Mortification begun in the Foot may spread upwards to the destruction of the nobler parts of the Body" (P, 4:486). As a parent, England, like Josiah Franklin, should give its child freedom; as elsewhere, the image of parenthood which Franklin uses is one of enlightened indulgence, not control. But the plaintive way in which the hope is expressed implies also the helplessness of the child in the face of parental arbitrariness, just as Franklin himself had been helpless when his own father pulled him out of grammar school and destined him to be a tradesman.

But to be an American meant an embrace of diversity, not ethnic solidarity, as Franklin knew when he was not trying to be English. And to be an American also meant to be independent, in the way Polly Baker was independent or that the disciples of Father Abraham would be.

Franklin was clearly drawn to that ideal even as he was working on his identity as a deferential child of empire. In the 1750s, however, the diversity of America appeared more as dispersion and disunity. Much of Franklin's political life in America had been spent in fruitless efforts to unite elements that insisted on remaining irreconcilably apart.

One important disillusioning experience in his effort to coordinate American and English identities had been the Albany Congress of 1754, his first effort to establish the nation physically. Franklin had long been an advocate of military cooperation among the English colonies, and it was not long before the French and Indian War would begin. A month before the congress convened, Franklin published the famous snake cartoon in the *Pennsylvania Gazette*. The cartoon represents a snake broken into pieces labeled with the names of colonies, and the caption reads, "Join, or Die." The cartoon appeared above news of French incursions in the west; the snake suggests the thinness and disunity of English settlement. It is an oddly ambiguous symbol.[5] At the congress Franklin was in strange company. Already he had been inclined to favor elements in Pennsylvania politics that defended local prerogatives and freedom of action. Yet the representatives to the Albany Congress were as a whole strongly loyalist. James De Lancey and William Smith of New York, Thomas Hutchinson of Massachusetts, John Penn and Richard Peters of Pennsylvania—all were prominent defenders of British policy toward the colonies. Perhaps in distrust of its originators, the colonial legislatures rejected the Albany Plan of Union as an infringement on local autonomy. "Every Body cries, a Union is absolutely necessary," Franklin wrote in disgust to Peter Collinson at the end of the year; "but when they come to the Manner and Form of the Union, their weak Noddles are presently distracted. So if ever there be an Union, it must be form'd at home by the Ministry and Parliament. I doubt not but they will make a good one, and I wish it may be done this Winter" (P, 5:454). But the ministry was no more interested in the Albany Plan then were the suspicious American legislators. The frustration of seeing his plan ignored remained with him for many years after; over thirty years later he would defend the proposal in his *Autobiography*. Frustration took the form of anger against his fellow Americans, whose "weak Noddles" could not see the need to unite.

The small-mindedness and preoccupation with local issues—traits which are dubbed "provincial"—tended to make Franklin's countrymen ill at ease when they visited Great Britain, regardless of their political loyalty. At around the same time that Franklin arrived in London, the young John Dickinson was also visiting. Dickinson was as close to an aristocrat in America as anyone could be, but in London he found himself a bumpkin. "After his recovery from this mortifying discovery," he wrote back to his father, describing the fate of the provincial in London, "he considers the nature of the things which make this difference between himself and others, and since he can't attract the admiration of mankind, the same pride...that made him desire it now prevents his paying it to others. Thus a titled coward, or a gilded scoundrel he laughs at and despises."[6] In Philadelphia there was a real prejudice against "the evil of overvaluing Foreign parts"; Philadelphians did not approve of the "London tricks and St. James customs" of wealthy young Samuel Powel, who would spend several years traveling in Europe and receiving audiences with George III and the Pope.[7] (At the same time, of course, they were helplessly in the cultural orbit of Great Britain, adopting its fashions and manners as standards.)

Franklin himself never shared those provincial suspicions. He had lived in England himself as an adolescent; he had developed a series of friendships by correspondence with a few somewhat prominent Englishmen, Peter Collinson and William Strahan in particular. When he arrived in London, he made himself right at home. There were numerous satisfactions available to him in England that America could scarcely afford. He was never so emotionally integrated into Philadelphia that he could share its citizens' fear of the metropolis. Earlier he had overcome the original disadvantages of social class not by loudly affirming an unsatisfying identity but by implicitly denying that such an identity could apply to him. Once he was in London again he could see how much larger the world was than what he had left behind. As a fellow of the Royal Society and recipient of the Copley medal, Franklin was received immediately into a cultural and intellectual context that dwarfed his former surroundings. He had brought his son William along to study at the Middle Temple. To his fiancée, William writes soon after arriving about the attractions of the capital.

> For some Time after my Arrival at this great Metropolis, the infinite Variety of new Objects; the continued Noise and Bustle in the Streets; and the Viewing such Things as were esteem'd most curious, engross'd all my Attention. Since then, frequent Engagements amongst the Politicians, Philosophers, and Men of Business; making Acquaintances with such Men as have it in their Power to be of Service in settling our unhappy Provincial Disputes; and now and then partaking of the publick Diversions and Entertainments of this bewitching Country, have found full Employment for almost every Hour.[8]

As a Briton Franklin might escape more than just the provinciality of colonial Philadelphia. Society in the home country was civil and gentle compared to the climate of mutual aggression in America. "Of all of the enviable Things England has, I envy it most its People," Franklin wrote back to his hostess's daughter Polly Stevenson during his brief return to America in 1763.

> Why should that petty Island, which compar'd to America is but like a stepping Stone in a Brook, scarce enough of it above Water to keep one's Shoes dry; why, I say, should that little Island, enjoy in almost every Neighbourhood, more sensible, virtuous and elegant Minds, than we can collect in ranging 100 Leagues of our vast Forests. (P, 10:232)

Visiting Scotland with his son in 1759, he was officially welcomed in Edinburgh, Glasgow, and St. Andrew's and granted an honorary degree at St. Andrew's. Harvard and Yale had previously recognized him, but here was public recognition from a European university. "On the whole," he wrote to Lord Kames,

> I must say, I think the Time we spent there, was Six Weeks of the *densest* Happiness I have met with in any Part of my Life. And the agreable and instructive Society we found there in such Plenty, has left so pleasing an Impression on my Memory, that did not strong Connections draw me elsewhere, I believe Scotland would be the Country I should chuse to spend the Remainder of my Days in. (P, 9:9–10)

The concept of empire allowed Franklin to make himself comfortable anywhere in Britain. He had grown up in a society of loose and fragile traditions, where fame was an almost unimaginable idea, but now he seemed to be coming into the inheritance of public acknowledgment he had sought as a young man in London. England presented itself to him as a family of which he had always been a member. He visited Ecton in Northamptonshire where his father was born, and had the parish rector trace his ancestry back to the sixteenth century. There no longer seemed to be any need, here at "home," for the outsider status he had preserved back in Philadelphia.

Living in England also meant escaping from his wife, the shrill, dumpy, and semiliterate Deborah. William Strahan wrote a jovial letter to her urging her to come over to join her husband; a month later Franklin wrote himself, telling her he was sure she would not want to come and vaguely hinting that he might return to Philadelphia soon (P, 7:295–97, 359–60). Not that Franklin was interested in philandering.

He moved in as a lodger with a respectable woman in a comfortable house near Charing Cross and took up an avuncular relationship with his landlady's daughter. This was one of a series of cheerful self-limited relationships with bright and pretty younger women that he developed from his forties onwards—Catherine Ray, Polly Stevenson, Georgiana Shipley, Madame Brillon. Franklin did not want to get sexually involved, though he tended to make gallant gestures in that direction. Something in him knew how encumbering a sexual relationship with a young woman could be, and he always found women who could be relied on to hold him at arm's length. A widespread mythology has grown up recently about Franklin which seeks to portray him as vastly lecherous and quite prolific of illegitimate children. There is no basis for this characterization.[9] (We do, of course, learn from this misconception something about our apparent need to beef up the sexuality of the Founding Fathers.)

In England Franklin was looking for something rather more emotionally fulfilling than sexuality. He wanted to belong. It seemed at first to make no difference that he was really a transplanted American living in London, because the English identity he imagined for himself was an abstract identity, having nothing to do with habitation of the island of Great Britain. In his headiest moments Franklin even saw the American as a further extension of English identity, the Englishman of the future. During the controversies of the late 1760s Franklin was accused of advocating the eventual removal of the seat of government from London to America (P, 14:325). "No one can rejoice more sincerely than I do on the Reduction of Canada," he wrote to Lord Kames from London shortly after Wolfe's victory at Quebec;

> and this, not merely as I am a Colonist, but as I am a Briton. I have long been of Opinion, that the Foundations of the future Grandeur and Stability of the British Empire, lie in America; and tho', like other Foundations, they are low and little seen, they are nevertheless, broad and Strong enough to support the greatest Political Structure Human Wisdom ever yet erected. (P, 9:6–7)

Franklin's uneasiness with his own rhapsodic picture of empire reveals itself when he breaks off at the end of the paragraph. "But I refrain, for I see you begin to think my Notions extravagant, and look upon them as the Ravings of a mad Prophet" (P, 9:7). But, why, after all, should it not be possible to change the very nature of England in order to make himself, the American Englishman, central?

America, in his eyes at this point, was an organic extension of England. The British Empire of his imagination lacked any subordination of parts, any hierarchy of importance, and central focus. When he discussed in the *Increase of Mankind* the relation of parts of an empire to each other, he chose as his illustration a polyp, a rudimentary plantlike animal.

> In fine, a Nation well regulated is like a Polypus; take away a Limb, its place is soon supply'd; cut it in two, and each deficient Part shall speedily grow out of the Part remaining. Thus if you have Room and Subsistence enough, as you may by dividing, make ten Polypes out of one, you may of one make ten Nations, equally populous and powerful; or rather, increase a Nation ten fold in Numbers and Strength. (P, 4:93)

Franklin had described the morphology of the polyp in a recent *Poor Richard's Almanack*, so that implications possible in the image were fresh in his mind; the polyp's unusual characteristics, which had been recently discovered, were a subject for much contemporary discussion in Europe.[10] The polyp renews itself through division, each severed piece developing by itself the missing parts, so that there is no head or heart at the basis of its existence. Its life extends throughout history because of this constant renewal. Its divisions and replacements suggest evolution without change. Most significantly, to compare a nation to a polyp is to deny any binding and permanent parent-child relationship between England and America, since America was then an independent entity that had developed from a fragment of Great Britain.

Images of dismemberment recur in Franklin's writing about politics. The American colonies had been compared to a snake and chopped in pieces. The British empire was compared to a polyp. Later we shall see further developments of Franklin's preoccupation with this image. The recurrence suggests the ways in which more than the morality or the power relationships of political questions figured into Franklin's thinking. He was concerned about continuity, wholeness, and the interrelation of parts, all questions relating to the nature of group identity. In England in the 1750s and 1760s he was trying to engraft himself into the political community as he never had before.

The attempt was, of course, unsuccessful. Franklin conceived of a British empire that would not be based on a hereditary hierarchy—this in a century in which noble birth was preeminently valued even by comparison with other periods in English history. His version of empire required the possibility of a shift in center toward America—at a time when there was a revival of interest in America as a neglected national estate to be profitably exploited. Franklin was comfortable living in England, but he was by no means content to settle there as a private person. The need for public acknowledgment that had driven him so far impelled him to seek a special and privileged place in relation to his imagined empire. He saw himself in a favored place; as his father had exhorted him to diligence so he could stand before kings, he sought a special attachment to George III. His whole perception of Great Britain was a mixture of fact and fantasy, and the fantasy was to collapse most humiliatingly in the years before the Revolution.

In 1760 George III began his long reign. Franklin attended his coronation, which took place in 1761 amid heady imperial triumphs for Britain; British armies on three continents were drawing toward victory in the Seven Years' War. Franklin developed a strong sense of allegiance to the young king, an abstract rather than a personal attachment, needless to say, since there is no record that he ever spoke to the king or saw him except on public occasions. In the character of his attachment to the king Franklin was different from both his English and his American contemporaries.

The young king, first of the House of Hanover to be wholly English, was widely popular in England upon his accession, but his popularity declined abruptly when his favorite, the Earl of Bute, proved an inadequate and bungling successor to the elder Pitt. From that time on—or until a sense of general pity for him in his madness overtook the country forty years later—he was the object of a mixed response. More actively involved in the details of government than his predecessors, he soon became associated with certain policies, so he was honored or vilified in association with those policies. For Americans the king was far away, hardly imaginable except as a symbol. In New England especially, ideas of a republican commonwealth persisted among the descendants of the Puritans. The king was part of an articulated social structure that most Americans could not altogether comprehend from the vantage of their own societies. To illustrate this incomprehension during the period before the Revolution, Horace Walpole told a popular story "that a wealthy merchant in one of the provinces had said, 'They say King George is a very honest fellow; I should like to smoke a pipe with him,' so little conception had they in that part of the world of the majesty of an European monarch!"[11]

The imagery of parent-child relations was used by both sides in the quarrel between Britain and America before the American Revolution.

Different definitions of the right relations that should exist between parent and child were used by opposing factions on both sides of the Atlantic, and of course the imagery expressed the potent emotions stirred up by the breach.[12] But Franklin's own use of the images of parenthood differs from that of his American countrymen. For them, until Lexington and Concord, the parent was England, a country, which was seen as acting collectively. Franklin, on the other hand, recurrently referred to the king himself as the protective father of the empire. On several occasions this feeling of loyalty to the king even provoked Franklin to indignation toward the English, who seemed to him disloyal to their prince. During his two-year interval in America from 1762 to 1764, Franklin wrote indignantly about the abuse the king was receiving in the press from John Wilkes and others.

> The Glory of Britain was never higher than at present, and I think you never had a better Prince: Why then is he not universally rever'd and belov'd? I can give but one Answer. The King of the Universe, good as he is, is not cordially belov'd and faithfully serv'd by all his Subjects. I wish I could say that half Mankind, as much as they are oblig'd to him for his continual Favours, were among the truly loyal. Tis a shame that the very Goodness of a Prince, should be an Encouragement to Affronts. (P, 10:302–3)

Around the same time his good friend William Strahan wrote to describe the political situation in England. Strahan, by this time a member of Parliament, offered a decidedly negative assessment of the new king's abilities and his selection of ministers. To this political judgment Franklin responded in the language of apocalyptic prophecy.

> You now fear for our virtuous young King, that the Faction forming will overpower him, and render his Reign uncomfortable. On the contrary, I am of the Opinion, that his Virtue, and the Consciousness of his sincere Intentions to make his People happy, will give him Firmness and Steadiness in his Measures, and in the Support of the honest Friends he has chosen to serve him; and when that Firmness is fully perceiv'd, Faction will dissolve and be dissipated like a Morning Fog before the rising Sun, leaving the rest of the Day clear, with a Sky serene and cloudless. Such, after a few of the first Years, will be the future Course of his Majesty's Reign, which I predict will be happy and truly glorious. (P, 10:407)

Through the 1760s, amid the controversies over the Stamp Act and the Townshend Acts, Franklin's loyalty to the virtuous young king persisted, despite all indications of the king's disapproval of the colonies' insubordinate attitude. In 1767 he visited France and as an eminent scientist was presented to Louis XV. Writing to England about his audience, he says "I would not have you think me so much pleas'd with this King and Queen as to have a Whit less Regard than I us'd to have for ours. No Frenchman shall go beyond me in thinking my own King and Queen the very best in the World and the most amiable" (P, 14:253). During the 1768 riots in London over "Wilkes and Liberty," he was deeply upset at the actions of the mob, which he linked with the corruption and instability of the government as an offense against the king.

> What the Event will be God only knows; But some Punishment seems preparing for a People who are ungratefully abusing the best Constitution and the best King any Nation was ever blest with, intent on nothing but Luxury, Licentiousness, Power, Places, Pensions and Plunder. (P, 15:129)

As late as 1770, in a letter to Samuel Cooper of Boston in response to the news of the Boston Massacre, Franklin persists in his loyalty to the king, a loyalty which he found consistent with circumventing government measures in the colonies.

> Let us therefore hold fast [our] Loyalty to our King (who has the best Disposition toward us, and has a Family-Interest in our Prosperity) as that steady Loyalty is the most probable Means of securing us from the arbitrary Power of a corrupt Parliament, that does not like us, and conceives itself to have an Interest in keeping us down and fleecing us. (P, 17:163–64)

These professions of devotion go well beyond the decorum of public loyalty to the sovereign. The professions in fact are not contained in writings for the press but rather are generally addressed to private friends. They could not have gained him preferment, nor did they serve especially to advance the political projects he was undertaking. Since the 1750s he and his allies in the Pennsylvania Assembly had been maneuvering to replace the proprietaries with a royal governor; later on, deference to the king became a corollary to the colonial strategy of defiance to Parliament and the ministry. But these political reasons do not sufficiently account for Franklin's sincere and reiterated feelings toward the virtuous young king.

Such feelings associated Franklin with odd company. In England the real devotees of royalty before the French Revolution were Jacobites or Tories. Dr. Johnson was greatly moved by his unexpected interview with King George in the Queen's library, but this feeling of loyalty caused him to denounce the American rebels. Franklin's associates, defenders of America like John Wilkes, William Pitt, and Joseph Priestley, were either indifferent or actively hostile toward the king. In general the House of Hanover was tolerated because it was Protestant, but it was not the focus for much real feeling during the eighteenth century. The previous century's controversies over the Stuarts had thrown the institution of kingship into an ambiguous shadow. The first two Georges were politically tied to the Whigs, the party that was less affectively tied to royalty. When Franklin writes to Strahan about how the king's firmness will cause faction to dissolve, he expresses a political sentiment unlike those of either patriot or loyalist Americans. He sounds like Bolingbroke, the Tory political theorist of the early eighteenth century—surely one of the most unlikely political writers for any American to echo. George III in Franklin's eyes was a Patriot King, the father of his people. "The true image of a free people, governed by a Patriot King," writes Bolingbroke, "is that of a patriarchal family, where the head and all the members are united by one common interest, and animated by one common spirit."[13] Here is the alternative during the eighteenth century to Locke's conception of society as a freely gathered collection of independent selves. In both English and American contexts Franklin was excessive in his expressions of loyalty to the king. His search for a British imperial identity led him to overidentification. He deserted his previously guarded independence and submerged himself in the royal symbol of family order and love.

For Franklin the special relation to the king meant more than just a counterargument in a constitutional controversy. To affirm the king's fatherhood meant to assume the protected status of a favored child, something Franklin had known in his childhood. This status involved more than just honorary degrees from Oxford and St. Andrew's, the respect of the British scientific and intellectual community, and ready access to the press. Although he was well received in England, he looked for more than the alien status he found. Franklin sought to be not merely a curious American freak—not merely an ingenious tradesman and publicist. He sought ultimately that special greatness that compels public acknowledgment, that frees the self from the status relationships of its society. He wanted to be like Cato in Busy-Body 3, whose virtue alone is sufficient to earn him the respect of the powerful. He wanted to be free from the contempt of the great and from the helpless frustration of the commoner.

So he turned to propaganda for an expanded empire as the Seven Years' War was coming to a close. A decision would have to be made about whether to keep Canada or the sugar-producing island of Guadeloupe after the war; Franklin joined into the pamphlet war on behalf of keeping Canada. In his most important pamphlet, *The Interest of Great Britain Considered,* he disposed of a number of opposing arguments, particularly having to do with the lessened dependence on Britain in America if the French threat from Canada was removed. Franklin maintains that Americans would have no desire for independence; prominent and wealthy Americans, he suggests, would naturally be drawn to live in England. "And there will always be in the conveniences of life, the politeness, the pleasures, the magnificence of the reigning country, many other attractions besides those of learning, to draw men of substance there, where they can, apparently at least, have the best bargain of happiness for their money" (P, 9:87). The real pleasures of civilized life were in England.

Another objection to annexing Canada was that the Americans might unite against England. Franklin had tried to unite America himself; he knew better.

> Those [colonies] we now have, are not only under different governors, but have different forms of government, different laws, different interests, and some of them different religious persuasions and different manners. Their jealousy of each other is so great that however necessary an union of the colonies has long been, for their common defence and security, against their enemies, and sensible soever each colony has been of that necessity, yet they have never been able to effect such an union among themselves, nor even to agree in requesting the mother country to establish it for them. (P, 9:90)

The Americans were hopelessly disunited by themselves, Franklin asserts with detachment. Canada was of course turned over to Britain in the peace of 1763, and Franklin credited the "Canada Pamphlet" with swaying those in power to that decision. "The People in Power here do now seem convinc'd of the Truth of the Principles I have inculcated, and incline to act upon them," he wrote to Josiah Quincy in America (P, 9:299). In fact, the pamphlet war probably had little effect on the decision. No pamphlet writer working on his own could sway ministerial policy in England in the 1760s in the way Franklin believed.

The Franklin who plumped for empire saw no contradiction between being American and being English. He perceived himself as a kind of interpreter between the two: advocating American needs to England, explaining English interests in America. But there were problems with his identity. He needed to have a public identity in England, of a sort comparable to his public identity in Pennsylvania, but there his status was the rather ambiguous one of colonial agent. To the American colonial legislators who delegated that responsibility to him, that was a public function, involving payment, regular correspondence with legislators, and specific issues he was to advocate. But in London there was an assortment of colonial agents, who lobbied for the sometimes conflicting interests of their American constituents and whose influence varied considerably as the ministerial climate of opinion changed.[14]

Moreover, Franklin was slow to grasp how insignificant he was in England. He could not transform English society or the nature of the empire. In political terms his affirmation of the king instead of Parliament as sovereign over the colonies ran counter to the prevailing tradition of English political theory, which affirmed the unlimited sovereignty of Parliament.[15] Besides, the king himself did not have good intentions for America. He was alienated from the Rockingham Whigs and others who favored conciliation of the Americans. Franklin found himself in England, particularly from 1764 on, a man caught in the middle. He had to keep the allegiance of the Americans back home, at a time when colonial leaders were being radicalized by confrontation with the mother country. Yet he was living in London, a short walk from Parliament. It is important to realize that Franklin was the only one of the future Founding Fathers to have had any direct experience in dealing with the British ministry. What was for John Adams or Thomas Jefferson an abstract conflict of legal interpretations was for Franklin a direct clash of personalities. He had sought tranquility in England; instead he found conflict. His illusion of having a special and protected status slowly wore away, dissolved by the brutal contempt of powerful adversaries to his aims as a colonial agent.

The Stamp Act crisis of 1765 revealed suddenly the vulnerability of Franklin's position and of his illusions. George Grenville, the king's first minister, was determined to get money out of the colonies to reduce the national debt left over from the war, and one of his measures was a stamp required on newspapers and various documents. Franklin resisted the proposal, along with other colonial representatives, but soon concluded there was no realistic chance of overcoming it. The measure was popular in England; Grenville had the votes in Parliament; a mere three weeks after the annual budget for 1765 was introduced, the Stamp Act passed the House of Commons. By temperament Franklin had always been one to bow to the inevitable. "Depend upon it my good Neighbour," he wrote to Charles Thomson, a political associate in Pennsylvania, in a letter which was soon after published, "I took every Step in my Power, to prevent the passing of the Stamp Act; no body could be more concern'd in Interest than my self to oppose it, sincerely and Heartily. But the Tide was, too strong against us. The Nation was provok'd by American Claims of Independance, and all Parties join'd in resolveing by this Act to Settle the Point" (P, 12:207). So he made the best of things and angled to get his friend John Hughes the lucrative post of stamp distributor for Philadelphia. "We might as well have hinder'd the Suns setting" (P, 12:207).

But Franklin had seriously miscalculated the American situation, however accurate he may have been about the English. Resistance to the stamps was universal and violent. "The Sun of Liberty is indeed fast setting, if not down already, in the American colonies" (P, 12:279), Thomson wrote back, and his apocalyptic words pointed to perceptions that had nothing to do with Franklin's resignation to political realities in England. A mob gathered around Hughes's house in Philadelphia and threatened to tear it down and Franklin's as well. To give in to the Stamp Act, even while protesting, was treason to the colonists. Franklin's standing as an American spokesman was in great danger of collapsing, leaving him an expatriate former Pennsylvania politician with a place in the colonial post office.

He salvaged his reputation in the colonies by redoubled efforts at repealing the Act, particularly through his widely publicized testimony before the House of Commons. The *Examination* was widely reprinted on both sides of the Atlantic as a central document in the conflict; it was even translated into French.[16] Now Franklin was the herald and defender of American intransigence.

Q. Don't you think they would submit to the stamp-act, if it was modified, the obnoxious parts taken out, and the duty reduced to some particulars, of small moment?
A. No; they will never submit to it. (P, 13:136)

In part the examination was carefully staged, with series of questions planted among friendly members for Franklin to answer. But the character of other questions revealed a basic problem: the two sides of the conflict were not speaking the same political language. Franklin was facing the same problem he had faced when he first arrived in England in 1757 and had been told by Lord Granville, President of the Privy Council, that American pretensions to legislative autonomy were legally unfounded.

To follow the course of questions and answers in the Examination and the pamphlet controversies on both sides that continued through the years before the Revolution is to see that the apparent issues—internal or external taxation, virtual representation in Parliament, the sovereignty of king or Parliament over the colonies—are argumentative counters in some more basic conflict. Franklin was caught flat-footed at the beginning of the conflict because of his vision of empire, and he had not yet grasped the strange rhetoric of the disagreement. The nature of the situation made it necessary for him to voice as profound conviction opinions rather lately arrived at. Franklin was not the dogmatist that both John Adams and Thomas Jefferson were; in the debates preceding the Revolution he was always a pragmatist, adapting his ideas to the shifts in the debate. But his pragmatism did not mean that there was no principle of consistency in his stance. He may not have been concerned about abstract legal or constitutional principles in the way that others were, but he was deeply concerned about the perceived status of Americans. He considered himself their spokesman and exemplar; it was his own self-definition that he was defending.

Worse than ignorance was involved in the English attitude toward the Americans. The contempt which moved his countrymen to fury at an ocean's distance Franklin felt first hand. Much of his polemical writing in this period was devoted to the task of convincing his English audience that the American colonies were of some importance. For example, in response to one adversary, "Vindex Patriae," he wrote a defense of American Indian corn under the pseudonym "Homespun." "JOHN BULL shews in nothing more his great veneration for good eating. and how much he is always thinking of his belly, than in his making it the constant topic of his contempt for other nations, that *they do not eat so well as himself*" (P, 13:45). The piece is a defense of American cuisine, a humorous exercise in the serious cause of dealing with the suspicion that the Americans were a race of primitives unworthy of being listened to. One continuing subject Franklin agitated about was the practice of transporting felons to the colonies. As if America were a fitter place for them than England! His political satire before the Revolution adopts the tactic of cajoling his audience into seeing the American side. In his *Edict of the King of Prussia* he imagines Frederick the Great as dictating the same measures to England that the English were dictating to America on the basis that the Anglo-Saxons were originally German emigrants.

But humor would not help Franklin in the direct confrontations he was to have with ministers of the king who were determined to impose their will on America. Earlier, when he had been obliged to negotiate personally with the Penn brothers, he had gotten a taste of the helplessness of the commoner in the face of highborn insolence. Thomas Penn denied directly that the privileges in his father's charter had been legally granted.

> [T]hat He [Thomas Penn] said with a Kind of triumphing laughing Insolence, such as a low Jockey might do when a Purchaser complained that He had cheated him in a Horse. I was astonished to see him thus meanly give up his Father's Character and conceived that Moment a more cordial and thorough Contempt for him than I ever before felt for any Man living—A contempt that I cannot express in Words, but I believe my Countenance expressed it strongly. And that his Brother was looking at me, must have observed it; however finding myself grow warm I made no other Answer to this than that the poor People were no Lawyers themselves and confiding in his Father did not think it necessary to consult any. (P, 7:362)

Tensions with the proprietary family were longstanding for Franklin's party in the Assembly as well as for Franklin himself. Here, however, had been his first direct confrontation with personal contempt for him, a contempt that his subordinate status prevented him from retaliating against. The reader of the *Autobiography* can have little sense of Franklin's capacity for anger, so rigorously does that work bring his past emotions into control. But he could become very angry indeed, his habitual assertions of geniality notwithstanding. "One of the great difficulties in knowing Franklin through the written word left behind him," write the editors of the Franklin *Papers*, "is that he rarely, on paper, lost his temper. He sometimes did in his marginalia, his most private comments; but in his correspondence with others he preserved a calm that was undoubtedly more Olympian than the flesh-and-blood man could maintain" (P, 18:73). There were numerous provocations to this sort of anger during the period in England.

This same helplessness recurs again in his dealings with Lord Hillsborough, Secretary of State for the American Colonies. In January 1771 Franklin waited upon Lord Hillsborough to present his credentials as agent of the Massachusetts House of Representatives. Hillsborough curtly denied that Franklin could have been legitimately appointed without the concurrence of Governor Hutchinson, a denial of Franklin's status that carried personal as well as political implications. Franklin tried to reason, as he described in an account of the interview sent to Samuel Cooper in Boston.

> B.F. I cannot conceive, my Lord, why the Consent of the *Governor* should be thought necessary to the Appointment of an Agent for the *People*. It seems to me, that——
> L.H. (*With a mix'd Look of Anger and Contempt*) I shall not enter into a Dispute with YOU, Sir upon this Subject. (*P,* 18:14)

The discussion concluded as Franklin received back the copy of his appointment. "I beg your Lordship's Pardon for taking up so much of your time," he said as he was leaving.

> It is I believe of no great Importance whether the Appointment is acknowledged or not, for I have not the least Conception that an Agent can *at present* be of any Use, to any of the Colonies. I shall therefore give your Lordship no farther Trouble. *Withdrew.* (*P,* 18:15–16)

In his satire *Rules by Which a Great Empire May Be Reduced to a Small One* he includes a reference to confrontations like the Hillsborough affair.

> Let the Parliaments flout their Claims, reject their Petitions, refuse even to suffer the reading of them, and treat the Petitioners with the utmost Contempt. Nothing can have a better effect in producing the Alienation proposed; for though many can forgive injuries, *none ever forgave Contempt*. (*P,* 20:394)

The relations between England and America are thus seen as a presentation of selves. To the other colonists the controversies with England were fought more at a distance, with only the royal governors and their coteries to stand as surrogates for the parliamentary opposition. To Franklin the enemies of America and the opponents of his concept of empire were close at hand, so that confrontation of personality became inseparable from the confrontation of ideas.

Two episodes were crucial during Franklin's English years. The first was the Stamp Act crisis. There Franklin discovered the necessity of aligning himself with the Patriot side in the colonies if he was to retain his credibility there as an American spokesman. Whatever his natural disposition to be a compromiser, go-between, and detached observer, he was henceforth obliged to act as an advocate in a series of increasingly irreconcilable confrontations. He had left Boston as a youth because he had felt himself the vulnerable man in the middle. He had always hated altercation; he found it sickening rather than invigorating. But now he could not escape it, except by retiring from his coveted role as the representative American. The second crucial episode was the Hutchinson letters controversy in 1773 and 1774. In it Franklin's last illusions of empire were rudely and publicly crushed.

The most touchy part of Franklin's public role was his services as colonial agent for the Massachusetts Assembly. For three-quarters of a century the Assembly had quarreled with its royal governors; the mood of confrontation was stronger there than anywhere else in the colonies. The Assembly's Committee on Correspondence was not altogether comfortable with Franklin as their representative because they suspected him of being less intransigent than they. They were of course right; Franklin often had reservations about the radical elements in Boston and toned down the most inflammatory of the Assembly's petitions, though he did conduct his own vigorous writing and lobbying campaign for them. The royal governor of Massachusetts since 1771 had been Thomas Hutchinson, a Massachusetts man and one-time associate in various intercolonial projects with Franklin. Hutchinson and Andrew Oliver, the lieutenant governor, had written a series of letters to an English associate of Grenville in which they urged strong and even repressive measures against the present climate of Massachusetts opinion: abridgment of liberties, independent salaries for royal officials, perhaps the use of troops. Franklin got hold of the letters and sent copies to the Committee on Correspondence for their information, making it clear that the letters should not be widely seen. Once there, however, the letters created a stir that could not be kept secret; they were soon published and led to a petition for the removal of Hutchinson and Oliver.

In England Franklin publicly accepted responsibility for sending the letters to Massachusetts. He was obliged to; a duel had already been fought between two other men over the responsibility, and Franklin stepped in to prevent further bloodshed. The petition for Hutchinson's removal, which he then had to present to the government, became enmeshed in the controversy over the leaking of the letters. Franklin had been by 1774 a longtime irritant to the ministry, and the Hutchinson letters seemed a perfect opportunity to cut him down.

The petition from Massachusetts for Hutchinson's removal was to be presented to the Privy Council, but the focus was quickly turned from the petition to one piece of evidence it cited, the letters. When the

Privy Council met on 29 January 1774 in the Cockpit, the rumors of the confrontation between the assembled ministry and Franklin attracted a packed house, including Arthur Lee, Lord Shelburne, Edmund Burke, and Jeremy Bentham. Present in the Council itself were the Archbishop of Canterbury, the Bishop of London, and the Earl of Dartmouth, Lord Hillsborough, the Earl of Sandwich, Lord North, and Sir Jeffrey Amherst, almost a roll call of the dominant political figures in England.[17] There the Solicitor General, Alexander Wedderburn, a Scot with a reputation for scurrilous abuse, responded after Franklin's counsel had presented the Assembly's petition. The confrontation turned out to be a carefully staged scene of public humiliation. For over an hour Franklin stood as petitioner while Wedderburn denounced him as a felon, knave, upstart, traitor, and inciter to insurrection.

"Dr. Franklin," Wedderburn announced, ". . . stands in the light of the first mover and prime conductor of this whole contrivance against His Majesty's two Governors; and having by the help of his special confidents and party leaders, first made the Assembly *his* Agents in carrying on his own secret designs, he now appears before your Lordships to give the finishing stroke to the work of his own hands" (*P,* 21:47–48). Franklin was at least free of the taint of obscurity. His denouncer accused him of masterminding the entire colonial resistance to royal government in Massachusetts. Twice in the speech Franklin was called the "prime conductor" of the conspiracy, a sneering reference to his research in electricity. It was he who, with his minions, had deluded the simple rustic Americans into their posture of resistance to authority, perhaps because he aspired to be governor himself. Wedderburn summarized the events leading up to the duel and Franklin's subsequent letter admitting the transmission of the letters. "After the mischiefs of this concealment had been left for five months to have their full operation, at length comes out a letter, which it is impossible to read without horror; expressive of the coolest and most deliberate malevolence" (*P,* 21:490). Likening the impassive Franklin to Zanga, the villain in Edward Young's play *Revenge,* Wedderburn declared, "I ask, my lords, whether the revengeful temper attributed, by poetic fiction only, to the bloody African; is not surpassed by the coolness and apathy of the wily American?" (*P,* 21:50). More than personal abuse went with such words; the qualities attributed to Franklin—coolness, apathy, wiliness—were the supposed characteristics of the American Indian, according to current biological theories that judged America and its inhabitants to be unhealthy and inferior to the old world.

Franklin, cried Wedderburn, had "forfeited all the respect of societies and of men. Into what companies will he hereafter go with an unembarrassed face, or the honest intrepidity of virtue?" (P, 21:48–49). By forwarding Hutchinson's letters, Franklin was acting as the receiver of stolen goods, not accidentally but deliberately. "Other receivers of goods dishonourably come by, may plead as a pretence for keeping them, that they don't know who are the proprietors: In this case there was not the common excuse of ignorance; the Doctor knew whose they were, and yet did not restore them to the right owner. This property is as sacred and as precious to gentlemen of integrity, as their family plate or jewels are" (P, 21:51). Why did Franklin do it? "My Lords, Dr. Franklin's mind may have been so possessed with the idea of a Great American Republic, that he may easily slide into the language of the minister of a foreign independent state" (P, 21:58–59).

In the account of the proceedings that Franklin prepared anonymously for the *Pennsylvania Gazette*, he emphasized the deliberately humiliating character of the proceedings. The Solicitor-General

> in a virulent Invective of an Hour, filled with Scurrility, abused him personally, to the great Entertainment of Thirty-Five Lords of the Privy-Council, who had been purposely invited as to a Bull-baiting, and not one of them had the Sense to reflect on the Impropriety and Indecency of treating, in so ignominious a Manner, a Public Messenger, whose Character in all Nations, savage as well as civilized, used to be deemed sacred, and his Person under public Protection, even when coming from an Enemy; nor did one of them check the Orator's Extravagance, and recall him to to the Point under Consideration, but generally appeared much delighted, chuckling, laughing, and sometimes loudly applauding. (P, 21:112–13)

Franklin's description underlines the problem of status or identity which he was having: in his own eyes his status as a "public messenger" should have left him immune from such attacks. Wedderburn's snide insinuations that Franklin imagined himself the diplomatic representative of a republic proved oddly prophetic; three years later Franklin would in fact be an ambassador from America to a foreign state. For now, however, Wedderburn meant only that Franklin was a deluded and traitorous man. Franklin claimed to be the colonial agent for Massachusetts. "But, my Lords, the rank in which Dr. Franklin appears is not even that of a Province Agent; he moves in a very inferior orbit" (P, 21:59). He represented only the Assembly, and really only a party in the Assembly. It was the same denial of Franklin's public standing that Hillsborough had made. This time, though, something more was going on than a mere attack in the press or a personal snub. Franklin was undergoing a ritual expulsion from society.

It was the public quality of the event that affected Franklin most. Discouraged by his own helplessness and disoriented by the dissolution of his ideas of empire, Franklin had frequently written in the months before about returning to private life. The episode in the Cockpit closed off that escape. He was trapped forever in the public world, forced to retaliate against his tormentors. Any retreat into private life now would only mean acceptance of his humiliated and discredited status. The Wedderburn incident stayed in his mind. The story is told that four years later when he was to sign the treaty of alliance with France he would deliberately take out the suit he had worn at the Cockpit and wear it at the ceremony. Franklin's biographers disagree about whether the episode took place, but certainly the existence of the story suggests the continued importance of the Privy Council humiliation.[18]

Though they chose here to humiliate him, the ministry indicated several times that they were ready to buy him off, partly because they seemed to share the opinion declared by Wedderburn that the colonial resistance somehow originated from Franklin. Indeed the ministry apparently considered his son's appointment as royal governor of New Jersey as some sort of pledge of the father's good behavior. Even though bribery was endemic through the highest ranks of British public life, Franklin seems to have been genuinely revolted by these approaches; to accept them would have meant that he was no better than his venal adversaries, no better than a peer of the realm and minister of the king.[19] Allegiance to king above country, England above America had never really been an imaginative possibility for him, nor could he escape from public life into some position of neutrality.

To deny America would have meant denying the continuity of his own character, a continuity which he was affirming by beginning the *Autobiography* in 1771. The *Autobiography* was always intended for publication—it was written at a time when Franklin could hardly have kept any of his writings private—and it must have motivated him to keep his life consistent and intact for the inspection of posterity. Already in the 1770s it was longer than any of his published works, and though he did not resume it until 1784 it must have been on his mind.

There were also private provocations to Franklin, instances of unconscious British arrogance he could bitterly recall ten years later. In England Franklin had no closer friend than William Strahan, like himself a printer who had risen to prominence, a member of Parliament and friend to Dr. Johnson and his circle. They had corresponded on matters both of business and of mutual interest for years before Franklin arrived in England; once united, their friendship became even closer, to the point where they imagined marrying their children to each other. But Strahan remained an Englishman, and in his hostility to the English identity which events had denied him, Franklin even turned on his own friend. In 1784 Franklin would harshly remind Strahan of the opinions current in London about the Americans just before the war. "You believ'd rather the Tales you heard of our Poltroonery and Impotence of Body and Mind. Do you not remember the Story you told me of the Scotch sergeant, who met with a Party of Forty American Soldiers, and tho' alone, disarm'd them all, and brought them in Prisoners?" A British general "had the Folly to say in my hearing" that by force or a little coaxing a thousand British grenadiers could easily castrate all the males in America. It was folly indeed to make such remarks in Franklin's hearing; Franklin did not forget insults. "It is plain he took us for a species of Animals very little superior to Brutes. The Parliament too believ'd the stories of another foolish General, I forget his Name, that the Yankeys never *felt bold*. Yankey was understood to be a sort of Yahoo, and the Parliament did not think the Petitions of such Creatures were fit to be received and read in so wise an Assembly." Franklin goes on to remind Strahan of the pathetic performance of British arms in America and the incompetence of British diplomacy: there is a note of unconcealed and exultant hostility in his summary. He concludes with a final and characteristically American insult.

> I am too well acquainted with all the Springs and Levers of our Machine, not to see, that our human means were unequal to our undertaking, and that, if it had not been for the Justice of our Cause, and the consequent Interposition of Providence, in which we had Faith, we must have been ruined. If I had ever before been an Atheist, I should now have been convinced of the Being and Government of a Deity! It is he who abases the Proud and favours the Humble. (W, 9:261–62)

Horace Walpole coined a suggestive epigram to describe the effects of Franklin's encounter with Wedderburn at the Cockpit:

> Sarcastic Sawney, swol'n with spite and prate,
> On Silent Franklin poured his venal hate.
> The calm philosopher, without reply,
> Withdrew, and gave his country liberty.[20]

The epigram points to Franklin's pattern of withdrawing from hostile confrontations.[21] It represents the intimate connection between private motives and public action which was characteristic of Franklin. It notes both Franklin's apparent calmness and his possession of mythic powers.

In the face of British rejection of his own self-defined identity as an Englishman, Franklin had to redefine himself in the early 1770s, systematically rejecting the British elements. In the 1750s the polyp had been his image for the British Empire, replication by division. Back during the Stamp Act crisis he had had a cartoon drawn depicting Great Britain as a mutilated woman, her arms and legs identified as the American colonies. The moral which Franklin pointed to still implied that the Empire was organically one nation: "History affords us many instances of the ruin of states by the prosecution of measures ill suited to the temper and genius of their people" (P, 8:71). The home country loses the colonies in an act of self-mutilation. The responsibility for the dismemberment of the Empire lay with England; a 1775 letter written from America recalls the image in the cartoon. "'Tis a million of pities so fair a plan as we have hitherto been engaged in, for increasing strength and empire with *public felicity,* should be destroyed by the mangling hands of a few blundering ministers. It will not be destroyed; God will protect and prosper it, you will only exclude yourselves from any share in it (P, 22:217). Franklin employs still a third image for the disintegration of the Empire in a letter written in 1776 to Lord Howe in response to gestures of conciliation:

> Long did I endeavour, with unfeigned and unwearied Zeal, to preserve from breaking that fine and noble China Vase, the British Empire: for that I knew that being once broke, the separate Parts could not retain even their Share of the Strength or Value that existed in the Whole, and that a perfect Re-Union of those Parts could scarce even be hoped for. (P, 22:520)

America now appeared as healthy, upright, and vigorous; England as corrupt and in decline. Shortly before leaving for America in 1775 he wrote in disgust to Joseph Galloway, "when I consider the extream Corruption prevalent among all Orders of Men in this old rotten State, and the glorious publick Virtue so predominant in our rising Country, I cannot but apprehend more Mischief than Benefit from a closer Union" (P, 21:509). The reasons for England's rottenness were centered in its aristocratic character: "Numberless and needless Places, enormous Salaries, Pensions, Perquisites, Bribes, groundless Quarrels, foolish Expeditions, false Accompts, or no Accompts, Contracts and Jobbs, devour all Revenue, and produce continual Necessity in the Midst of natural Plenty" (P, 21:509).

In the 1770s Franklin dwells more and more on what he considers the characteristic American industry and frugality. The Americans were self-sufficient, while the British were debased by luxury and dependence upon the government. Franklin encouraged nonimportation agreements in the colonies to pressure British merchants and to lessen American reliance on "English Modes and Gewgaws." In the winter of 1771–72 when he toured Scotland and Ireland, he observed the desperate poverty of the rural poor. This poverty for him was the inevitable result of a society given over to luxuries, trade, and manufacture.

> Farther, if my Countrymen should ever wish for the Honour of having among them a Gentry enormously wealthy, let them sell their Farms & pay rack'd Rents; the Scale of the Landlords will rise as that of the Tenants is depress'd, who will soon become poor, tattered, dirty, and abject in Spirit. Had I never been in the American Colonies, but was to form my Judgment of Civil Society by what I have lately seen, I should never advise a Nation of Savages to Admit of Civilisation: For I assure you, that in the Possession and Enjoyment of the various Comforts of Life, compar'd to these People every Indian is a Gentleman: and the Effect of this kind of Civil Society seems only to be the depressing Multitudes below the Savage State that a few may be rais'd above it. (P, 19:7)

A remarkable misunderstanding of the character of English society underlies this passage. The social organization of agriculture is seen as the product not of tradition and local circumstances but of conscious choice. What had once been British amiability was now the abjectness of spirit inevitable in an aristocratic society. To demonstrate the superiority of America over British society, Franklin invokes a basic Enlightenment standard. Britain is inferior to tribes of savages living in the state of nature.

Franklin rejected England in the 1770s with as much vehemence as he had identified with it ten years earlier. His anger and despair reached a point by the time he left for America in 1775 where he could no longer act effectively as a mediator between English and Americans even if such mediation had been possible. His tactic before had always been to ignore attacks on him, anticipating that hostility would be checked by silence. Now he counterattacked, vigorously and ineffectually.[22] He defended himself through reports written in the third person about the Cockpit incident, which he had published anonymously in American newspapers. Franklin had long carried on an anonymous campaign defending the American position in newspapers on both sides of the Atlantic. His writing in 1774 and 1775 reveals a man deprived of his most effective mode of expression. Genial irony turned to sarcasm. Franklin was no Swift; savage indignation he preferred to reject as impolitic. But now he no longer had confidence in his capacity to convince. In one representative piece, taking as his inspiration the boastful general's suggestion he had heard at Strahan's, he suggested to Lord North in the *Public Advertiser* that the proliferation of the American population be stopped.

> It is humbly proposed, and we do hereby give it as Part of our Instructions to our Representatives, that a Bill be brought in and passed, and Orders immediately transmitted to G——l G—e, our Commander in Chief in North America, in consequence of it, that all the Males there be c—st——ed. He may make a Progress thro' the several Towns of North America at the Head of five Battalions, which we hear our experienced Generals, who have been consulted, think sufficient to subdue America if they were in open Rebellion; for who can resist the intrepid Sons of Britain, the Terror of France and Spain, and the Conquerors of America in Germany. Let a Company of Sow-gelders, consisting of 100 Men, accompany the Army. On their Arrival at any Town or Village, let Orders be given that on the blowing of the Horn all Males be assembled in the Market Place. If the Corps are Men of Skill and Ability in their Profession, they will make great Dispatch and retard but very little the Progress of the Army. (P, 21:221)

Franklin had been hurt deeply by insults to America, too deeply to respond with anything better than spluttering rage to this sort of contempt for his manhood.

Attempts at conciliation still went on in England, led most prominently by the ailing William Pitt, Lord Chatham. Chatham met with Franklin to share ideas for a peaceful resolution of the conflict, including even a visit to Franklin's own lodgings on Craven Street on 29 January 1775. Franklin later described the meeting: "Such a Visit from so great a Man, on so important a Business, flattered not a little my Vanity; and the Honour of it gave me the more Pleasure, as it happen'd on the very Day 12 month, that the Ministry had taken so much pains to disgrace me before the Privy Council" (P, 21:579). A few days later, Chatham offered his plan in the House of Lords, with Franklin in the spectator's gallery. In the debate following the introduction of Chatham's motion, Lord Sandwich denounced the motion as having been in fact drafted by some American, looking at Franklin. Responding later to that insinuation, Chatham replied that he would be happy to consult with "one, he was pleas'd to say, whom all Europe held in high Estimation for his Knowledge and Wisdom, and rank'd with our Boyles and Newtons; who was an Honour not to the English Nation only but to Human Nature" (P, 21:581–82). Listening to the House of Lords's rejection of Chatham's plan, Franklin recalls later, "gave me an exceeding mean Opinion of their Abilities, and made their Claim of Sovereignty over three Millions of virtuous sensible People in America, seem the greatest of Absurdities, since they appear'd to have scarce Discretion enough to govern a Herd of Swine. Hereditary Legislators! thought I. There would be more Propriety, because less Hazard of Mischief, in having ([as] in some University of Germany,) Hereditary Professors of Mathematicks!" (P, 21:583). Actually, Franklin's reflections shortly after Chatham's plan was voted down were more positive, since he realized then that the plan had done well given that the ministry controlled a considerable majority of the seats (P, 21:463–64). But by the time he organized his reflections on this whole period, he could feel only contempt for the whole scheme of British government and a society based on hereditary distinctions. The House of Commons was no better, he added; its legislators could be bought and sold by the highest bidder.

In the meantime, Deborah Franklin died in Philadelphia, in December 1774. The Continental Congress had met and was speaking for the colonies as a whole, so his former status as representative of individual colonies was somewhat irrelevant. On 20 March 1775 he sailed for America. On board ship he wrote a long letter to his son explaining and justifying his conduct in the recent peace negotiations. While he was at sea, the skirmishes at Lexington and Concord took place. Soon after came Bunker Hill, and the news of it caused him to write a short wrathful note to Strahan:

> Look upon your Hands! They are stained with the Blood of your Relations!—You and I were long Friends!—You are now my Enemy,—and I am
>
> Yours,
> B. Franklin
>
> (W, 6:407)[23]

The letter was never sent, but his anger at Strahan, who now sat in Parliament and supported the war policy, was genuine. For Franklin the Revolution was as much a personal as a political struggle.

13 Revolutionary Years

Franklin left England in 1775 for a variety of reasons. His wife had died in Philadelphia, so no one was managing his affairs there. His attempts to engineer compromise in London had failed. What influence he had attained in England was collapsing; he had lost his position in the post office. There was a chancery suit pending against him connected to the Hutchinson letters case.

He had returned to Pennsylvania between 1762 and 1764, losing during the last year a bitter mud-slinging election to the Pennsylvania Assembly. So that interlude within his English years had reminded him vividly of the confusion and vicissitudes of political life in America; he had returned to his pleasant London lodgings on Craven Street with a renewed sense of English comforts. Eleven years later, those comforts had not kept him from humiliation and disillusionment.

When he returned to Philadelphia in May 1775 the Continental Congress was about to meet. He was immediately elected as a delegate from Pennsylvania. He found political life greatly changed. The old Pennsylvania issues that had preoccupied the colony earlier had been superseded by the confusing new problems of accelerating Revolution. His former opponents were now silent, dead, or transformed by new circumstances into allies. In Congress Franklin stood out as a national figure more than a Pennsylvanian, by far the best known American in the world. Without seeking it, he moved immediately into a leading role in Congress, where his associates deferred to his experience and prestige.

In Congress Franklin did not participate extensively in the debates, but he was continually selected for committees on establishing a postal service, on petitions to the king, on manufacturing saltpetre, on Indian affairs, on protecting American trade, and so on. He had reached his own conclusions about the inevitability of conflict and American independence in his last months in England, so he no longer entertained the hopes of reconciliation that some others did.

The spectacle of a freshly committed revolutionary who is seventy years old will seem strange unless we recognize how inevitable that role was for Franklin. The alternative would have meant withdrawal from public life entirely. Writing a long memoir in the form of a 196-page letter to his son on the voyage back to Philadelphia, he set forth his own role in the failed conciliation negotiations of 1774 and early 1775. He could not negotiate directly with any of the ministry after Wedderburn had assulted him before the Privy Council. "From the Time of the Affront given me at The Council Board in January 1774, I had never attended the Levee of any Minister. I made no Justification of my self from the Charges brought against me: I made no Return of the Injury by abusing my Adversaries; but held a cool sullen Silence, reserving my self to some future Opportunity" (P, 21:545–46). Evidently the future opportunity he imagined involved the reversal of the current course of British policy, and Franklin had worked hard to negotiate a peaceful resolution of the issues between Britain and America. But the lingering resentment at the injury he had received is obvious in his choice of words. Withdrawal from public activity would have meant an indefinitely prolonged and embittered "cool sullen Silence."

The return to America meant a return to public life, to the acknowledgment he had sought since he had contributed to his brother's newspaper fifty-three years earlier. Several of his letters register his delight at having been immediately elected to Congress.

Ironically, during the same period when he was struggling to preserve or recover a public role he was urging a more private one to members of his own family. In 1771 and 1772 his son-in-law Richard Bache had visited him in London in hopes that Franklin could find him a government job. Even at that point Franklin saw political patronage as an unpromising future, and his own influence was unsteady, so Bache was sent back to Philadelphia with the advice that he be a storekeeper there. Since 1762 William Franklin had been royal governor of New Jersey. Gradually his father came to realize in the years following the Stamp Act crisis that William, who had once been his henchman in London and Philadelphia, had developed an allegiance to the Empire that was grounded in the royal office he held. Yet William had also remained apparently loyal to his father and continued to write encouraging letters to London. William's continuing loyalty was certainly connected to the money Franklin kept providing to supplement the governor's salary. After the Privy Council humiliation and the loss of his post office position, Franklin at first wrote to William to suggest that he resign his governorship, especially since William's chances for advancement were lost and he had never made ends meet on his salary there. "I wish you were well settled in your Farm. 'Tis an honester and a more honourable because a more independent Employment" (P, 21:75). But a few weeks later Franklin wrote to warn his son that William might be pressured to resign and suggested that instead he wait to be fired. But eventually Franklin warned that William should resign. "I think Independance more honourable than any Service, and that in the State of American Affairs, which from the present arbitrary measures is likely soon to take place, you will find yourself in no comfortable Situation, and perhaps wish you had soon disengaged yourself"(P, 21:212). His son-in-law should become a storekeeper, his son an independent farmer. But Franklin was not interested in such private roles for himself. As in the case of the *Poor Richard* sayings on industry and frugality, Franklin preached a doctrine he thought applied to others, not to himself. Still, his views on the merits of independence and patronage had not really shifted since his youth. In part his *Autobiography* tries to ascribe his success both to his own independent efforts and also to well-earned benevolence from more-established figures. The potential contradiction would never fully resolve itself in his life in the direction of either patronage or independence, but certainly he was shifting in the direction of independence after the disillusionment of his English years.

His perceptions of America had changed also. Twenty years earlier, in the aftermath of the Albany Congress's failure to engineer American unity, he had resigned himself to fragmentation as an inevitable feature of political life in the colonies, and when he had argued for the addition of Canada to the British Empire, he had listed chronic American disunity as one of the reasons why the addition of another colony would not lead to any potential combined resistance to Britain. But now he insisted on the unity of the colonies in defense of their freedoms. To David Hartley in England he writes, "I arrived here last Night, and have the Pleasure to learn that there is the most perfect Unanimity throughout the Colonies; and that even N York, on whose Defection the Ministry so confidently rely'd, is as hearty and zealous as any of the rest" (P, 21:31).

In fact, that perfect unanimity in the colonies did not include certain people of special importance to Franklin. One was Joseph Galloway, longtime lieutenant of Franklin's in Pennsylvania politics and still the leader of the anti-Proprietary party in the colony, who was now withdrawing from political life. As a delegate to the First Continental Congress in 1774 Galloway had proposed a plan of colonial union within the Empire. In fact Galloway had even opposed Pennsylvania participation in the Congress and favored separate dealings for redress by the colony.[1] Another exception to the consensus Franklin claimed to see in America was his son William, who was still trying to function as the royal governor of New Jersey in the midst of the public uproar after the battles of Lexington and Concord. Galloway seems to have perceived Franklin as not yet committed to the radical cause; at least the account he gave to Thomas Hutchinson in 1779 suggested that Franklin may have been wavering. As Hutchinson reports the conversation in his diary,

> When D[r]. Franklyn first arrived from England in America, after the revolt was begun, he came to Galloway, they having been long friends; that Galloway opened his mind to him, and hoped he was come to promote a reconciliation: that the Doctor was reserved, and kept upon his guard; that the next morning they met again, and the D[r]. said—'Well M[r]. Galloway, you are really of the mind that I ought to promote a reconciliation?' Galloway said 'Yes'—and no more passed: that for five or six weeks Franklyn kept much at home, [and] people seemed at a loss what part he would take. S. Adams opened against him as a suspicious person, designing to betray the cause. At length a more full conversation was proposed between F. & G., and the D[r] read to him three fourths of his Journal while he was in England, but company interrupted . . . that soon after, Galloway and the two Franklyns met together, and the glass having gone about freely, the Doctor, at a late hour, opened himself, and declared in favour of measures for attaining to Independence:— —exclaimed against the corruption and dissipation of the Kingdom, and signified his opinion, that from the strength of Opposition, the want of union in the Ministry, the great resources in the Colonies, they would finally prevail. He urged Galloway to come into the Congress again; and from that time, united in the closest connection with Adams, broke off from Galloway, who lost the remaining part of his Journal, which probably was the most interesting.[2]

This extended recollection is certainly inaccurate in some details, and the circumstances of the conversation undoubtedly colored Galloway's memory. By this time an exiled loyalist in England, conversing with Hutchinson, who had his own grievance with Franklin, Galloway recalls a more undecided and suggestible Franklin. There is some reason to believe the suggestion that radicals like Samuel Adams were at first leery of Franklin in the Congress. The journal Galloway describes hearing was Franklin's long account of his failed peace negotiations. After the meeting which Galloway describes, both Galloway and William Franklin came to be politically and thus personally alienated from Franklin. The long letter written at sea about his peace negotiations, though ostensibly addressed to his son, was, like the first part of the *Autobiography*, never sent to William Franklin.

The time Franklin spent in America in 1775 and 1776 was extremely busy, but it is not easy to guess what was going on in his mind. As the editors of his *Papers* put it,

> Members of a group in day-to-day contact leave at most a record of their joint decisions, and whatever we know about who said what comes only by accident. Franklin's role in Philadelphia, far more than his role in London, was played orally. The only evidence that survives is in other men's letters, diaries, and later memoirs, which give nothing more than glimpses, often unreliable and sometimes contradictory, of what that role was. As a consequence, although his political activities in this period were more important than ever before, we know less about them. (P, 22:xliii)

Where the detailed evidence is so lacking, an investigation like this one, which seeks the personality behind public acts, must not drift into speculation. We know from Franklin's American letters of 1775 and 1776 that his spirits were high and that he was active in a variety of ways in organizing the colonial resistance and the post office. To Bishop Jonathan Shipley, his host when he had begun the *Autobiography*, he writes, "I met with a most cordial Reception, I should say from all Parties, but that all Parties are now extinguish'd here. Britain has found means to unite us" (P, 22:42). Franklin was active both in Congress and in Pennsylvania matters; he served on Congressional committees to consult with General Washington outside of Boston and to negotiate with Canada. He was included, of course, in the committee to draft the Declaration of Independence. Increasingly in the months from June through October 1776, Franklin was involved with plans to secure assistance from France. Already Silas Deane had been dispatched to France to lobby the French. By September, Congress was ready to designate commissioners to France. On 27 October 1776, Franklin set sail with two grandsons for France.

Though he was nominally one of three American commissioners sent to negotiate with France, Franklin's reputation far overshadowed his colleagues' so that he came eventually to be named the sole American representative. Even while he had been in England his European reputation had been growing. The implications of his discoveries in electricity were gradually being understood and publicized; those discoveries came to be compounded with his reputation as a defender of America and prophet of thriftiness. The *Oeuvres de M. Franklin* in two volumes had been handsomely produced and lovingly edited in France by Jacques Barbeu-Dubourg, appearing in 1773. "Learned and ingenious foreigners that come to England, almost all make a point of visiting me," he had written to his son, "for my reputation is still higher abroad than here; several of the foreign ambassadors have assiduously cultivated my acquaintance, treating me as one of their *corps*, partly I believe from the desire they have from time to time of hearing something of American affairs" (P, 19:259). Franklin had been practically alone in acting as an interpreter of America to the European continent. He was an inveterate traveler while Parliament was not in session, and wherever he went he described America to the learned community with which his scientific discoveries put him in ready contact. "I do not doubt," wrote Gottfried Aschenwall, a German university professor who in 1767 drafted a long sketch about social life in America based on an interview with Franklin,"that other men of letters in this country have enjoyed the conversation of this honored man just as much as I.... Indeed I found in him not only every readiness to answer my questions, but he even expressed a special pleasure that people here were no less eager to learn something of the New World than he, who came from there, was to become acquainted with the Old" (P, 13:377).

The position of interpreter and ambassador was one Franklin had long trained for. Once he was out of England, he was free of the threats and complications he had experienced there. During the war years in America and France, Franklin was not subjected to the sort of experiences that would force him to alter his sense of his own identity. Americans and Frenchmen were eager to confirm his fame. The role of America could never be denied him by an insolent lord. In France he would be able in fact to create the role, and a lifetime of self-study had prepared him to perform magnificently in the part. There he could even set aside the role for a while, ignore industry and frugality, flirt with pretty women, and write literary trifles on the side. There were conflicts in the American embassy with Arthur Lee and John Adams, but those conflicts could do no more than annoy him. To one who had faced the wrath of English peers, the hurt feelings of American provincials like John Adams were not especially threatening. They were merely Americans, while he was *the* American.

The story of how Franklin came to be a cultural phenomenon in France from 1776 to 1785 has already been told well and does not need to be repeated here.[3] Perhaps it will be sufficient to quote again the testimony of his adversary John Adams, writing in 1811 in a general context of denunciation of what Adams saw as the insufficiency of Franklin's diplomatic activities and the shallowness of his political ideas:

> His reputation was more universal than that of Leibnitz or Newton, Frederick or Voltaire, and his character more beloved and esteemed than any or all of them. Newton had astonished perhaps forty or fifty men in Europe; for not more than that number, probably, at any one time had read him and understood him by his discoveries and demonstrations. And these being held in admiration in their respective countries as at the head of the philosophers, had spread among scientific people a mysterious wonder at the genius of this perhaps the greatest man that ever lived. But this fame was confined to men of letters. The common people knew little and cared nothing about such a recluse philosopher. Leibnitz's name was more confined still. Frederick was hated by more than half of Europe as much as Louis the Fourteenth was, and as Napoleon is. Voltaire, whose name was more universal than any of those before mentioned, was considered as a vain, profligate wit, and not much esteemed or beloved by anybody, though admired by all who knew his works. But Franklin's fame was universal. His name was familiar to government and people, to kings, courtiers, nobility, clergy, and philosophers, as well as plebeians, to such a degree that there was scarcely a peasant or citizen, a *valet de chambre*, coachman, or footman, a lady's chambermaid or a scullion in a kitchen, who was not familiar with it, and who did not consider him as a friend to human kind. When they spoke of him, they seemed to think he was to restore the golden age.[4]

Franklin seems almost to have stumbled into the opportunities for this sort of adoration. Apparently he had once opposed even the idea of American solicitation of French assistance. As he often did when great honors or opportunities presented themselves, Franklin seems to have remembered the place of Modesty in his list of virtues. In Congress he apparently had declared "that a Virgin State should preserve the Virgin Character, and not go about suitering for Alliances, but wait with decent Dignity for the Applications of others. I was overruled; perhaps for the best" (P, 23:511). America might have been a Virgin State, but Franklin himself knew something of the world. The pretense of artless naiveté is one of the most common devices of eighteenth-century fictions. Don Giovanni flirts with the peasant girl Zerlina; Lovelace poses as the noble-minded protector of Clarissa Harlowe; Valmont seduces the Présidente de Tourvel by displays of generosity.[5] All of those had some wicked scheme afoot, whereas Franklin's courtship seemed to him wholly virtuous. The reversal of sexual roles (Franklin playing the Virgin State) permitted him to act the disguised coquette. He realized soon that the French expected him to be a Philadelphia Quaker, and though in London he had kept up with the fashion in wigs and dress, he played to the French expectations.[6] To a woman who had been a friend during his English days he writes, describing himself, "Figure me in your mind as jolly as formerly, and as strong and hearty, only a few Years older, very plainly dress'd, wearing my thin grey strait Hair, that peeps out under my only Coiffure, a fine Fur Cap, which comes down my Forehead almost to my Spectacles. Think how this must appear among the Powder'd Heads of Paris" (P, 23:298). An extended dalliance was required before France would sign a treaty of Alliance on 6 February 1778.

Once he was established in Passy, then a suburb of Paris, Franklin developed a circle of local acquaintances including particularly Madame Brillon and Madame Helvetius. With these two women Franklin carried on elaborate flirtations, secure in the knowledge that Madame Brillon was too pious and innocent and Madame Helvetius too satisfied with the freedom of her widowed status to become physically entangled with him. These charming women provided him with an audience for gallant letters and literary bagatelles which he even printed up in a small private press of his own. The negotiations with Vergennes, the king's first minister, were burdensome, and his little flirtations in Passy served as a respite from public business. On the other hand John Adams felt that Franklin was rather lazy and dilatory in the conduct of the embassy's business.

I found that the Business of our Commission would never be done, unless I did it. My two Colleagues would agree in nothing. The Life of Dr. Franklin was a Scene of continual discipation. I could never obtain the favour of his Company in a Morning before Breakfast which would have been the most convenient time to read over the Letters and papers, deliberate on their contents, and decide upon the Substance of the Answers. It was late when he breakfasted, and as soon as Breakfast was over, a crowd of Carriges came to his Levee or if you like the term better to his Lodgings, with all Sorts of People; some Phylosophers, Accademicians and Economists; some of his small tribe of humble friends in the litterary Way whom he employed to translate some of his ancient Compositions, such as his Bonhomme Richard and for what I know his Polly Baker &c.; but by far the greater part were Women and Children, come to have the honour to see the great Franklin, and to have the pleasure of telling Stories about his Simplicity, his bald head and scattering strait hairs, among their Acquaintances.[7]

Adams also realized, however, that it had been Franklin who had achieved the treaty of alliance. In Adams's view Franklin was a shameless self-promoter, always using "his small tribe of humble friends in the litterary Way" to advance his own reputation. In his own mind Adams was torn between the claims of self-denial and a sense of the reputation which the worthy deserve. Adams's most perceptive biographer, Peter Shaw, has shown that "Franklin posed Adams with the deepest personal challenge of his life."[8] By use of means that Adams deplored and was unsuited to, Franklin had achieved far more than Adams.

The Franklin whom Adams saw in "continual discipation" in Paris had never enjoyed such gratification in London (and certainly not in Philadelphia). London had offered him solid comforts, but much of his work had had to be done behind the scenes—anonymous press contributions, consultations with prominent people at their pleasure, preserving the good will of his often uncomprehending and unsympathetic colonial constituents. Now Franklin was a celebrity wherever he went, meeting with Voltaire on public occasions. And he was so far away from Congress that he could operate to a great extent on his own.

Though Franklin was highly conscious of the admiration he inspired in France and though there was much work to be done as ambassador, the conflicts of his English years did not simply evaporate. He had pretty much cut off correspondence with his English friends even before the treaty with France was signed, in part because he knew that the English authorities were probably opening both his own letters and the letters of his English friends (P, 24:412; 25:64–65). The rejection of England and English life which had begun to appear in his writings as early as 1772 had now become a state of war.

And the king became a symbol for the identity which was being rejected. All of Franklin's anger at being snubbed, disregarded, and abused for years by the British ministry he now focussed on George III. (Franklin's hostility was perhaps returned in kind. George III ordered that blunt lightning rods be erected for the royal residence in defiance of Franklin's arguments against them.) Adams tells a curious story about how a mysterious letter addressed specifically to Franklin appeared in June 1778, suggesting a reconciliation between England and America through a special appeal to the king with the provision that American revolutionary leaders be made British peers.[9] Franklin composed an emphatic rejection of the whole elaborate scheme, indicating in his letter his belief that the originator of this intricate procedure of mediation was the king himself (W, 7:172). Adams comments in a passage in his autobiography written in 1806,

> The Reasons for believing that [the letter] came with the Privity of the King, were derived wholly from Dr. Franklin, who affirmed to me that there were in the Letter infallible Marks, by which he knew that it came from the King, and that it could not have come from any other without the Kings Knowledge. What these Marks were he never explained to me. I was not impertinently inquisitive, and he affected to have reasons for avoiding any more particular devellopement of the Mystery. Many other hints have been dropped by Franklin to me, of some Mysterious Intercourse or correspondence between the King and him, personally.... He often and indeed always appeared to me to have a personal Animosity and very severe Resentment against the King. In all his conversations and in all his Writings, when he could naturally and sometimes when he could not, he mentioned the King with great Asperity. He wrote certain Annotations on Judge Fosters discourse on the Legality of the Impressment of Seamen, in the Margin of the Book, and there introduced his habitual Accrimony against his Majesty.[10]

Adams was too well-bred to have been "impertinently inquisitive" about the strange letter, but his antagonism to Franklin sharpened his awareness of the senior diplomat.[11] For Franklin the virtuous young king was now a tyrant and a madman. In 1779 he wrote to Lafayette that he had no early expectation of peace "at least while the present Ministry continues, or, rather, while the present Madman has the Choice of Ministers" (W, 7:367).

As the peace negotiations were getting quietly under way in 1782, Franklin contrived a propaganda hoax, a supposed Supplement to the Boston *Independent Chronicle* to set the British at a disadvantage in the negotiations and to even a few old scores. One article reported the discovery of hundreds of American scalps on their way to England. Included with the scalps was a message from a Seneca chief to the governor of Canada. "We wish you to send these Scalps over the Water to the great King, that he may regard them and be refreshed; and that he may see our faithfulness in destroying his Enemies, and be convinced that his Presents have not been made to ungrateful people" (W, 9:440). Elsewhere in the Supplement Franklin has John Paul Jones defend himself from the charge of piracy; the letter concludes with an extended comparison between George III and Nero.

> [Nero] put to death a few of his courtiers, placemen, and his pensioners, and among the rest his *tutor*. Had George the Third done the same, and no more, his crime, though detestable, as an act of lawless power, might have been as useful to his nation, as that of Nero was hurtful to Rome; considering the different characters and merits of the sufferers. Nero indeed wished that the people of Rome had but one neck, that he might behead all of them by one stroke; but this was a simple wish. George is carrying the wish as fast as he can into execution; and, by continuing in his present course a few years longer, will have destroyed more of the British people than Nero could have found inhabitants in Rome. Hence the expression of Milton, in speaking of Charles the First, that he was "*Nerone Neronior*" is still more applicable to George the third. (W, 9:446)

The comparison continues with more of Franklin's persisting obsession with pensions, placemen, and courtiers. "Impartial history" will survive bribery and servility, however; "and this King will, therefore, stand foremost in the list of diabolical, bloody, and execrable tyrants"(W, 9:447). The "Supplement to the Boston *Independent Chronicle*" was published supposedly to reinforce the American position at the peace negotiations, but that position hardly needed reinforcing after Yorktown. Franklin was releasing the unavoidable feelings of rage he felt at a former object of love and admiration who had betrayed him.

Interestingly enough, some vestiges of the disposition to revere a king appeared while Franklin was in France, to the distress of John Adams. Adams believed that Franklin was so close to the French that he was ready to sacrifice vital American interests. "He thinks, as he tells me himself," Franklin writes in 1780 to Congress,

> that America has been too free in Expressions of Gratitude to France; for that she is more oblig'd to us than we to her; and that we should show Spirit in our Applications. I apprehend that he mistakes his Ground, and that this Court is to be treated with Decency and Delicacy. The King, a young and virtuous Prince, has, I am persuaded, a Pleasure in reflecting on the generous Benevolence of the Action in assisting an oppressed People, and proposes it as a Part of the Glory of his Reign. I think right to encrease this Pleasure by our thankful Acknowledgements, and that such an Expression of Gratitude is not only our Duty, but our Interest. (W, 8:127)

Franklin's capacity to judge character and to see the demands of self-interest was normally excellent, but when he dealt with authority figures he remained vulnerable to the same frustration he had experienced with Governor Keith—he assumed that the authority figure would act out of a spirit of disinterested benevolence. In the last months of his life, as the first reports of the French Revolution were reaching Philadelphia, Franklin would be disturbed. "The Troubles you have had in Paris have afflicted me a great deal," he would write to his old friend Le Veillard, "I hope by this Time they are over, and everything settled as it should be, to the Advantage both of the King and Nation" (W, 10:70).

Undoubtedly Franklin's antipathy to George III was exacerbated by his son William's allegiance to the king. After escaping from the custody of the American rebels, William Franklin had gone on to head the Associated Loyalists in New York, taking the furthest possible position in opposition to his father.

During the peace negotiation of 1782, Franklin was implacably opposed to satisfying the damage claims of American loyalists, more so than either Adams or John Jay, his fellow negotiators. In the meantime William had taken refuge in England. Eventually he wrote to his father in 1784 suing for peace in the family after the victory of the United States.

In the return letter his father's habitual self-control was not sufficient to overcome nine years of accumulated anger.

> I received your Letter of the 22d past, and am glad to find that
> you desire to revive the affectionate Intercourse, that formerly
> existed between us. It will be very agreable to me; indeed noth-
> ing has ever hurt me so much and affected me with such keen
> Sensations, as to find myself deserted in my old Age by my
> only Son; and not only deserted, but to find him taking up
> Arms against me, in a Cause wherein my good Fame, Fortune
> and Life were all at Stake. (W, 9:252)

A long life of avoiding harsh and dogmatic statements, and a literary
style that disarms hostility could not suppress Franklin's feelings; he
had been deserted by the son he loved. He gestures unconvincingly at
explaining or excusing, but his concessions only stir him to greater bit-
terness:

> You conceived, you say, that your Duty to your King and Re-
> gard for your Country requir'd this. I ought not to blame you
> for differing in Sentiment with me in Public Affairs. We are
> Men, all subject to Errors. Our Opinions are not in our own
> Power; they are form'd and govern'd much by Circumstances,
> that are often as inexplicable as they are irresistible. Your Situ-
> ation was such that few would have censured your remaining
> Neuter, *tho' there are Natural Duties which precede political
> ones, and cannot be extinguish'd by them.*
>   This is a disagreable Subject. I drop it. And we will endeav-
> our, as you propose mutually to forget what has happened re-
> lating to it, as well as we can. (W, 9:252)

Choked with anger, he breaks off. The rest of the letter avoids public
matters. No private act of disobedience could ever have provoked the
father so deeply, because his public commitments carried all the force
of his whole identity. In his final will, Franklin left his son only the
books and papers already in his possession and some worthless property in Nova Scotia. "The part he acted against me in the late war,
which is of public notoriety, will account for my leaving him no more
of an estate he endeavoured to deprive me of" (W, 10:494). The item regarding his son comes first in the will. It was a calculated and bitter rebuke.

14 Final Return to America

B y the time he was relieved as ambassador by Thomas Jefferson, Franklin was seventy-nine and in poor health. For years he had suffered from gout and kidney stones, brought on, probably, by hyperuricemia. He no longer used his carriage for social occasions, though society continued to come to him. To one friend he wrote wishing that he had a balloon such as the Montgolfier brothers were currently experimenting with so he could get around without pain (W, 9:572–73). He had toyed with the idea of remaining in France; he proposed marriage to Madame Helvetius in one of his bagatelles. In a letter he writes from Le Havre just before sailing, he stresses that he is not sure of being happy in America, but he has to go ("Je ne suis sur d'etre heureux in Amerique; mais il faut que je m'y rende" (W 9:346). For the fourth time in his life he set sail for Philadelphia from Europe.

By the time he left France many of his old friends on both continents were dead. In the last letter he had received from his old London landlady Margaret Stevenson, he wrote that she had died half a year after writing the letter. "This good Woman my dear Friend died the first of January following. She was about my age." He reflected somberly that the previous year had carried away many of his closest friends in England: ". . . this has begun to take away the rest and strikes the hardest. Thus the ties I had to that country and indeed to the World in general are loosen'd one by one and I shall soon have no Attachment left to make me unwilling to follow."[1] Franklin was not one, however, to dwell on such depressing realizations. He had to get back to America, where he knew there was still important work for him to do which he had already begun.[2]

He had been a citizen of the world in France, enjoying there a fame and acceptance that utterly eclipsed that of his highborn adversaries in England. At times he could echo the cosmopolitan sentiments of the Enlightenment. "God grant that not only the Love of Liberty, but a thorough Knowledge of the Rights of Man, may pervade all the Nations of the Earth," he would write to David Hartley in 1789, "so that a Philosopher may set his Foot anywhere on its Surface and say, 'This is my Country' " (W, 10:72). But he himself was finally an American and a believer in the providential destiny of his own country. His cosmopolitan fame paradoxically depended upon his status as an American. He had represented in Europe the promise of a new nation, a rugged, agrarian, and uncultured place that had nevertheless advanced human freedom beyond anything known before. What remained for him was to shape the newly created American self in the right image.

The 1780s was a decade of uncertainty about American political and cultural life.[3] The European diplomats who had negotiated the peace ending the war anticipated that this client state of France would soon collapse of inner conflicts, leaving them to redivide the pieces. [4] Republics were notoriously unstable. Classical republican political theory dictated that citizens quite different from those of any state in previous history would be needed to hold the country together. "The eighteenth-century mind," writes Gordon Wood, "was thoroughly convinced that a popularly based government 'cannot be supported without *Virtue*' "[5]

The leaders of the successful Revolution now had to create a virtuous foundation for the new country. Most of them were anxious about the people who now were to govern themselves without any resistance from royal appointees. In *Federalist 10* Madison would warn that factiousness was built into man's nature. "As long as the connection subsists between his reason and his self-love, his opinions and his passions will have a reciprocal influence on each other; and the former will be objects to which the latter will attach themselves."[6] The solution to these problems of human nature, in the view of most American leaders, was a system of carefully adjusted constitutional restraints on political behavior: frequent elections, short terms of office, prescribed powers, and so forth. In his old age John Adams would read through the plays of Shakespeare and comment only "that the balance of powers had been lacking in [Shakespeare's] time."[7] The obtuseness of such a comment is only explainable by the range of Adams's intellectual preoccupations.

Franklin, however, differed from his fellow Revolutionary leaders about the means of establishing a virtuous nation. Despite all the time he had spent in assemblies, congresses, and conventions, he had less faith than the others in the final efficacy of constitutional arrangements. He was more concerned about the methods of upbringing, the disposition to accommodate to others, and the awareness of genuine motivation regarding political questions. It mattered less to him how many houses a legislature should include than what sort of person should sit in them. His preoccupations, in the largest sense, were literary—character, motivation, social behavior.

He was less worried than other revolutionary leaders about contemporary signs of American anarchy. A long career of publicly justifying the Americans at an ocean's distance from them had prepared him to discount negative symptoms. By the time he returned to Philadelphia, his health prevented extensive overland travel. He could no longer see much of the country at first hand, so he was all the more dependent upon his memories and his own projections to provide a sense of America.

He had read in English newspapers reports of American divisiveness, and he contemptuously denounced them. He felt a personal stake in the harmony and prosperity of America. Writing to David Hartley after arriving back in Philadelphia, he denied the reports of dissatisfaction and disunion. "As to the contentment of the inhabitants with the change of government, methinks a stronger proof cannot be desired, than what they have given in my reception. You know the part I had in that change, and you see in the papers the addresses from all ranks with which your friend was welcomed home" (W, 9:473). Naturally Franklin believed that an enthusiastic welcome for him meant that the country was healthy. As for faction, he was inclined to think it might be good. "It is true, that in some of the States there are Parties and Discords; but let us look back, and ask if we were ever without them? Such will exist wherever there is Liberty; and perhaps they help to preserve it. By the Collision of different Sentiments, Sparks of Truth are struck out, and political Light is obtained. The different Factions, which at present divide us, aim all at the Publick Good; the Differences are only about the various Modes of promoting it" (W, 10:120).

While he was still in France, the fresh prestige of the newly independent United States had attracted many inquiries about immigration. To some of these inquirers he wrote back recommending Hector St. John de Crevecoeur's recently published *Letters From an American Farmer*. For the same purpose he wrote *Information to Those Who Would Remove to America*. Coming from one who had always lived in cities,

Franklin's characterization of American society in this publication, and in the other writings of his last period, may seem strange. America, he says, is fundamentally and properly agrarian. It affords no patrons of the arts, no profitable offices to be filled, and no respect for eminent birth. Consequently there can be little demand for "Strangers, possessing Talents in the Belles-Lettres, fine Arts, &c." (W, 8:603). For Franklin, the sculptor, artist, and architect could only flourish in a condition of dependence upon leisure and wealth, so he willingly consigned them to Europe. Twenty years earlier, Franklin had held out hope for the flourishing of arts in America, duplicating their status in England. Now he was ready to dispense with such amenities. The essay offers a tough-minded view of life in America. "The Husbandman is in honor there, and even the Mechanic, because their Employments are useful. The People have a saying, that God Almighty is himself a Mechanic, the greatest in the Univers; and he is respected and admired more for the Variety, Ingenuity, and Utility of his Handyworks, than for the Antiquity of his Family" (W, 8:606).

If he was less concerned about faction than his colleagues were, Franklin was quite determined that the distinctive features of English society he remembered from his disastrous stay there should not get a foothold in America. He was particularly attached to one provision in the Pennsylvania state constitution: the prohibition of payment to elected or high appointed public officials. The English system of bribery and patronage had destroyed any possibility for disinterested public service, he felt. However pragmatic he may have been, he never really relinquished the ideal of the United Party for Virtue that he had envisioned as a young man.

He also worked to frustrate what he saw as efforts to establish any sort of hereditary honors in the new American republic. After the Revolution, retired officers of Washington's army formed the Society of the Cincinnati, membership of which in the future would be hereditary. In its first few years the Society seemed likely to exert considerable influence on American social and political life. Hearing in France of its establishment, Franklin wrote his daughter in disapproval. Honor, he maintained, is "in its Nature a *personal* Thing, and incommunicable to any but those who had some Share in obtaining it" (W, 9:162). Properly speaking, honors could ascend to the parents—so that Josiah Franklin, for example, might be distinguished by having such a son—but they could never descend to children.[8] There was thus no truly important thing that William Franklin could ever have inherited from his father. The concept of hereditary distinction he subjected to a mathematical

Ben Franklin

reductio ad absurdum which showed how little of the original Revolutionary officer's blood could be left to any descendant after a few generations.

A variety of tactics, both serious and comic, were brought into play to undercut the Society's aristocratic pretensions. Franklin lightly ridiculed the ribbons, badges, and emblems of the Cincinnati, all of which he called a childish affectation borrowed from the French. Reviewing the emblems, he digresses about the American eagle, which looks like a turkey in the Society's medal.

> For my own part, I wish the Bald Eagle had not been chosen as the Representative of our Country; he is a Bird of bad moral Character; he does not get his living honestly; you may have seen him perch'd on some dead Tree, near the River where, too lazy to fish for himself, he watches the Labour of the Fishing-Hawk; and, when that diligent Bird has at length taken a Fish, and is bearing it to his Nest for the support of his Mate and young ones, the Bald Eagle pursues him, and takes it from him. (*W*, 9:166)

Franklin rambles on about the bald eagle's moral failings, which include cowardice as well as laziness. Indeed the turkey would not make a bad symbol for America. "For in Truth, the Turk'y is in comparison a much more respectable Bird, and withal a true original Native of America. . . . He is, [though a little vain and silly, it is true, but not the worse emblem for that,] a Bird of Courage, and would not hesitate to attack a Grenadier of the British Guards, who should presume to invade his Farmyard with a red Coat on" (*W*, 9:167).

Behind the sly garrulousness of Franklin's digression on symbolic birds is a serious attempt to alter the Americans' perception of their relation to the nation. The perception he encourages is personal and critical rather than communal and ritualistic. Something more basic than even the attack on heredity is involved in this debate over eagles and turkeys. The turkey's peculiar qualities—its barnyard ordinariness, its vanity and silliness, its readiness to fight back when its vital space is encroached upon—those qualities are Franklin's own credentials as an American. He never sought the hieratic poses before posterity of his colleagues Adams, Jefferson, and Washington; the immortality he sought was not the static finality of the marble bust. He was not indifferent to posterity in this pose as the talkative and comical old man. He knew that his letter would be published in America, and he even took steps to have it published in France. (Abbé Morellet, his translator, persuaded him that its arguments against hereditary nobility would be officially disapproved of.[9])

Much of Franklin's late writing is colored by the particular humor of this encomium to the turkey. What distinguishes this humor is a sense of detachment from his own understood limitations. The inevitable disparity between intentions and actions is now a subject of amusement rather than frustration. As he approached his eighties, he wrote to an elderly friend about how often he had sung the refrain to a drinking song about the good life.

> May I govern my Passions with an absolute sway,
> Grow wiser and better as my Strength wears away,
> Without Gout or Stone, by a gentle Decay.
>
> (W, 9:333)

The song expresses Franklin's continuing good intentions from as far back as the project of arriving at moral perfection. "But what signifies our Wishing? Things happen after all, as they will happen. I have sung that *wishing Song* a thousand times, when I was young, and now find, at Fourscore, that the three Contraries have befallen me, being subject to the Gout and the Stone and not being yet Master of all my Passions" (W, 9:333). Mastering his own passions had once been a means to independence, an assertion of ego control over the intransigent resistance of the body. In the end, though, he could accept as inevitable his own slothfulness, his taste for women and good food, and his own abiding preoccupation with himself.

Franklin's disposition to accept himself as he was, however unsatisfactory, led him toward different sources for comparison by which to describe and judge American society. Earlier, through his projects in Philadelphia, he had worked to bring about a complex and sophisticated urban society, complete with college, hospital, fire protection, clean streets, and so on. This had even an urban ideal, to which he graduated toward the imperial conceptions of his English period. His sense of a desirable social life had been posited upon expansion, improvement, and change.

But his psychological return to America implied for him an acceptance of his country, and ultimately of human nature, as it was. He never really abandoned his belief in the value of continual adjustment and experimentation, but his attitude toward such changes shifted. To his old friend Jonathan Shipley he wrote, "We are, I think, in the right Road of Improvement, for we are making Experiments. I do not oppose all that seem wrong, for the Multitude are more effectually set right by Experience, than kept from going wrong by Reasoning with them. And I think we are daily more and more enlightened; so that I have no doubt of our obtaining in a few Years as much public Felicity, as good Government is capable of affording" (W, 9:489). A chill can perhaps be felt behind this last line. Most of human happiness, it is implied, lies beyond the powers of governments to bring about. Even such perfectibility as he had tried to achieve in his own life had been greatly inadequate. "Human Felicity is produc'd not so much by great Pieces of good Fortune that seldom happen, as by little Advantages that occur every Day," he wrote around the same time in his *Autobiography* (A, 207). As for government, expediency and chance are likely to produce as good results as careful and rational calculation. "The Best public Measures are therefore seldom *adopted from previous Wisdom*, but *forc'd by the Occasion*" (A, 212).

Despite all his activity for public improvement, his attitude toward human nature was not especially flattering. "Men I find to be a Sort of Beings very badly constructed," he wrote to Joseph Priestley in 1782,

> as they are generally more easily provok'd than reconciled, more disposed to do Mischief to each other than to make Reparation, much more easily deceiv'd than undeceiv'd, and having more Pride and even Pleasure in killing than in begetting one another; for without a Blush they assemble in great armies at NoonDay to destroy, and when they have kill'd as many as they can, they exaggerate the Number to augment the fancied Glory; but they creep into Corners, or cover themselves with the Darkness of night, when they mean to beget, as being asham'd of a virtuous Action. A virtuous Action it would be, and a vicious one the killing of them, if the Species were really worth producing or preserving; but of this I begin to doubt. (W, 8:451–52)

In part Franklin was indulging in one of the most common of Enlightenment rhetorical exercises, the denunciation of the entire human species.[10] There is a kind of Voltairean irony in the juxtaposition of war and sex; the sentiments expressed seem to come out of no immediate and personal provocation, beyond Franklin's occasional sense of war-weariness. He was often given to echoing the commonplace notions of his time, not insincerely but also not freshly. Here, however, he seems freed from political and cultural responsibilities; to his English scientist friend he could set aside his allegiance to Americans and express his underlying sense of detachment from human beings in general. It is not merely men in the mob or men in ill-governed societies whom he disdains; his detachment is more radical than that sustained by most of the Founding Fathers. In his weariness with humanity he expresses something almost akin to a religious perception, like Augustine's sense of alienation from human communities.

Yet even in this profound emotional detachment from others, Franklin saw himself as an American. Numerous passages in the last major sections of the *Autobiography* take a cool view of mankind. About Whitefield's preaching during the Great Awakening he remarks, "it was matter of Speculation to me who was one of the Number, to observe the extraordinary Influence of his Oratory on his Hearers, and how much they admir'd & respected him, nothwithstanding his common Abuse of them, by assuring them they were naturally *half Beasts and half Devils*" (A, 175). Franklin's position in this case, as the silently ironic observer in the midst of a crowd of differently disposed people, recurred throughout his life. But passages such as this appear in the midst of a multitude of practical suggestions for the good of individuals and the country as a whole. The nation is not formed as a community of intimates. It is clear from the *Information to Those Who Would Remove to America* that America is a country where everyone looks out for himself.

By the 1780s Franklin had come so far from the urban and imperial ideals of America that he could hold up the Indians as a society in many ways preferable to the supposedly civilized inhabitants. "Savages we call them, because their Manners differ from ours, which we think the Perfection of Civility; they think the same of theirs," (W, 10:97) he writes at the beginning of his *Remarks Concerning the Savages of North America*. Civility is Franklin's real subject; the stories he tells of Indian civility reveal the rudeness and high-handedness of the whites. A Swedish missionary goes among the Susquehannah Indians and tells them the Genesis story of creation; an Indian spokesman in turn tells him their own account, which he angrily dismisses as mere fables. "The Indian, offended, reply'd 'My Brother, it seems, your Friends have not done you Justice in your Education; they have not well instructed you in the Rules of common Civility. You saw that we, who understand and practise those Rules, believ'd all your stories; why do you refuse to believe ours?"(W, 10:101). Franklin's Indians, like Montesquieu's Persians, are outsiders who perceive the basic character of a society better than the insiders do. The last anecdote tells of the Mohawk Canassatego, who had recently visited Albany to sell furs and been denied a fair price by a conspiracy of Dutch traders. The price goes down, Canassatego has noticed, after the traders had all gathered in a meeting where a man in black had talked to them of *Good Things*; he concludes that the meetings "are only to contrive the *Cheating of Indians in the Price of Beaver*" (W, 10:104). Franklin's Indian sees through the pretense of worship and realizes that religion serves primarily to sharpen the white people's acquisitive instincts. Like the letter on the Cincinnati, the *Remarks Concerning the Savages of North America* was intended to prod Franklin's fellow Americans into a more detached perspective on their own lives. In the last years of his life as never before Franklin turned to satires directed at his own countrymen: in the "Account of the Supremest Court of Judicature in Pennsylvania, Viz the Court of the Press" he noted the growing irresponsibility of American newspapers; in another letter to the press in 1790 published only days before his death he parodied the defense of slavery of a Georgia Senator by describing a bogus historical incident in which the roles of whites and blacks had been reversed (W, 10:36–41; 86–91). The public humor of his last years was no longer the bland and simpering note he had employed earlier in *Poor Richard* or the *Pennsylvania Gazette*. Secure in his reputation, he felt at last free to say what he was thinking.

He relaxed some of his former attitudes on industry and frugality. In *The Way to Wealth* luxury had been a dangerous seduction; it was not to be hoped for by the great majority of his countrymen if they valued their own prosperity. Luxury was also a classic danger to the life of republics; Jefferson speaks of trade, manufactures, and luxuries as a cancer that must be surgically removed.[11] For the late Franklin luxury could have more than one connotation: it could mean either dissipation and dependence or the reward for hard work. The appearance of luxury in his own household in the form of a china bowl and a silver spoon had signaled his attainment of economic success. In the largest view luxury could not be dangerous in America, he wrote to Benjamin Vaughan in 1784. Bringing the American wilderness under cultivation would keep Americans busy for the imaginable future; the American seaport towns are not the basis of the nation's strength or prosperity. History indicates that civilization has developed in Europe despite wars, luxuries, and the absence of concerted design, simply because "upon the whole, the Quantity of Industry and Prudence among Mankind exceeds the Quantity of Idleness and Folly" (W, 9:247). Others might fret over the theoretical dangers of luxury; Franklin could never confine himself within any theoretical system at the expense of his own observations or his recollected personal experience.

Franklin's differences from the generation of American leaders in the 1770s and 1780s appeared most prominently in the Constitutional

Convention of 1787. Franklin was naturally asked to serve as a Pennsylvania delegate; he had been the dominant figure in that state's political life since before most delegates were born, and he continued to serve as the President of Pennsylvania's Supreme Executive Council. But even his long association with Pennsylvania left him an ambiguous figure in the eyes of many of the other delegates. Pennsylvania's state constitution, with which—rightly or wrongly—he was associated, had a unicameral legislature, thus not providing the sort of balanced representation that most of his colleagues believed in.[12] William Pierce of Georgia, in drawing up sketches of the delegates, notes about Franklin, of course, that he was, "the greatest phylosopher of the present age.... But what claim he has to the politician, posterity must determine. It is certain that he does not shine much in public Council,—he is no Speaker, nor does he seem to let politics engage his attention. He is, however, a most extraordinary Man, and tells a story in a style more engaging than anything I have ever heard....He is 82 years old, and possesses an activity of mind equal to a youth of 25 years of age."[13]

Franklin was honored in the Convention but little heeded. Nearly all his colleagues were lawyers, with the lawyer's concern for cautious consideration of all imaginable outcomes. They were, moreover, a peculiarly pragmatic and unimaginative group; there were no orators or professional revolutionaries like John or Samuel Adams or Thomas Jefferson. Early in the convention, when the subject of salaries for executive officers in the new government was being discussed, Franklin offered one of his infrequent contributions. His English experience had left him suspicious of paid public officials, so he composed a speech proposing that federal officials receive no pay at all. "He said," noted James Madison in his journal of the proceedings, "that being very sensible of the effect of age on his memory, he had been unwilling to trust to that for the observations which seemed to support his motion, and had reduced them to writing."[14] James Wilson, his Pennsylvania colleague, volunteered to read the speech for him. By this time Franklin was eighty-one and rather feeble, hardly fit for delivering the speech himself, much less contributing actively to the movement of the debate. His carefully prepared speeches, however, fell on ears conditioned to the greater immediate impact of *extempore* presentation. When Wilson finished reading his motions, there was no rush to discuss the proposal, which the delegates clearly saw as preposterous. Alexander Hamilton politely seconded it, "with the view he said merely of bringing up so respectable a proposition before the Committee, and which was besides enforced by arguments that had a certain degree of weight."[15] The motion was quickly postponed, to get it out of the way.

"It was treated with great respect," Madison observed, "but rather for the author of it, than from any apparent conviction of it is expediency or practicability."[16]

Franklin was not profoundly concerned about the constitutional niceties the others were debating. He was in favor of compromise and mutual harmony whatever the issue in question. "When a broad table is to be made, and the edges of planks do not fit," he remarked, "the artist takes a little from both and makes a good joint. In like manner here both sides must part with some of their demands in order that they may join in some accommodating proposition."[17] The homely similitude implicitly undercuts the final importance of constitutional structures. Franklin was more of a fix-it man than an architect at the Convention, ready to adapt to arrangements imposed by circumstance. Arguing on one occasion for the lower house's power of initiating money bills, he fell back on the common sense notion that the more popularly elected house would listen more closely to the general public. "As to the danger or difficulty that might arise from the negative in the 2d. [house] where the people wd. not be proportionally represented, it might easily be got over by declaring that there should be no such Negative: or if that will not do, by declaring that there shall be no such branch at all."[18] No such branch at all! Franklin was casually admitting indifference to structural questions about which his colleagues had debated for weeks.

On the last day of the Convention's deliberations, Franklin spoke up to urge that all the delegates sign the resulting document. He himself, he said, had some reservations, but he had changed his mind often in the past.

> It is therefore that, the older I grow, the more apt I am to doubt my own judgment of others. Most men, indeed, as well as most sects in religion, think themselves in possession of all truth, and that wherever others differ from them, it is so far error. . . . But, though many private Persons think almost as highly of their own infallibility as of that of their Sect, few express it so naturally as a certain French Lady, who, in a little dispute with her sister, said 'But I meet with nobody but myself that is always in the right.' 'Je ne trouve que moi qui aie toujours raison.' (W, 9:607)

Others in the convention might have cited Montesquieu or Thucydides; Franklin, as always intrigued by vanity, quoted the "certain French lady," a reminder also to the delegates of his own cosmopolitan experience. Hamilton also urged all to sign, and when he later drafted the first number of the *Federalist*, he described the convention's work as one of the triumphs of human reason. "It has been frequently remarked that it seems to have been reserved to the people of this country, by their conduct and example, to decide the important question, whether societies of men are really capable or not of establishing good government from reflection and choice, or whether they are forever destined to depend for their political constitutions on accident and force."[19] Franklin's view of the achievement of the convention, expressed in his last speech, was more modest and skeptical.

> I doubt... whether any other Convention we can obtain, may be able to make a better constitution; for, when you assemble a number of men, to have the advantage of their joint wisdom, you inevitably assemble with those men all their prejudices, their passions, their errors of opinion, their local interests, and their selfish views. From such an assembly can a *perfect* production be expected? It therefore astonishes me, Sir, to find this system approaching so near to perfection as it does; and I think it will astonish our enemies, who are waiting with confidence to hear, that our councils are confounded like those of the builders of Babel, and that our States are on the point of separation, only to meet hereafter for the purpose of cutting one another's throats. Thus I consent, Sir, to this Constitution, because I expect no better, and because I am not sure that it is not the best. (*W*, 9:608)

The Constitution had been like Franklin's own "bold and arduous Project of achieving moral Perfection," a noble enterprise which had produced something flawed, but about as good as any human contrivance can be. The important point for Franklin was that something at least had emerged; the English skeptics about America would be confounded.

Earlier in the convention Franklin had used the same illustration about the builders of Babel. When the delegates seemed hopelessly snarled in disagreement over the question of representation by state or by population, Franklin had moved that prayers "imploring the Assistance of Heaven and its Blessing on our Deliberations" be held every morning in the Convention.[20] Franklin, whose religious position was ambiguous at the time in the eyes of his contemporaries, made a fervent plea for a consciousness of divine guidance. Their prayers had been answered in their contest with England; divine aid would now be necessary if the delegates were to control faction and local interests, the confounding of wills that brought an end to the town of Babel. "I have lived, Sir, a long time; and the longer I live, the more convincing proofs I see of this Truth, *that GOD governs in the affairs of Men*."[21] Pious Roger Sherman of Connecticut seconded the motion. Hamilton tactfully suggested that it was a little late to start praying at this point and that a sudden beginning would look bad outside the convention. (It was also mentioned that the Convention had no funds to pay a minister.) "After several unsuccessful attempts for silently postponing the matter by adjourng [sic]," Madison recorded in his journal, "the adjournment was at length carried, without any vote on the motion." [22]

Here the difference between Franklin and his colleagues was most striking. For him the real assurance of the nation's preserved integrity was based not on law but on destiny. More and more in his later years Franklin fell back on the inherited rhetoric of his childhood, the Puritan rhetoric of a national covenant. Even at this time he was not formally religious. When his old friend Ezra Stiles wrote inquiring about his religious convictions, he wrote back tactfully suggesting his doubts about the divinity of Christ, praising Christianity as an ethical system, and setting down again the all-purpose creed. But somehow he insisted on believing in the existence of a God who had the United States under his special care. When he turned later to defend the Constitution in a letter to the *Pennsylvania Gazette*, he spun out an elaborate typological argument for ratification based on the parallels between the Constitution and the Ten Commandments. According to these parallels, there were among the thirteen tribes of Americans many who were still secretly loyal to the land that had enslaved them (England–Egypt). The dissident followers of Corah, the anti-federalists, accused Moses and Aaron of conspiring against their liberties and of embezzling public funds. The article bristles with footnotes to passages in Numbers and Exodus. Franklin's use of typology is not Cotton Mather's. He finds the parallels suggestive rather than divinely ordained, and the article sounds somewhat like Dryden's *Absalom and Achitophel*, another playful adaptation of scripture to contemporary political events. But the issues were urgent to Franklin. He concludes by denying that he thinks the Constitution divinely inspired but affirming that his faith in the providential government of the world had taught him that matters of such importance to the nation were subject to the direction of "that omnipotent, omnipresent, and beneficent Ruler, in whom all inferior Spirits live, and move, and have their Being" (*W*, 9:703).

Franklin used the language of traditional belief because that language was associated with the great rhetoric of promise. For despite his readiness to prod and cajole his countrymen, he was at the end content with America. Unlike most other national leaders during the 1780s, he believed the national promise had been fulfilled in his own times. Back when the war was still going on in America he had prophesied the nation's imminent recovery and prosperity in a letter to Washington.

> I must soon quit the Scene, but you may live to see our Country flourish, as it will amazingly and rapidly after the War is over. Like a Field of young Indian Corn, which long Fair weather and Sunshine had enfeebled and discolored, and which in that weak State, by a Thunder Gust, of violent Wind, Hail, and Rain, seem'd to be threaten'd with absolute Destruction; yet the Storm being past, it recovers fresh Verdure, shoots up with double Vigour, and delights the Eye, not of its Owner only, but of every observing Traveller. (W, 8:29)

Franklin's image of the field of corn suggests that the Revolution was invigorating for Americans, just as it had reinvigorated and rescued him from the delusion of imperial dependency. American is likened to Indian corn, a native product; the final emphasis is on the aesthetic recovery, the delight to the eye, not just to its American owners but to the observing world. Franklin did not quit the scene so soon as he thought—for the last thirty years of his life he thought of himself recurrently as an old man in his last days. In the post war years he spoke up for the essential soundness of his country as it was.

His countrymen in this period were inclined to consider him a sort of tutelary figure, a national institution in a country lacking in institutions. "In physics we have produced a Franklin, than whom no one of the present age has made more important discoveries, nor has enriched philosophy with more, or more ingenious solutions of the phaenomena of nature," wrote Jefferson in his *Notes on the State of Virginia*, defending the country against the charge of producing no great men.[23] Franklin graciously acceded to this idolization. His letters, articles, and speeches of this period reveal an assured grace and good humor; in no other period of his life had he seemed so comfortable with his achieved identity.

Franklin achieved in these last years of his life the psychological condition that Erik H. Erikson refers to as "ego integrity." Describing that state of mind Erikson says,

It is the acceptance of one's one and only life cycle as something that had to be and that, by necessity, permitted of no substitutions; it thus means a new, a different love of one's parents. . . . Although aware of the relativity of all the various life styles which have given meaning to human striving, the possessor of integrity is ready to defend the dignity of his own life style against all physical and economic threats. For he knows that an individual life is the accidental coincidence of but one life cycle with but one segment of history; and that for him all human integrity stands or falls with the one style of integrity of which he partakes. [24]

Erikson characterizes the other possible response to old age as despair, the surrender to a mass of small annoyances while feeling frustrated that time is running out. Franklin had more than small annoyances to bother him in his last years. His letters indicate that for much of the last two years of his life he was in so much pain from gout and the stone that he could do very little.

Yet in those years he still had thoughts to share with the public. He observed, for example, what had happened to the Philadelphia Academy since he had helped to found it and wrote a sharply worded criticism of its divergence from first purposes (W, 10:9–32).

And it was near the end of his life that he finally returned to writing his *Autobiography*. Though he had resumed writing it in France and looked forward there to continuing when he had access to his papers in Philadelphia, he had delayed writing it for several years, despite his intentions. In 1786 he writes, "having been persuaded by my Friends, Messrs. Benjᵃ Vaughan, M. Le Veillard, Mr. James of this Place, and some others, that such a *Life*, witten by myself, may be useful to the rising Generation, I have made some Progress in it, and hope to finish it this Winter" (W, 9:550–51). However, only after he was finally retired from public office in 1788 did he start writing the third section of the work. By late October 1788 he could write to the duc de La Rochefoucauld that he had carried the narrative to his fiftieth year. "What is to follow will be more important Transactions: But it seems to me that what is done will be of more general Use to young Readers; as exemplifying strongly the Effects of prudent and imprudent Conduct in the Life of Business" (W, 9:665). Writing at the same time to Benjamin Vaughan, he says,

> To shorten the work, as well as for other reasons, I omit all
> facts and transactions, that may not have a tendency to benefit
> the young reader, by showing him from my example, and my
> success in emerging from poverty, and acquiring some degree
> of wealth, power, and reputation, the advantages of certain
> modes of conduct which I observed, and of avoiding the errors
> which were prejudicial to me. If a writer can judge properly of
> his own work, I fancy, on reading over what is already done,
> that the book will be found entertaining, interesting, and use-
> ful, more so than I expected when I began it. (W, 9:675–76)

He talks about finishing the *Autobiography* in the coming winter, then
sending a copy to Vaughan for suggested revisions. Though he might in
other contexts describe himself as in his last days, when it came to put-
ting his life in its final draft, he could imagine a more indefinite period
of composition and revision. In the letters to La Rochefoucauld and
Vaughan he also refers without much concern to the recent disputes
about the ratification of the Constitution. "The first Congress will
probably mend the principal ones, & future Congresses the rest.... We
are making Experiments in Politicks; what Knowledge we shall gain by
them will be more certain, tho' perhaps we may hazard too much in
that Mode of acquiring it" (W, 9:666).

Of course he did not finish the *Autobiography*, and in fact reached
only a little farther in time than the point he reports in October 1788, a
year and a half before his death. His life had been a long experiment,
like his country's experiments in politics. Frequently in the letters of
his last years he expressed the wish to live longer, even hundreds of
years more. He wanted to see the future developments in technology
which he was sure would come. He had no further plans for his own
involvement, though. He would be an onlooker, a spectator.

One of his final descriptions of his native county, written obviously
as a sort of valedictory, was *The Internal State of America*. The little essay has been generally neglected, but it summarizes well his final attitudes toward America. It appeared for the first time in the last
collection of writings over which he had any sort of control, along with
the *Advice to those Who Would Remove to America*, the *Remarks Concerning the Savages of North America*, and a few other pieces. [25] He began by evoking the severity of life in the first Puritan settlements and
the tradition of the jeremiad. "Being piously dispos'd, they sought Relief from Heaven, by laying their Wants and Distresses before the Lord,
in frequent set Days of fasting and Prayer. Constant Meditation and
Discourse on these Subjects kept their Minds gloomy and discon-

tented; and, like the Children of Israel, there were many dispos'd to that Egypt, which Persecution had induc'd them to abandon" (W, 10:116). At length, however, a sensible farmer in the assembly proposed that things were not so bad and were getting gradually better: the land was productive, the waters were full of fish, and they enjoyed civil and religious liberty. They should rather give thanks than fast. If the jeremiad called upon the people to rededicate themselves to an exacting national calling, Franklin was proposing instead an attitude of acceptance.

"The great Business of the Continent is Agriculture" (W, 10:117), he states. So it would always be. The scarcity of labor would mean that labor would always be highly paid, so exploitative manufacturers could never take hold. There were neither the wealthy nor the abject, half-starved poor of Europe; a "happy Mediocrity... generally prevails throughout these States" (W, 10:120). ("Mediocrity" was of course not a pejorative term.) Some Americans worried over the temptations of faction and luxury; Franklin asserts that the spirit of political liberty and the dominant activity of agriculture would keep these in check. If Americans kept in mind the land and oceans from whence their wealth came, they would see their present situation in right proportion. "We are Sons of the Earth and Seas, and, like Antaeus, if, in wrestling with Hercules, we now and then receive a Fall, the Touch of our Parents will communicate to us fresh Strength and Ability to renew the contest. Be quiet and thankful" (W, 10:122).

Franklin wrote his *Autobiography* to record how far he had come from his own origins, but in the end he returned home and asserted the continuity of his life with the simple, provincial people he had grown up among. If the nation turned out not to be the static and separate place he had at last imagined, if his own image was later enlisted to serve the cause of expansion, change, and empire, we would do well to remember how different his last vision of America really was.

Notes

Preface

1. For examples of such specialized studies, see I. Bernard Cohen, *Franklin and Newton* (Philadelphia: American Philosophical Society, 1956); Lewis J. Carey, *Franklin's Economic Views* (New York: Doubleday, 1928); Kemp Malone, "Benjamin Franklin on Spelling Reform," *American Speech*, 1 (1925), 96–100; Gerald Stourzh, *Benjamin Franklin and American Foreign Policy* (Chicago: University of Chicago Press, 1965); Paul W. Connor, *Poor Richard's Politicks: Benjamin Franklin and His New American Order* (New York: Oxford University Press, 1965); Alfred O. Aldridge, *Benjamin Franklin and Nature's God* (Durham, N.C.: Duke University Press, 1967); Lawrence D. Wroth, "Benjamin Franklin: The Printer at Work," *Journal of the Franklin Institute*, 239 (1942), 105–32.

2. See Richard Bushman, "On the Uses of Psychology: Conflict and Conciliation in Benjamin Franklin," *History and Theory*, 5(1966), 225–40; John F. Lynen, *The Design of the Present: Essays on Time and Form in American Literature* (New Haven: Yale University Press, 1969), 123–52; David Levin, "The Autobiography of Benjamin Franklin: The Puritan Experimenter in Life and Art," *Yale Review*, 53 (1964), 258–75; James M. Cox, "Autobiography and America," *Virginia Quarterly Review*, 47(1971), 252–77.

3. Leo Braudy, *Narrative Form in History and Fiction* (Princeton: Princeton University Press, 1970) and *The Frenzy of the Renown* (New York: Oxford University Press, 1986); Peter Shaw, *The Character of John Adams* (Chapel Hill: University of North Carolina Press, 1976); Fred Weinstein and Gerald

M. Platt, *The Wish to Be Free: Society, Psyche and Value Change* (Berkeley: University of California Press, 1969); Edwin Burrows and Michael Wallace, "The American Revolution: The Ideology and Psychology of National Liberation," *Perspectives in American History*, 6 (1972), 167–306; Jay Fliegelman, *Prodigals and Pilgrims: The American Revolution against Patriarchal Authority, 1750–1800* (Cambridge: Cambridge University Press, 1982); Mitchell R. Breitwieser, *Cotton Mather and Benjamin Franklin: The Price of Representative Personality* (Cambridge: Cambridge University Press, 1984).

Chapter 1

1. The Founding Fathers were not hindered from making more exalted claims by a lack of imagination or by defects in sensibility. Jefferson, for example, was certainly not a less gifted literary stylist than Franklin; his passionate appreciation of music and architecture suggests that he was probably more artistically sensitive than Franklin, and he was also more self-consciously an intellectual. Yet Jefferson's life, as he saw it, had no comprehensive direction and shape, as Franklin's did; Jefferson's autobiography was not written to serve as an independent work, but rather as a sort of memorandum. He omits to describe, for example, his career as governor of Virginia, for the explicit reason that public documents can adequately present that period in his life (*Autobiography* in Thomas Jefferson, *Writings* [New York: Library of America, 1984], 45).

2. See Ormond Seavey, "D. H. Lawrence and Benjamin Franklin as Conflicting Modes of Consciousness," in *Critical Essays on Benjamin Franklin*, ed. Melvin H. Buxbaum (Boston: G.K. Hall, 1987), 60–80.

3. The literature on identity is ample and affords subtleties of meaning beyond what are necessary for my purposes. Freud makes the distinction between personal identity and object-choice (*Group Psychology and the Analysis of the Ego*, trans. and ed. James Strachey, rev. ed. [New York: Liveright, 1967], 38–39). Erik H. Erikson uses the term *identity* to refer to the results of a simultaneous process: the self achieves a sense of its own consistency and integrity and thereby recognizes its own association with culture ("The Problem of Ego Identity," *Journal of the American Psychoanalytic Association*, 4[1956], 57, and elsewhere in Erikson's writings). When I speak of national identity, then, I seek to formalize the question of the self's consciousness of being related to an encompassing group. Object-choice and personal identity become a continuum of involvement. For the *sabra*, national identity may be close to personal identity. For the urban intellectual, national identity may be object-choice, if that.

4. The critical literature on autobiography has become in recent years considerable. See, for example, Robert F. Sayre, "The Proper Study—

Autobiographies in American Culture," *American Quarterly*, 29 (1977), 241–62; Albert E. Stone, " Autobiography and American Culture," *American Studies: An International Newsletter*, 11 (1972), 22–36; William C. Spengemann, *The Forms of Autobiography: Episodes in the History of a Literary Genre* (New Haven: Yale University Press, 1980) [in particular the bibliographic essay, pp. 170–245]; James Olney, ed., *Autobiography: Essays Theoretical and Critical* (Princeton: Princeton University Press, 1980); James Olney, *Metaphors of Self: The Meaning of Autobiography* (Princeton: Princeton University Press, 1972); Karl Joachim Weintraub, *The Value of the Individual: Self and Circumstance in Autobiography* (Chicago, University of Chicago Press, 1978); Mutlu Konuk Blasing, *The Art of Life: Studies in American Autobiographical Literature* (Austin: University of Texas Press, 1977); Elizabeth W. Bruss, *Autobiographical Acts: The Changing Situation in a Literary Genre* (Baltimore: Johns Hopkins University Press, 1976); Janet Varner Gunn, *Autobiography: Toward a Poetics of Experience* (Philadelphia: University of Pennsylvania Press, 1982); James M. Cox, "Autobiography and America," *Virginia Quarterly Review*, 47 (1971), 252–77; Patricia Meyer Spacks, *Imagining a Self: Autobiography and Novel in Eighteenth-Century England* (Cambridge:Harvard University Press, 1976); Roy Pascal, *Design and Truth in Autobiography* (Cambridge: Harvard University Press, 1960); Donald Greene, "The Uses of Autobiography in the Eighteenth Century," in *Essays in Eighteenth-Century Literature*, ed. Philip B. Daghlian (Bloomington: Indiana University Press, 1968); Georges May,"Biography, Autobiography and the Novel in Eighteenth-Century France," in *Biography in the Eighteenth Century*, ed. J. D. Browning (New York: Garland, 1980).

5. Robert M. Sayre, for example, uses those circumstances to account for the differences in Franklin's approach from one section to another (*The Examined Self: Benjamin Franklin, Henry Adams, Henry James* [New Haven: Yale University Press, 1964], 17–26).

6. Levin, *Yale Review*; Daniel B Shea, *Spiritual Autobiography in Early America* (Princeton: Princeton University Press, 1968), 234–48.

Chapter 2

1. The editors of the Yale edition sensibly note that Franklin must have written rapidly indeed to have completed the first part at Twyford. I think it would have been quite impossible for him to have done so without locking himself in his room and writing furiously for many hours a day, something so sociable a man as Franklin was most unlikely to do. The first part of the *Autobiography* runs to eighty-three manuscript pages and prints out (in the Yale edition) at ninety-one pages. The superscription has led many critics to assume that the whole first section was written at Twyford; internal evidence

indicates, however, that Franklin consulted papers of his that could not have been available on holiday, the journal of his voyage back to America in 1726, for example (A, 106). J. A. Leo Lemay and P. M. Zall, in the introduction to their genetic text edition of the *Autobiography*, refuse to go beyond the observation that it "may seem unlikely that even Franklin could have written so much, so well, in so short a time—in addition to carrying on an active social life with the Shipley family" (*The Autobiography of Benjamin Franklin: A Genetic Text*, ed. J. A. Leo and P. M. Zall [Knoxville: University of Tennessee Press, 1981], xx). During the months following the August visit to Twyford Franklin did a great deal of leisurely traveling and wrote an unusually small number of surviving letters, only eight from mid-August to mid-December. However, letters may well have been lost; he remarks in a letter to Jonathan Shipley on 14 December 1771 that he had "Heaps of Letters to answer" (*P*, 18:267). He wrote neither political pamphlets nor scientific papers during that period. It seems reasonable to conjecture that the writing of the *Autobiography* could have extended at least through this six-month period preceding the Parliamentary session that met in January 1772, when the press of business closed in on him again.

2. Alan Rannie, *The Winchester Countryside: A Guide to the Country Surrounding Winchester* (London: Allen & Unwin, 1947), 12–13, 172–73; *P*, 18:137.

3. *P*, 4:504; *W*, 7:64; *W*, 8:454. In a letter to his young grandson Benjamin Bache, Franklin laid down as an absolute requirement this kind of beginning: "You should . . . when you write, acknowledge the receipt of letters that have come to your hands, mentioning their dates" (*A Benjamin Franklin Reader*, ed. Nathan G. Goodman [New York: Crowell, 1945], 769).

4. On the Quakers and autobiography, see Daniel B. Shea, *Spiritual Autobiography in Early America* (Princeton: Princeton University Press, 1968), 3–84. Herbert's work, written perhaps in the 1640s, was first printed privately by Walpole at Strawberry Hill in 1764.

5. Donald A. Stauffer, *The Art of Biography in Eighteenth-Century England* (Princeton: Princeton University Press, 1941), 65–131.

6. *Autobiography of Edward Gibbon*, ed. Dero A. Saunders (New York: Meridian, 1961), 27.

7. Leo Lemay has pointed out that Franklin had come to expect that his letters would be passed around and even published; even as a letter, then, the *Autobiography* could hardly have been a private document (Leo Lemay, "Benjamin Franklin," *Major Writers of Early American Literature*, ed. Everett Emerson [Madison: University of Wisconsin Press, 1972], 218).

8. *The Life of Edward Lord Herbert of Cherbury Written by Himself*, 3d ed. (London: J. Dodsley, 1778), 1–2.

9. The latter was the express motive of Letitia Pilkington, friend of Swift, aspiring poetess, and eventually public scandal. "Although it has been the common practice with writers of Memoirs to fill their volumes with their own praises, which, whatever pleasure they may have afforded to the authors by indulging their vanity, are seldom found to give any to the readers, I am de-

termined to quit this beaten track, and, by a strict adherence to truth, please my enemies, by presenting them with a lively picture of all my *Faults*, my *Follies*, and the *Misfortunes* which have been consequential to them." In the next paragraph, however, she begins the abuse of her malicious enemies which is the more prevalent substance of her autobiography (*Memoirs of Mrs. Letitia Pilkington 1712–1750 Written by Herself* [New York: Dodd, Mead, 1928], 25).

10. In the manuscript Franklin originally wrote "Fame," a more assertive word than the less specific phrase he used instead (*Benjamin Franklin's Memoirs: Parallel Text Edition*, ed. Max Ferrand [Berkeley: University of California Press, 1949], 2).

11. *Memoirs of Benvenuto Cellini* trans. Anne McDonnell (New York: Dutton, 1952), 1.

12. *An Apology for the Life of Colley Cibber, with an Historical View of the Stage during His Own Time*, ed. B. R. S. Fone (Ann Arbor: University of Michigan Press, 1968), 7.

13. Gibbon, 27.

14. This episode is discussed revealingly in Richard Bushman's important article "On the Uses of Psychology: Conflict and Conciliation in Benjamin Franklin," *History and Theory*, 5 (1966), 225–40.

Chapter 3

1. Alfred O. Aldridge, "The First Published Memoir of Franklin," *William & Mary Quarterly*, 27 (1967), 624–28.

2. Carl Becker, "Benjamin Franklin," *Dictionary of American Biography*.

3. John Locke, *Two Treatises of Government*, ed. Peter Laslett (New York: New American Library, 1965), 309.

4. Adam Smith, *The Wealth of Nations* (Homewood, Ill.; Richard O. Irwin, 1963), I, II.

5. Charles Secondat, Baron de Montesquieu, *The Spirit of the Laws*, trans. Thomas Nugent (New York: Hafner, 1959), 316.

6. David Hume, *Writings on Economics*, ed. Eugene Rotwein (Madison: University of Wisconsin Press, 1970), 79.

7. Joseph Addison and Richard Steele, *Selections from the Tatler and the Spectator*, ed. Robert J. Allen (New York: Holt, Rinehart, 1957), 117–18.

8. Voltaire, *Philosophical Letters*, trans. Ernest Dilworth (Indianapolis: Bobbs-Merrill, 1961), 26.

9. George Lillo, *The London Merchant*, III, i, in Ricardo Quintana, ed., *Eighteenth-Century Plays* (New York: Random House, 1952), 311–12.

10. Among the strangest corollaries for us in this rendition of society is the treatment of social groups between the self and the state. (See Otto Gierke, *Natural Law and the Theory of Society 1500 to 1800*, trans. Ernest Barker

[Cambridge: Cambridge University Press, 1950], 114–17.) Locke and his contemporaries virtually deny any authority or permanent character to such groups, except the Church. Yet these individualist theories were in some ways based on valid sociological observation. Peter Laslett has shown that European society before the coming of industry was virtually without that body of social groups that bind and direct twentieth-century lives (Peter Laslett, *The World We Have Lost: England before the Industrial Age* [New York: Scribners, 1965], 8–10).

11. Georges Louis Leclerc, comte de Buffon, *Natural History*, trans. William Smellie (London: T. Cadell & W. Davis, 1812), III, 294–95; Otis E. Fellows and Stephen F. Milliken, *Buffon* (New York: Twayne, 1972), 125.

12. Etienne Bonnot abbé de Condillac, *Treatise on the Sensations*, trans. Geraldine Carr (Los Angeles: University of Southern California, School of Philosophy, 1930), 224.

13. See also Locke, *Essay Concerning Human Understanding*, Books I and II, *passim*. Gibbon parodies this general belief in his *Autobiography* when describing his own birth: "Our fancy may create and describe a perfect Adam, born in the mature vigor of his corporeal and intellectual faculties; far different is the origin and progress of human nature, and I may confidently apply to myself the common history of the whole species. Decency and ignorance cast a veil over the mystery of generation, but I may relate that after floating nine months in a liquid element I was painfully transported into the vital air.

"Of a newborn infant it cannot be predicated 'he thinks therefore he is'; it can only be affirmed 'he suffers, therefore he feels.' But in this imperfect state of existence I was still unconscious of myself and of the universe; my eyes were open without the power of vision; and according to M. de Buffon, the rational soul, that secret and incomprehensible energy, did not manifest its presence till after the fortieth day" (Gibbon, *Autobiography*, 52).

14. Jean le Rond d'Alembert, *Preliminary Discourse to the Encyclopedia*, trans. Richard N. Schwab and Walter E. Rex (New York: Bobbs-Merrill, 1963), 8.

15. Voltaire, *Philosophical Letters*, 53–54.

16. Louis-Alexandre, duc de La Rochefoucauld d'Anville, *Eloge de Franklin* in *L'Apothéose de Benjamin Franklin*, ed. Gilbert Chinard (Paris: Librairie Orientale et Américaine, 1955), 99.

17. Georges Gusdorf, *La Découverte de soi* (Paris: Presses Universitaires de France, 1948), vi–vii.

18. Michel de Montaigne, *The Complete Essays of Montaigne*, trans. Donald Frame (Stanford: Stanford University Press, 1969), 611.

19. *Julius Caesar* V: iv: 73–75.

20. Denis Diderot, *The Encyclopedia: Selections*, trans. Stephen J. Grendzier (New York: Harper, 1967), 204.

21. Denis Diderot, *Oeuvres de Diderot*, ed. André Billy (Paris: Gallimard, 1946), 1091 (my translation).

22. Philip Dormer Stanhope, 4th. Earl of Chesterfield, *Letters to His Son* (Washington: M. Walter Dunne, 1901), I, 126–31, 148–49, 244–48, and *passim*.

23. Gibbon, *Autobiography*, 134.

24. Jean-Jacques Rousseau, *Confessions*, trans. J. M. Cohen (Harmondsworth: Penguin, 1953), 327.

25. James Boswell, *Boswell's London Journal, 1762–1763*, ed. Frederick A. Pottle (New York: McGraw-Hill, 1950), 166, 173.

26. Ibid., 269–70.

27. Gibbon, *Autobiography*, 30.

28. Quoted in Braudy, *Narrative Form in History and Fiction*, 58.

29. Ibid., 31–90.

30. Alexander Pope, *Essay on Man* I. 289–92.

31. P, 1:62; Franklin then proceeds to use the century's frequent simile comparing the universe to an immense clock.

32. Voltaire, *Candide, Zadig, and Selected Stories*, trans. Donald M. Frame (New York: New American Library, 1961), 286.

33. *The Yale Edition of the Works of Samuel Johnson*, ed. E. L. McAdam et al. (New Haven: Yale University Press, 1958–1971), II, 262.

34. Henry Fielding, *Joseph Andrews and Shamela*, ed. Martin C. Battestin (Boston: Houghton Mifflin, 1961), 157.

35. Johnson, *Yale Edition*, III, 318–23.

36. Quoted in J. Salwyn Schapiro, *Condorcet and the Rise of Liberalism* (New York: Harcourt, Brace, 1934), 69.

37. James Boswell, *Life of Johnson* (London: Oxford University Press, 1953), 19–23.

38. Johnson, *Yale Edition*, II, 263.

39. Gibbon, *Autobiography*, 30.

40. Rousseau, *Confessions*, 17.

41. David Hume, "My Own Life" in *Hume on Religion*, ed. Richard Wollheim (New York: Meridian, 1963), 278–79.

Chapter 4

1. The most recent discussion of the development of the manuscript and its provenance can be found in Lemay and Zall, *Genetic Text*, xvii–lviii. Earlier discussions of importance include the introduction to the Yale edition of the *Autobiography* (A, 22–37); Max Farrand, ed., *Benjamin Franklin's Memoirs: Parallel Text Edition* (Berkeley: University of California Press, 1949).

2. See the discussion of P. M. Zall, "The Manuscript and Early Texts of Franklin's Autobiography," *Huntington Library Quarterly*, 39 (1976), 375–84.

3. This reference to his journal book, one of several allusions, suggests that the journal provides much of the material for his *Autobiography*, including details and dates.

4. R. Jackson Wilson discusses this episode suggestively in his introduc-

tion to the *Autobiography* (*The Autobiography of Benjamin Franklin* [New York: Modern Library, 1981], xix–xxi).

5. John F. Lynen, *The Design of the Present*, 136.

6. A vertical line in the "Notes," possibly drawn in when Franklin picked up the project in 1784, extends down to the note for "Library erected. Manner of conducting the Project. Its plan and Utility" (*A*, 267–69).

Chapter 5

1. On theories of audience, see for example Wolfgang Iser, *The Art of Reading: A Theory of Aesthetic Response* (Baltimore: Johns Hopkins University Press, 1978); Susan R. Suleiman and Inge Crosman, ed., *The Reader in the Text: Essays on Audience and Interpretation* (Princeton: Princeton University Press, 1980).

2. Ernest C. Mossner, *The Life of David Hume* (Oxford: Clarendon Press, 1954), 592.

3. The whole tortured process by which Franklin's *Autobiography* was written is laid out in Max Farrand, "Benjamin Franklin's Memoirs," *Huntington Library Bulletin*, 10 (1936), 49–78. See also Lemay and Zall, *Genetic Text*, xix–xxiii.

4. Owen Jenkins, "Richardon's *Pamela* and Fielding's 'Vile Forgeries,' " *Philological Quarterly*, 44 (1965), 20. The letters were satirized by Fielding in *Shamela*.

5. There is a pronounced element of play in Franklin's scientific work, which can be seen in the kind of experiments he constructed and in his readiness to mix those experiments with practical jokes. Carl Becker has stated that science was the only thing Franklin gave himself to wholeheartedly ("Franklin, Benjamin," *DAB* [1934]). If so, it was with a devotion rather different in character from that of most fulltime scientists.

6. Examining the developing structure of the *Autobiography*, Hugh Dawson argues persuasively that Franklin, unsure of whether he would be able to continue to work, brings it here to what serves as a conclusion. ("Franklin's 'Memoirs' in 1784: The Design of the *Autobiography*, Parts I and II," *Early American Literature*, 12 (1977), 286–93.

Chapter 6

1. For references in his letters to his intentions for completing the *Autobiography*, see *W*, 9:497; 9:371; 9:533; 9:550; 9:559; 9:637; 9:645; 9:657; 9:665.

2. The history of Franklin's religious opinions is dealt with in Alfred O. Aldridge, *Benjamin Franklin and Nature's God* (Durham, N.C.: Duke University Press, 1967). See also Melvin H. Buxbaum, *Benjamin Franklin and the Zealous Presbyterians* (University Park: Pennsylvania State University Press, 1975).

3. Lemay and Zall, *Genetic Text*, xxii.

4. See in particular W, 10:32 and 10: 35, letters he wrote in June and September 1789 to Vaughan and Le Veillard.

5. Max Farrand and, after his death, his associates at the Huntington Library assembled what they called the "First Authoritative Edition," supposedly reconstructing Franklin's final intentions; this text is in print in the Signet paperback. On this edition, see the review by Donald H. Mugridge, *William & Mary Quarterly*, 3d ser., 6 (1949), 649–59; the introduction to the Yale *Autobiography*, 36–37; and Zall, "Manuscript and Early Texts."

Chapter 7

1. Lemay and Zall, *Genetic Text*, 87–88.

2. Quoted, A, 10–11. See also Richard D. Miles, "The American Image of Benjamin Franklin," *American Quarterly*, 9 (1957), 121–28, and Louis B. Wright, "Franklin's Legacy to the Gilded Age," *Virginia Quarterly Review*, 22 (1946), 268–79.

3. Lawrence, *Studies in Classic American Literature* (1923; rpt. New York: Viking, 1964), 10. See Ormond Seavey, "D. H. Lawrence and 'The First Dummy American,' " *Georgia Review*, 39 (1985), 113–28.

4. Ibid., 16.

5. Carl Van Doren, *Benjamin Franklin* (New York: Macmillan, 1938), 782.

Chapter 8

1. Several of those eulogies, in an edited form, appear in translation in Gilbert Chinard, "The Apotheosis of Benjamin Franklin, Paris 1790–1791," *Proceedings of the American Philosophical Society*, 99 (1955), 440–73. See also Alfred O. Aldridge, *Franklin and His French Contemporaries* (New York: New York University Press, 1957).

2. As John Lynen notes, "the 'many-sided Franklin'. . . is not one person but several, and this typically modern preference has the advantage of flattering our taste for believing that selfhood is a closetful of masks. But one need only ask what a mask may be to recognize the evasion. Franklin's roles are,

we say, 'Franklin's.' They must form a system defining some true identity at the center, and that self can be described only as a state or mode of consciousness" (Lynen, 125–26).

Chapter 9

1. Douglass Adair in his brilliant essay "Fame and the Founding Fathers" remarks that "there are only two of the great generation who we know set themselves very 'lofty aims' (in the de Tocqueville sense) before the Revolution. One is the oldest of the major leaders, Benjamin Franklin, who as a young man wrote down among the rules by which he tried to govern his behavior: 'Imitate Jesus and Socrates' " (*Fame and the Founding Fathers* [New York: W. W. Norton, 1974], 7. (The other person Adair cites is Alexander Hamilton.)

2. *The Diary of Samuel Sewall*, ed. M. Halsey Thomas (New York: Farrar Straus, 1973), I, 603. On the backgrounds of Josiah Franklin's Puritanism, see Arthur Bernon Tourtellot, *Benjamin Franklin: The Shaping of Genius, the Boston Years* (Garden City, N.Y.: Doubleday, 1977), 21–113.

3. Franklin's interest in his own ancestry was life-long. One of the last surviving letters to him from his father is in response to questions about family history (P, 2:229–32). Numerous letters to his younger sister Jane Mecom discuss ancestry. He went to some trouble in England to look up Franklin family records and to collect anecdotes about his ancestors. See John W. Jordan, "Franklin as a Genealogist," *Pennsylvania Magazine of History and Biography*, 23 (1899), 1–22. It should be mentioned that in New England Josiah Franklin would have found a vigorous Puritan practice and belief. See Robert G. Pope, *The Half-Way Covenant: Church Membership in Puritan New England* (Princeton: Princeton University Press, 1969).

4. A, 51; *The Letters of Benjamin Franklin and Jane Mecom*, ed. Carl Van Doren (Princeton: Princeton University Press, 1950), 72.

5. *Diary of Samuel Sewall*, I, 482.

6. See the extensive Franklin genealogy compiled in P, 1:l–lxv.

7. See Alfred O. Aldridge's discussion in *Benjamin Franklin: Philosopher and Man* (Philadelphia: Lippincott, 1965), 29.

8. *Letters of Benjamin Franklin and Jane Mecom*, 126.

9. *Franklin's Wit and Folly: The Bagatelles*, ed. Richard E. Amacher (New Brunswick, N. J.: Rutgers University Press, 1953), 45. Mitchell R. Breitwieser discusses the whistle bagatelle perceptively in *Cotton Mather and Benjamin Franklin: The Price of Representative Personality* (Cambridge: Cambridge University Press, 1984), 298–99.

10. Freud, *Group Psychology*, 67–69; Lawrence, *Studies*, 14.

11. Emory Elliott, *Power and the Pulpit in Puritan New England* (Princeton: Princeton University Press, 1975), 80.

12. *W*, 10: 30–31; "Excerpts from the Papers of Dr. Benjamin Rush," *Pennsylvania Magazine of History and Biography*, 29 (1905), 27.

13. Ebenezer Turell, *The Life and Character of the Reverend Benjamin Colman, D. D.* (1749; rpt. Delmar, N. Y.: Scholar's Facsimiles & Reprints, 1972), 167–68; see also Larzer Ziff, *Puritanism in America: New Culture in a New World* (New York: Viking, 1973), 272–79.

14. Bernard Bailyn, *The New England Merchants in the Seventeenth Century* (Cambridge: Harvard University Press, 1955), 189–90.

15. Bernard Bailyn, *Education in the Forming of American Society: Needs and Opportunities* (New York: Random House, 1960), 22–26; Carl and Jessica Bridenbaugh, *Rebels and Gentlemen: Philadelphia in the Age of Franklin* (New York: Oxford University Press, 1962), 207–12; James Axtell, "The White Indians of Colonial America," *William and Mary Quarterly*, 3d ser., 32 (1975), 55–88.

16. To see how that different model of sonship worked, see Emory Elliott, *Power and the Pulpit in Puritan New England*. It is, by the way, striking to note how many of the Revolutionary leaders had fathers who were either socially insignificant or who died when their sons were young—Washington, Jefferson, both Adamses, Franklin, Hamilton, and Hancock. James Otis, Jr., and John Dickinson, whose fathers were prominent in their lives, both proved psychologically incapable of leading the revolutionary turmoil to the point of revolution. On the other hand, Kenneth S. Lynn offers the astonishingly reductionist argument in *A Divided People* (Westport, Conn.: Greenwood Press, 1977) that the differences between Patriots and Loyalists can be largely explained in terms of the different patterns of relationship to fathers between the two groups. For a more sophisticated treatment of attitudes toward parent-child relations in the Revolutionary era, see Jay Fliegelman, *Prodigals and Pilgrims: The American Revolution Against Patriarchal Authority, 1750–1800* (New York: Cambridge University Press, 1982).

17. Locke was prompted to his major theorizing on politics by Sir Robert Filmer's *Patriarcha*, a defense of paternal power. He is uncharacteristically vehement and sarcastic as he denounces "This strange kind of domineering Phantom, call the *Fatherhood*, which whoever could catch, presently got Empire, and unlimited power" (*Two Treatises*, 179). On the psychology of fatherless groups, see Freud, *Group Psychology*; W. R. Bion, *Experience in Groups* (New York: Basic Books, 1959); Philip E. Slater, *Microcosm: Structural, Psychological and Religious Evolution in Groups* (New York: John Wiley, 1966).

18. Harry M. Ward, "The Search for American Identity: Early Historians of New England" in *Perspectives on Early American History: Essays in Honor of Richard B. Morris*, ed. Alden T. Vaughan and George A. Billias (New York: Harper, 1973), 52–53.

19. *P*, 1:161. In the *Autobiography* Franklin notes how well this passage was received: "some spirited Remarks of my Writing on the Dispute then going on between Govr. Burnet and the Massachusetts Assembly, struck the principal People, occasion'd the Paper and the Manager of it to be much talk'd of, and in a few Weeks brought them all to be our Subscribers" (*A*, 121).

20. *New-England Courant,* 5 February 1722.

21. *Ibid.,* 4 December 1721.

22. *Ibid.,* 22 January 1722.

23. Elizabeth C. Cook, *Literary Influences in Colonial Newspapers* 1704–1750 (New York: Columbia University Press, 1912), 15; Samuel Johnson, "Life of Addison," in *The Works of Samuel Johnson, LL. D.* (Oxford: Talboys & Wheeler, 1825), VII, 473.

24. Franklin's inspiration for vegetarianism came from a book by Thomas Tryon, a prolific and bizarre seventeenth-century Pythagorean who left radical Protestantism for mysticism and a successful career as a merchant. Franklin himself would later dabble in freemasonry and religious rites of his own devising. In Tryon's work Franklin found the mixture of ascetic capitalism, humanitarianism, dietary prohibitions, and organizing schemes for self-improvement that he could similarly link together later himself. ("Tryon, Thomas," *DNB.*)

25. Bushman, 233.

26. *Letters of Benjamin Franklin and Jane Mecom,* 63–64.

27. Bushman, 233.

28. Perry Miller, *The New England Mind: From Colony to Province* (1953); rpt. Boston: Beacon, 1961), 342–43.

29. Leo Lemay has pointed out the role Gardner must have had as a writing model for Franklin (Lemay, "Benjamin Franklin," 205–6).

30. Addison and Steele, *Selections,* 71.

31. C. S. Lewis, "Addison," in *Eighteenth-Century English Literature: Modern Essays in Criticism,* ed. James L. Clifford (New York: Oxford University Press, 1959), 146.

32. For a different characterization of Mistress Dogood, see James A. Sappenfield, *A Sweet Instruction: Franklin's Journalism as a Literary Apprenticeship* (Carbondale, Ill.: Southern Illinois University Press, 1973), 35–37.

33. Lemay, "Benjamin Franklin," 208.

34. For a different characterization of James Franklin, see Perry Miller, *The New England Mind: From Colony to Province,* 333–42, and also his Introduction to *The New-England Courant, A Selection of Certain Issues Containing Writings of Benjamin Franklin or Published by Him During His Brother's Imprisonment* (Boston: American Academy of Arts and Sciences, 1956). Miller applauds the Couranteers in their campaign against smallpox inoculation, a curious attitude that can only be accounted for by his overwhelming dislike of Cotton Mather.

35. *New-England Courant,* 23 July 1722.

36. Bushman, 233–38.

37. Van Doren, 36.

Chapter 10

1. Aldridge, "First Published Memoir," 625.
2. Erik H. Erikson, *Young Man Luther: A Study in Psychoanalysis and History* (New York: W. W. Norton, 1962), 43.
3. Ibid., 98–104.
4. Van Doren, 70.

Chapter 11

1. Bridenbaughs, *Rebels and Gentlemen*, 195.
2. Ibid., 24–25.
3. Daniel J. Boorstin, *The Americans: The Colonial Experience* (New York: Random House, 1958), 59–61.
4. Sam Bass Warner, *The Private City: Philadelphia in Three Periods of Its Growth* (Philadelphia: University of Pennsylvania Press, 1968), 11.
5. P, 1:21–23; Miller, *The New England Mind: From Colony to Province*, 339–41.
6. I am unsure whether the extended self-defense against Keimer in *Busy-Body 5* is by Franklin or by his collaborator Joseph Breintnall. The file of the *American Weekly Mercury* in the Library Company of Philadelphia has a marginal note, probably by Franklin, indicating that Breintnall and Franklin together wrote the fifth letter. Stylistically, the section of that letter before the self-defense is superior, but Breintnall was a fairly graceful writer in his own right (P, 1:114, 130; Cook, *Literary Influences*, 74–76, 83–84). In either case, Franklin was involved in that passage, whether he wrote it or not.
7. Lemay, "Benjamin Franklin," 211–13.
8. On the sources for Franklin's proverbs, see Robert H. Newcomb, "The Sources of Benjamin Franklin's Sayings of Poor Richard," unpublished dissertation, University of Maryland, 1957, and four articles taken from that dissertation: "Benjamin Franklin and Montaigne," *Modern Language Notes*, 72 (1957), 489–91; Franklin and Richardson," *Journal of English and Germanic Philology*, 57 (1958), 27–35; "Poor Richard and the English Epigram" *Philological Quarterly*, 40 (1961), 270–80; "Poor Richard's Debt to Lord Halifax," *PMLA*, 70 (1955), 535–39. See also Van Doren, 110–14; John F. Ross, "The Character of Poor Richard: Its Source and Alteration," *PMLA*, 55 (1940), 785–94; Stuart A. Gallacher, "Franklin's *Way to Wealth*: A Florilegium of Proverbs and Wise Sayings," *Journal of English and Germanic Philology*, 48 (1949), 229–51.

9. Carl Bridenbaugh, *Cities in the Wilderness: The First Century of Urban Life in America 1625–1742* (New York: Knopf, 1955), 143–44.

10. The question of William Franklin's parentage has long been unresolved. In the eighteenth century it was accepted that he was illegitimate, and there was some resentment that Franklin should have obtained the governorship of New Jersey for a "base-born brat." Charles Henry Hart tried to argue in 1911 that his mother was Deborah Franklin, who conceived him before the parents moved in together. Hart seems to have been moved by an impulse to clear Franklin of the charge of immorality. ("Who Was the Mother of Franklin's Son: An Inquiry demonstrating that she was Deborah Read, wife of Benjamin Franklin," *Pennsylvania Magazine of History and Biography*, 35 [1911], 308–14). It seems more likely, however, that the mother was a woman named Barbara. See William Herbert Mariboe, "The Life of William Franklin, 1730(1)–1813: 'Pro Rege et Patria' " (Ph.D. dissertation, University of Pennsylvania, 1962).

11. *A*, 167. The Hemphill episode is discussed in Merton A. Christenson, "Franklin on the Hemphill Trial: Deism Versus Presbyterian Orthodoxy,"*William & Mary Quarterly*, 3d. ser., 10 (1953), 422–40, and by Melvin H. Buxbaum, *Benjamin Franklin and the Zealous Presbyterians*. 76–115.

12. Adams, *Works*, 1:661.

13. Private benevolence of his own he seems to have found amusingly out of character. A man named Hayes once gave him a hand out of the water he had fallen into while trying to board a stage-boat; Hayes then dunned him repeatedly for presents in return for saving his life. Franklin always obliged, though he notes that he had always been a strong swimmer and was in no danger. When Hayes died, his wife took up the requests. "He seems...to have left me to his Widow as part of her dowry" *W*, 10:75).

14. Franklin would hardly have accepted Milton's view of the end of learning, "to repair the ruins of our first parents by regaining to know God aright" (John Milton, *Prose Selections*, ed. Merritt Y. Hughes [New York: Odyssey, 1947], 31). He cites Milton's reason for the study of politics, "that they may not in a dangerous fit of the commonwealth be such poor, shaken, uncertain reeds, of such a tottering conscience, as many of our great counsellors have lately shown themselves, but steadfast pillars of the state" (Milton, 42). But Milton's emphasis is not particularly on political history, as Franklin's is. Parallels have been asserted between Franklin's ideas and the ideas of the Commonwealth educators. Of that group, Franklin was apparently only familiar with Milton's *Of Education*. The Commonwealth educators strongly believed in an innovative education as the basis for revolutionary changes in society; Milton's model student, for example, is clearly intended for public life. The radical Protestantism which was Franklin's background helps to explain why his ideas resemble those of the Commonwealthmen (see Robert Ulich, *History of Educational Thought* [New York: American Book Company, 1950], 180–87, 225–28). Charles Rollin, French educator and historian during the late reign of Louis XIV and the Regency, is another of Franklin's sources. Franklin quotes approvingly Rollin's remarks in favor of teaching history and

the vernacular languages (P, 3:406, 411). Yet despite Rollin's celebrity as a teacher, his ideas of curriculum are fundamentally traditional: he warns of the doctrinal dangers of French literature and he allows for no more than a half-hour a day away from Latin and Greek for the study of French; the history he would teach is ancient history and church history, leaving modern history to be read at the student's leisure (George Snyders, *La Pédagogie en France aux XVIIe et XVIIIe Siècles* [Paris: Presses Universitaires de France, 1965], 107–10, 94–95). Franklin is much more consistent with Locke than with any of his other sources, and he quotes Locke extensively, but Locke seems more to have coincided with Franklin's impulses than to have influenced him.

15. Robert Middlekauff, *Ancients and Axioms: Secondary Education in Eighteenth-Century New England* (New Haven: Yale University Press, 1963), 54–57.

16. The program also involves the study of oratory, not a capacity of Franklin's but a considerable interest. His fascination with the powers of George Whitefield is evident both in the *Autobiography* and in *Poor Richard's Almanack* (P, 3:336).

17. P, 4:108. As Bernard Bailyn points out, Franklin's idea of education was in no way narrowly utilitarian. "He wanted subjects and instruction that trained not for limited goals, not for close-bound, predetermined careers, but for the broadest possible range of enterprise" (*Education in the Forming of American Society*, 35).

18. Charles Coleman Sellers, *Benjamin Franklin in Portraiture* (New Haven: Yale University Press, 1962), 27. Sellers discusses the attribution of the painting to Feke, 24–25. The portrait is dated around 1746 based on what can be discovered about Feke's movements and the development of his art. See Louise Todd Ambler, *Benjamin Franklin: A Perspective* (catalogue to an exhibition held at the Fogg Art Museum, Harvard University, 1975), 36; R. Peter Mooz, "Robert Feke: The Philadelphia Story," in *American Painting to 1776: A Reappraisal.* Winterthur Conference Report, ed. I. M. Quimby (1971), 203.

19. P, 4:68. The editors of the Yale *Papers* contrast Franklin's admonition with Jefferson's attitude toward David Rittenhouse's involvement in revolutionary politics in the 1770s. "Nobody can conceive," Jefferson wrote, "that nature ever intended to throw away a Newton upon the occupations of a crown" (quoted in P, 4:68). Verner W. Crane briefly notes the contrast between the two letters to Colden in *Benjamin Franklin and a Rising People* (Boston: Little, Brown, 1954), 38–39.

20. Douglass Adair, discussing the attitude of the Revolutionary generation toward fame, quotes a letter from John Adams to Jefferson in 1813 on the modest extent of a Massachusetts colonist's ambitions before the Revolution—"to be worth ten thousand pounds Sterling, ride in a Chariot, be a Colonel of a Regiment of Militia and hold a seat in his Majesty's Council. No Man's Imagination aspired to anything higher beneath the skies" (quoted in Adair, 6).

21. Franklin's coining of such maxims strikes me as in some ways analo-

gous to the situation of the modern folksong writer, a person usually of considerable cultural and political sophistication who must somehow approximate in certain stylized ways the perceptions and diction of a person from the working class.

22. On the publication history of "The Speech of Polly Baker," see Max Hall, *Benjamin Franklin and Polly Baker: the History of a Literary Deception* (Chapel Hill: University of North Carolina Press, 1960); on its rhetoric, see J. A. Leo Lemay, "The Text, Rhetorical Strategies, and Themes of 'The Speech of Miss Polly Baker,'" in *The Oldest Revolutionary: Essays on Benjamin Franklin*, ed. J. A. Leo Lemay (Philadelphia: University of Pennsylvania Press, 1976). 91–120.

23. P, 1:19; Lemay, "Benjamin Franklin," 209.

24. *Letters of Benjamin Franklin and Jane Mecom*, 67.

25. Henri Bergson, *Laughter*, in *Comedy*, ed. Wylie Sypher (Garden City, N. Y.: Doubleday, 1956), 62–64.

Chapter 12

1. One measure of the relative importance of North America is the space given to it in William Robertson's important *History of America*, published first in 1777. Only one-seventh of the text of the original work was devoted to the English colonies. In his preface, however, Robertson registers that the balance of interest has shifted toward the British colonies. "The attention and expectation of mankind are now turned towards their future condition. In whatever manner this unhappy contest may terminate, a new order of things must arise in North America, and its affairs will assume another aspect." (*The Works of William Robertson, D. D.* [London: Longman, Brown, Green & Longmans, et al., 1851], V, v).

2. Max Weber, *The Protestant Ethic and the Spirit of Capitalism*, trans. Talcott Parsons (New York: Scribners, 1958), 54.

3. Lynen, 121.

4. Whitfield, Bell, "Benjamin Franklin and the German Charity Schools" *Publications of the American Philosophical Society*, 99 (1955), 383.

5. Franklin's responsibility for the cartoon is probable but not certain (P, 5:xiv). In 1775 and 1776 the snake appears again as an American symbol, this time with the caption, "Don't Tread on Me."

6. Quoted in Gordon S. Wood, *The Creation of the American Republic 1776–1787* (Chapel Hill: University of North Carolina Press, 1969), 106.

7. Bridenbaughs, *Rebels and Gentlemen*, 207, 295.

8. P, 7:289. Edward Shippen, a Philadelphian who had studied at the Middle Temple a few years earlier, expresses the forlorn corollary to this descrip-

tion: "How much we are excelled by those in Europe!" (quoted in Bridenbaughs, *Rebels and Gentlemen*, 137).

9. See in particular Claude-Ann Lopez and Eugenia W. Herbert, *The Private Franklin: The Man and His Family* (New York: Norton, 1975), which exhaustively discusses Franklin's personal relations.

10. Aram Vartanian, "Tremblay's Polyp, La Mettrie, and Eighteenth-Century French Materialism," *Journal of the History of Ideas*, (1950), 259–86.

11. Quoted in Bernard Bailyn, *The Ideological Origins of the American Revolution* (Cambridge: Harvard University Press, 1967), 303.

12. See Burrows and Wallace, *Perspectives in American History*, 6 (1972), 167–306.

13. Henry St. John, Viscount Bolingbroke, *The Idea of a Patriot King* (New York: Bobbs-Merrill, 1965), 46.

14. See Michael Kammen, *A Rope of Sand: The Colonial Agents, British Politics, and the American Revolution* (Ithaca, N.Y.: Cornell University Press, 1968).

15. Sir Lewis Namier, *England in the Age of the American Revolution*, 2d ed. (New York: St. Martin's, 1961), 37.

16. Paul Leicester Ford in his *Franklin Bibliography* (Brooklyn: n.p., 1889) numbers eleven editions of the *Examination*, seven in America including one in German. It also appeared in several collections in the eighteenth century in English, French, and German (127–33).

17. Van Doren, 467.

18. On the question of whether Franklin wore the coat, see Richard Meade Bache, "Franklin's Ceremonial Coat," *Pennsylvania Magazine of History and Biography*, 23 (1899), 444–52; Esmond Wright, *Franklin of Philadelphia* (Cambridge: Harvard University Press, 1986), 317.

19. Cecil B. Currey has argued in two books, *Road to Revolution: Benjamin Franklin in England, 1776–1775* (Garden City, N.Y.: Doubleday, 1968) and *Code Number 72: Ben Franklin; Patriot or Spy?* (Englewood Cliffs, N.J.: Prentice-Hall, 1972), that Franklin's own financial considerations explain his entire diplomatic career. In the latter book he sets forth the extraordinary suggestion that Franklin was a British agent in the Revolution.

20. Quoted in *Benjamin Franklin: Representative Selections*, rev. ed., ed. Chester E. Jorgenson and Frank Luther Mott (New York: Hill and Wang, 1962), xcix. Wedderburn was a Scot, hence "Sawney," an English epithet for the Scots.

21. Richard Bushman notes that pattern of withdrawal from confrontations in Franklin's life, "On the Uses of Psychology: Conflict and Conciliation in Benjamin Franklin," *History and Theory*, 5 (1966), 233–38.

22. *Benjamin Franklin's Letters to the Press, 1758–1775*, ed. Verner W. Crane (Chapel Hill: University of North Carolina Press, 1950), 245.

23. The conventions of publication in the Yale *Papers* dictate that dashes are replaced by what the editors see as appropriate marks of punctuation. In the case of this letter, however, the dashes that are preserved in the Smyth edition convey something of the fury of the letter, so I use that edition.

Chapter 13

1. On the relations between Franklin and Galloway, see Benjamin H. Newcomb, *Franklin and Galloway: A Political Partnership* (New Haven: Yale University Press, 1972).

2. Thomas Hutchinson, *The Diary and Letters of Thomas Hutchinson*, ed. Peter Hutchinson (1884–1886; rpt. New York: Burt Franklin, 1971), II, 237–38.

3. The historical scholarship on Franklin's French years has been particularly full. See, for example, Aldridge, *Franklin and His French Contemporaries*; Claude-Ann Lopez, *Mon Cher Papa: Franklin and the Ladies of Paris* (New Haven: Yale University Press, 1966); Edward Everett Hale and Edward Everett Hale, Jr., *Franklin in France*, 2 vols. (Boston: Roberts Brothers 1877–1888); Bruce Granger, "We Shall Eat Apples of Paradise," *American Heritage*, 10 (1959), 38–41, 103–4; Gilbert Chinard, "Franklin en France," *French Review*, 29 (1955–1956), 281–89; Jean Jules Jusserand, "Franklin in France," in *Essays Offered to Herbert Putman*, ed. William W. Bishop and Andrew Keogh (New Haven: Yale University Press, 1929), 226–47; David Schoenburn, *Triumph in Paris: The Exploits of Benjamin Franklin* (New York: Harper, 1976).

4. John Adams, *The Works of John Adams*, ed. Charles Francis Adams (Boston: Little, Brown, 1856), I, 660.

5. Wolfgang Mozart and Lorenzo da Ponte, *Don Giovanni*; Samuel Richardson, *Clarissa*; Choderlos de Laclos, *Les Liaisons dangereuses*.

6. Alfred Owen Aldridge, *Franklin and His French Contemporaries*, 21–38.

7. John Adams, *Diary and Autobiography of John Adams*, ed. L. H. Butterfield (Cambridge: Harvard University Press, 1961), 4:118.

8. Shaw, *The Character of John Adams*, 115; the political differences between Adams and Franklin are discussed in William B. Evans, "John Adams's Opinion of Benjamin Franklin," *Pennsylvania Magazine of History and Biography*, 92 (1968), 220–38.

9. B. F. Stevens, *Facsimiles of Manuscripts in European Archives Relating to America 1773–1783* (London: n.p., 1891), VIII, nos. 835–37.

10. Adams, *Autobiography*, 4:150.

11. Perhaps it should be noted that Adams also succeeded in getting under Franklin's skin, to the point where Franklin wrote to Robert Livingston in Congress of Adams, "I am persuaded . . . that he means well for his Country, is always an honest Man, often a wise one, but sometimes, and in some things, absolutely out of his senses" (W, 9:62).

Chapter 14

1. Lopez and Herbert, 264.

2. On the other hand, the indications of his intentions that Franklin gave in his letters written as he was leaving Europe suggest a readiness for retirement. Writing to his sister Jane Mecom on his way to Le Havre, he says, "I have continued to work till late in the Day; tis time I should go home and go to Bed" (Letters of Benjamin Franklin and Jane Mecom, 236; see also W, 9:359). As in 1775, he did not arrive in Philadelphia anticipating that a new set of political responsibilities would be thrust upon him, but he would state in the Autobiography that it was his policy not to turn down offices that were given to him. So he was not fully decided simply to "go home and go to Bed."

3. See Kenneth Silverman, A Cultural History of the American Revolution (New York: Crowell, 1976), 445ff.

4. Richard B. Morris, The Peacemakers: The Great Powers and American Independence (New York: Harper, 1965), 101–2, 149, 212.

5. Wood, 68.

6. The Federalist Papers (New York: New American Library, 1961), 78.

7. Shaw, 313.

8. The question of whether honors should ascend or descend, dealt with in Franklin's letter on the Cincinnati, was a frequent subject of discussion in the late seventeenth and early eighteenth centuries. See for example William Penn, No Cross, No Crown: Or several Sober Reasons Against Hat-Honour, Titular Respects...(1699), parodied lightly by Franklin in the New-England Courant in 1723 (P, 1:51–52); the debate between Whig Bishop Hoadly and Jacobite Charles Leslie (Bailyn, Ideological Origins, 310); Bolingbroke, The Idea of a Patriot King, 11.

9. Claude-Ann Lopez, Mon Cher Papa: Franklin and the Ladies of Paris (New Haven: Yale University Press, 1966), 288–89.

10. See Arthur O. Lovejoy, Reflections on Human Nature (Baltimore: Johns Hopkins University Press, 1961), 14–21.

11. Thomas Jefferson, Notes on the State of Virginia, in Writings, ed. Merrill D. Peterson (New York: Library of America, 1984), 290–91.

12. Wood, 163.

13. Max Farrand, ed., The Records of the Federal Convention of 1787 (New Haven: Yale University Press, 1911), III, 91.

14. Max Farrand, ed., The Records of the Federal Convention of 1787, rev. ed. (New Haven: Yale University Press, 1966), I, 81.

15. Ibid., 85.

16. Ibid., 85.

17. Ibid., 488.

18. Ibid., 546.

19. *Federalist Papers,* 33.

20. Farrand, *Records,* (1966), I, 452.

21. *W,* 9:601, In the manuscript *God* is underlined twice.

22. Farrand, *Records,* (1966), I, 452.

23. Thomas Jefferson, *Notes on the State of Virginia,* in *Writings,* ed. Merrill D. Peterson (New York: Library of America, 1984), 190.

24. Erik H. Erikson, *Childhood and Society,* 2d. ed. (New York: W. W. Norton, 1963), 268.

25. P. L. Ford, *Franklin Bibliography,* 177.

INDEX